'*England is Mine* is written with tact, wit and penetrating erudition. The book's importance lies in the fineness of its judgements. Bracewell knows where the bodies are buried in the garden of Post-Punk England. It's heartening to know someone's been keeping watch.'   *i-D*

'*England is Mine* is a wonderfully intriguing book, overflowing not only with examples and insights but with real verve and panache. Bracewell shows his intellectual and literary vivacity; summarising the impact of Elvis in the 1950s, for example, he concludes that in a drab, shabby England, "pop stood out like a sore thumb to be sucked". He also provides an inspired analysis of the Mods.
The competition is very strong but perhaps the best part of this book arrives when Bracewell takes an intelligent and sympathetic look at the English suburbs. He is at his impressive best when he is performing such intellectual riffs and playing with ideas. He has the knack of conjuring up a memorable turn of phrase. Evelyn Waugh is "rigid with neurotic snobbery".
Two superb paragraphs pinpoint the absurd appeal of Joanne Catherall and Susanne Sulley of The Human League – their banal yet disconcerting stage presence Bracewell brilliantly identifies as carrying "an independence and home-grown glamour", plus a feminist strength suggesting they "could either dance around a handbag or hit you with it". [This is] a bravura performance.'
                        HARRY RITCHIE, *Times Educational Supplement*

'Michael Bracewell's observations are astute and acutely accurate, making this an essential and enlightening read'
                        City Life

'Bracewell artfully diagnoses the black Gothicism and foment of revolt in the North, calling it in his chapter "Lucifer Over Lancashire" (a bravura text that swerves from Branwell Brontë to Mark E Smith) "a region of mythological darkness . . . a vernacular culture . . . quick-witted, yet steeped in despair and the history of protest".'   PHILIP HOARE, *Guardian*

'It takes a leap of the imagination to connect the idyllic and elegiac poetry of A E Housman or the "jolly hockey sticks" children's novels of Nancy Hayes with the lyrics of a Prefab Sprout album or the ramblings of the Fall's Mark E Smith, but Michael Bracewell is nothing if not imaginative. He also possesses one of the most wide-ranging minds in contemporary writing, as genuinely well-versed in the works of Auden and Waugh as he is steeped in the imagery of punk and its aftermath. His thesis, supported with reference to film, visual arts, poetry, television and pop music, is seductive, mainly because it is so well put: the writing is witty, vivid, occasionally acerbic. *England is Mine* is marvellously well-written; it is also very funny. No other cultural historian has Bracewell's gift for humour. He sets a new standard in cultural history, though he does so with a characteristically English modesty and wit.'   JOHN BURNSIDE, *Scotsman*

'Zeitgeisty effort to explain the English dream, more complex and uncharted than the American dream. A noble effort full of good things'   ROGER CLARKE, *Attitude*

'*England is Mine* knits together many threads from recent cultural life in its breakneck pursuit of English pop sensibility. [Bracewell's] cross-cultural enquiry leads to some eye-catching juxtapositions. I was particularly taken with a paragraph that somehow manages to skate from Dexy's Midnight Runners to the cast of *Auf Wiedersehen Pet*, and thence to the Angry Young Men and the Dominican order of friars, all with a couple of brisk sentences.
Bracewell is very good and his reflections are always worth thinking about.'   DJ TAYLOR, *Independent*

'Bracewell's account is eclectic, astute, often surprisingly and suitably contentious – not least in eschewing class analysis in favour of the idea of a general cultural impetus to explain social development. He takes us on a thought-provoking ride through our recent cultural history.'   PETER INGHAM, *The Times*

michael Bracewell

lives in Manchester and Surrey. He is the author of five works of fiction, the most recent being *Saint Rachel*.

from the reviews:

'As a gentle preamble to in-depth consideration of this weighty pan-cultural blockbuster, readers might like to play a little game. Who do the following sentences refer to? A singer and songwriter who "was covering the territory of Angela Carter's *Company of Wolves* in the guise of a Pre-Raphaelite raised on Jackie"; a poet whose work suggested "the bitter visions of the early Eliot, redefined in potent language of a working men's club, subverted by the sensual melancholy of the late Keats". Do not despair if your answers were other than Kate Bush and John Cooper Clarke. *England is Mine* may still have something for you.

The novelist and critic Michael Bracewell has set himself to consider the mysterious nature of the English dream, as opposed to the American one. His book starts and finishes with an evocative linkage. The first few pages describe the scene in Powell and Pressburger's 1946 propaganda landmark, *A Matter of Life and Death,* in which David Niven's dying flyer pours out his heart over his aeroplane wireless. The conclusion deals with Britain's jungle pirate radio stations of the 1990s, and their bid to transform the airwaves into an "outlaw, sonic sculpture". The author aims not just to join the cultural dots between these two ideas of what it is to be English, but to colour in the background as well. This is an ambitious project and there are many passages in this book that demand to be quoted. The extraordinary depth of Bracewell's erudition is matched by a lively sense of mischief. It is an invigorating tour of the high plains of cultural endeavour. There are enough good ideas to sustain four or five smaller volumes.'

BEN THOMPSON, *Independent on Sunday*

76903

'Appropriate that the novelist whose work has brought England most sharply into focus should chose it as the focus for this superb and sustained polemic. From CS Lewis to The Smiths, Evelyn Waugh to The Fall, here is pop culture filtered through the lens of highbrow history. Bracewell writes like an angel with an intellect that is as multifaceted as its subjects'
GRAHAM CAVENEY, *Arena*

'Bracewell's ambitious study provides a genealogy of the elements of the subversion and accommodation that have been the hall-marks of English popular music. He shows how defining motifs in the work of bands such as the Pet Shop Boys and The Smiths echo themes and attitudes embedded in a specifically English literary tradition (Wyndham Lewis's *Blast* is "a punk samizdat"). It's good on the suburbs as both citadel of boredom and hotbed of creativity, and on the sheer ordinariness of glam rock and is consistently witty and always stimulating.' GEOFF DYER, *Mail on Sunday*

'*England is Mine* should establish Bracewell as one of the most significant cultural commentators of the Nineties. Languid and labyrinthine, Bracewell tackles the hefty subject of Englishness in a style less sound bite than literary: the dream of Albion; the modernist's spotty, fast-paced hunger for the new; the dank, disaffected class-consciousness; the suburban tedium; the lugubrious tragi-comic approach of the northern working classes. Then, threading together examples as seemingly disparate as Benjamin Britten and Derek Jarman, John Cooper Clarke and Evelyn Waugh, Mark E Smith and George Orwell, Bracewell shows that all the themes which inform the English experience of popular music are deeply rooted in the national psyche: that pop is the inheritor of English artistic articulations and aspirations. If Bracewell's England is riddled with deep-rooted psychoses expressed in visionary and nightmare morphings, scratching the creative itch has produced an amazing rash of talent.'
The Big Issue

fiction by the same author:

england is mine

pop life in albion from wilde to goldie

michael bracewell

Flamingo

An Imprint of HarperCollins*Publishers*

FOR JOHN WILDE

Flamingo
An Imprint of HarperCollins*Publishers*
77–85 Fulham Palace Road,
Hammersmith, London W6 8JB

Published by Flamingo 1998
9 8 7 6 5 4 3 2 1

First published in Great Britain by
HarperCollins Publishers 1997

ISBN 0 00 655015 0

Set in Fairfield Light by
Rowland Phototypesetting Ltd,
Bury St Edmunds, Suffolk

Printed and bound in Great Britain by
Clays Ltd, St Ives plc

contents

'And I? May I say nothing, my lord?'

Oscar Wilde, on being sentenced to
two years hard labour, 25 May 1895

εnglanð as arcadу
Beſore þoþ

We can only be perched on the remains of an aircraft's wing because we are looking inside the cockpit of a badly damaged Lancaster bomber, which is limping its way back to England. The wind is roaring in our ears above the sickly, rising drone of the bomber's Rolls-Royce engines. The Skipper is alone now, having ordered the rest of the air crew to bail out. The friendly eyes of Flying Officer Trubshawe, his 'sparks', are open and staring in death; his epitaph is written in the confident curves of his magnificent handle-bar moustache. Later, in a Hun-free heaven that resembles a cross between Guildford Cathedral and a clerical division of the Home Civil Service, the revived owner of this moustache will perk up with boyish enthusiasm as he catches a line of Test Match commentary on the celestial wireless.

The bomber is losing height, and the young pilot is passing what he expects to be the last moments of his life in a valedictory radio conversation with a pretty young woman from Boston called

June, who is working for the airfield ground crew. With death
so close, intimacy accelerates. Before explaining that his parachute is shot to ribbons and the situation looks pretty hopeless,
the pilot, transcending formality, quotes some lines of verse by
Sir Walter Raleigh. 'I'd rather have written that,' he confides,
with a sudden grin of conviction, 'than flown through Hitler's
legs.' His cheerful bravery, in which the sporting frustration of
the bowled-out last bat is mixed with the courageous flippancy
of a wounded man refusing morphine, is almost too much to
bear. He is nobility itself in the lobby of the Ultimate Sacrifice,
admitting his fear but allowing no stain of bitterness to soil his
shroud as it descends. And, as June blinks back hot tears, love
– or something like it – is being forged, link by link and second
by second, in this desperately sad conversation between two
Allied strangers. It is a scene which brings together the stoical
suffering of Noël Coward's *Brief Encounter* with the luxurious
tragedy of certain poems written during World War One. 'Oh
what made fatuous sun-beams toil,' (we could recollect,) 'to
break earth's sleep at all?'

But this is the Higher Price to be paid by players in the greater
game; to protest, to do anything other than admire and mourn,
would be unthinkable. The young pilot is called Peter. He has
a neat, pencil-line moustache and dishevelled curly hair. In
peacetime he was probably useful in the slips. Now, to prevent
the risk of crashing his plane on to innocent Englanders, he
ditches it into the sea and bails out – without a parachute.
Slipping through the open trap-door behind his seat, into the
screaming mist that should pluck him from life, he leaves June
with tears in her eyes, frantically calling his name into the white
noise of the abandoned radio. Then she hears nothing but whist-
ling static, and her velvety Bostonian sobs close the scene.

What happens next is stranger in its details than its logic. Peter
comes to in the sandy shallows of an ebbing tide that is lapping
an empty beach; the sky is white with pale sunshine. Shedding

his flight-jacket, socks and boots he starts to walk, drawn by the sound of a rustic flute. The Afterlife has the air of the first day of the summer holidays. On a dune Peter comes across a naked little boy, who is playing the Pan Pipes while his goat champs at the salt grass beside him. The scene is Arcadian, drawn straight from the landscape of the Greek pastoral poets and echoed across the European centuries since. After the din of battle, the quotations from Raleigh and the sweet whiff of love coming off June, there is now a portentous mysticism wafting across the quiet sands. Peter, however, approaches heaven – for heaven it must be – with the sturdy formality of a new boy at prep school or barracks: 'I'm new,' he tells the startled shepherd boy. 'Where do I report?' Just then we see the wholly terrestrial figure of June cycling home along the coast road; she is still visibly shaken after the night-shift. We are in England, after all, with nothing more than a headache; and the little Hellenic shepherd, having played his ambiguous role, disappears.

This peculiar sequence of events takes place at the start of Michael Powell and Emeric Pressburger's fantastical propaganda film, *A Matter of Life and Death* (1946). The young pilot, David Niven, is both a warrior and a poet (though you get the impression that he would be a late Georgian rather than a follower of Auden) and he seems to represent a solid specimen of the English Classical Humanist tradition – troubled by the theology of Fair Play ('If only we'd listened to Plato and Aristotle and Jesus!') but unconnected to the modernist anxieties of paranoia and fragmentation. (It was a Frenchman, after all, who was 'sent' to fetch him to his rightful death, but who 'meezed 'im in an Eengleesh pee-zoopere'.) We would like to believe that Peter's subsequent tangle with the legislation of cosmic destiny is nothing that a glass of sherry won't put right; all things are still in their proper place, at this point in Englishness, even when you dodge a celestial emissary because of bad weather in the Channel.

It is telling that an incongruous Arcadian shepherd boy should be there to meet Peter at his point of crisis between England and heaven. Powell and Pressburger were tapping in to a spirit of Englishness, common enough before World War Two, that gambolled on the sunny meadow of pure and idealized pastoral. Arcady, in this particular theology of Englishness, is a quasi-mystical, historically vague notion of Ye Olde England as a benign rural democracy; it runs parallel but invisible to the English countryside, usually declaring itself at moments of crisis, emotional rapture or personal revelation. This happens to Ratty, in *The Wind in the Willows* (1908), as he and Mole are searching all through one short summer night for the baby otter, Portly. Ratty's close encounter is with Pan himself, and Kenneth Grahame's amicable prose makes a sudden shift into poetry, the official language of Arcadian England:

> Slowly, but with no doubt or hesitation whatever, and in something of a solemn expectancy, the two animals passed through the broken, tumultuous water and moored their boat at the flowery margin of the island. In silence they landed, and pushed through the blossom and scented herbage and undergrowth that led up to the level ground, till they stood on a little lawn of a marvellous green, set round with Nature's own orchard-trees – crab-apple, wild cherry, and sloe.
> 'This is the place of my song-dream, the place the music played to me,' whispered the Rat, as if in a trance. 'Here, in this holy place, here if anywhere, surely we shall find Him!'

'He', in an unexpected side-step from the Christian upper-case, is the Piper at the Gates of Dawn: pagan Pan, the protector of wild creatures and god of nature. And Ratty and Mole's experience of Arcardy in England finds an echo in Jerome K. Jerome's *Three Men in a Boat* (1889). Once again, the prose-style becomes charged with mystical fervour, exchanging Woosteresque bon-homie for pseudo-Keatsian poetics:

... till we laugh, and, rising, knock the ashes from our burnt-out pipes and say 'Good night', and, lulled by the lapping water and the rustling trees, we fall asleep beneath the great, still stars, and dream that the world is young again – young and sweet as she used to be, ere the centuries of fret and care had furrowed her fair face, ere her children's sins and follies had made old her loving heart – sweet as she was in those bygone days when, a new-made mother, she nursed us, her children, upon her own deep breast – ere the wiles of painted civilization had lured us away from her fond arms, and the poisoned sneers of artificiality had made us ashamed of the simple life we led with her, and the simple, stately home where mankind was born so many thousands of years ago.

Harris said:

'How about if it rained?'

There is a need within the psyche of Englishness to look back to an idealized past (think of the cult of domestic Edwardiana, pot pourri and cottage industry that flourishes in the marketing of 'Englishness' in the 1990s), and Arcady, as the mother and father of our prelapsarian innocence, is recalled with the sentimental nostalgia of infantilism: the adult reflex that yearns in crisis to re-create the remembered comfort and security of childhood. Communing with Arcady through the English countryside, we can become children again, echoing Blake's 'I am but two days old', or luxuriating in a spirit of nature as though it were amniotic fluid, postponing birth into a colder reality. Pan is father to Ratty and Mole; Night is the mother of the three men in their boat, dozing up the Thames towards Henley. For Powell and Pressburger, their England is a country whose stylized history as much as its Arcadian landscape is its greatest defence. Peter's bravery is sweetened by his love of Raleigh's poetry, and the ping-pong-playing neuro-surgeon who ends up defending his right to live in the celestial courtroom is a kind of Shavian Socrates, with the beard and perspicacity of a man who can marry philosophy to patriotism without flinching. English history, in the Arcadian idyll, is as strong, mystical and benign as the oak trees once used to build its ships and choirs.

This point had also been made (although contemporary critics were somewhat resistant) in Powell and Pressburger's earlier film of 1944, *A Canterbury Tale*. By wedding a plot that was pure Enid Blyton, revolving round a mysterious 'Glueman' who daubs thick gum in the hair of Land Army girls, to a meditation on pilgrimage, history and humility, the directors evoked a spirit of Englishness in which the idyll of Ye Olde England – its moral values and patriotism eclipsed by modernity and war – was another Arcady which we could rediscover through personal crisis. Temperament and moral sense were hereditary. All things were in their traditional place for the good of all – a sacrosanct arrangement given stern new purpose by the demands of war, in which medieval arcana, as much as the comedy of English country life, become symbolic of the deeper constitution of England. They are there to edify the American soldier Bob (who discovers at Canterbury that his girl is still writing to him), Alison, the Land Army girl with her 'London ways' (who discovers, also at Canterbury, that her fiancé is still alive) and even the cynical cinema organist, Peter Gibbs, who gets to realize his dream and play the cathedral organ at his battalion's service of departure. But the film turns into a moral conundrum with the fate of Mr Culpepper, local magistrate and Glueman, whose desire to attract an audience of soldiers to his lectures on Kentish archaeology (whose lesson is the vitality of Olde England) has driven him to his sticky crime; if he glues enough girls, he reasons, they'll be too scared to come out in the evening and offer the soldiers an alternative to his inspiring lectures. Despite being found out by the three modern pilgrims, they don't turn him in because of his good intentions; but he pays for this madness, we suspect, by being about to propose to Alison as she hears that her fiancé is alive and well in Gibraltar. The film also plays the virtues of country living off against the sterility or decadence of life in the capital, with a key line coming from a butch woman with a pitchfork, cheroot dangling from the corner of her mouth, who asks Alison about her London home: 'Was it a long street, with every house a different sort of sadness? The only man who ever asked me to marry him lived in a street like that.'

Short of resorting to a complex sexual sub-text, it is hard to make the film work as a story, but, as a piece of propaganda, *A Canterbury Tale* repeated sentiments that had been popular in England since the height of Empire. In H. V. Morton's gazeteer of 1928, *The Call of England*, we find him concluding his search for the heart of England with a peacetime version of Powell and Pressburger's soliloquy on Englishness:

> I can conceive no greater happiness than going out into England and finding it almost too English to be true: the little cottages, which vary from county to county, the churches with their naves in Norman England, the great houses, the castles, the incredible cathedrals, the strange little places which will, let us hope, never quite emerge from an earlier, and, I believe, happier world.

And there it is again: that tic in England's hymning of itself that believes the past to be a somehow better place, with its Englishness less diluted by progress or by what Jerome K. Jerome, somewhat viciously, had described as 'the poisoned sneers of artificiality' in his side-swipe at decadence in *Three Men in a Boat*, rehearsing the English distaste for Wildean philosophies of soul and sensuality that were contemporary to its composition. Indeed, the equation that makes moral decadence reveal itself through images and metaphors of physical illness will be a constant throughout the English retreat from Arcady. Sick children, in particular, denoting illness in the heart of infantilism, will come to stand for a national fall from grace and a cultural loss of Innocence. The right-wing writer Sir Arthur Bryant, in his essay of 1934, 'The National Character', had seen industrialism as the enemy of English morality and contentment, primarily because, in his opinion, all Englishmen recognized their real Utopia as 'a rose garden and a cottage in the country' of their birth – which was not, ironically, a million miles away from the late-nineteenth-century philosophy of the Arts and Crafts movement, with its basis in idealized socialism as cottage crafts-manship. Sentiments such as these, from both Kipling and the artsy-crafty romantic Left, would be a fetish with the so-called 'Georgian' thinkers and writers, such as Edward Marsh, Rupert Brooke or Andrew Young, and it is interesting that the trend would be revived in the 1970s and 1980s, when Harold Pinter's taut but luxurious screenplay for the film of L. P. Hartley's *The Go-Between* rehearsed the period confectionery of Merchant Ivory's heavily sweetened cinematic adaptations, in the 1980s, of the novels of E. M. Forster – thus responding to the dream world of both the Right and the Left. By that time, the English Arcadia would be a kind of National Trust disco, wherein flourished an equal desire to romanticize Englishness into a directory of soothing and picturesque cliché.

Over the last twenty years, despite the sub-contraction of the main-tenance of Arcady to the heritage industry, the Arcadian back-drop to Englishness has remained firmly in place. A useful tool, when linked to ecological awareness, for the advertising industry (pastoral serenity connotes health, a stable family unit and a positive credit rating), Arcady is also called upon, culturally, as a nostalgic state of mind. Even in English pop music, from the perversely Arcadian events in Hyde Park when Mick Jagger read Shelley in memory of Brian Jones, at the Rolling Stones' free festival in 1969 (Arcady as hippie paradise), to Donovan's 'Gift From A Flower To A Garden' with its setting of Shakespeare's 'Under the Greenwood Tree' and the psychedelic impulse to turn landscape inwards, Arcady has been called on to supply its quasi-mystical 'better world'. Hence the Pink Floyd's return to 'The Piper At The Gates of Dawn' in their acid landscapes of

English pastoralism. Transmitted through the English cult of the garden, Arcadian values could be tempered to the human scale, and thus the horticultural conceit would be joined to the etymology of the Arcadian England. Hence the pronouncement in Noël Coward's *This Happy Breed* (1944) (in which pride is synonymous with humility) that 'We've been called a nation of gardeners – and they weren't far from the truth; we like planting things.'

One of the most determined, if little noticed, journeys into Arcadian England was taken by Virginia Astley on her record *From Gardens Where We Feel Secure*. The title alone summed up the Arcadian stance, but the record was released by a record label (Rough Trade) at a time (1983) more concerned with apocalyptic dread and industrial soundscapes than pastoral minimalism. Astley's record was instrumental and ambient, enhancing Satie-esque piano pieces with the sounds of birdsong, sheep grazing, owls hunting and the soporific creak of rowing oars. There was even a track named after Auden's poem of 1933, 'Out on the Lawn I Lie in Bed', which pitted England's Arcady against personal despair. Not surprisingly, given its context, *From Gardens Where We Feel Secure* was seen as little more than the dew-soaked hem of Brian Eno's priestly robe of ambience experiments. But, in many ways, Astley had prefigured Michael Nyman's pastoral interludes in his soundtrack for Peter Greenaway's film *Drowning by Numbers* (1988), and brought back an eeriness which the Penguin Café Orchestra, on Eno's Obscure label, had somehow mislaid with their burgeoning popularity. This was not one woman's answer to *Tubular Bells*; rather, where Mike Oldfield had been a virtuoso with vision, and Michael Nyman's debt was to Mozart or Purcell, Astley's points of reference, it seemed, were Elgar and Vaughan Williams. It was a case of the shock of the old (an English speciality), occurring at a time when the new was locked in its own process of reinvention. Astley was neither fashionable nor unfashionable, and

From Gardens Where We Feel Secure was Sitwell-like in its eccentricity.

The music of Vaughan Williams is either loved or loathed as representative of a school of Englishness which has sympathy with the poetry of A. E. Housman and Walter de la Mare. It is charged, along with the entire Georgian sensibility, with being reactionary and Little Englander; it is too romantically English for some tastes, just as Wagner is too romantically German or Bernstein too romantically American. But this is rather like accusing Francis Bacon's paintings of not being easy on the eye. Vaughan Williams wrote music which articulated the love affair between England and Arcady, increasing in sublimity (or sentimentality, if you prefer) with his Pastoral Symphony (with its aching reference to the Last Post), The Lark Ascending, and the Serenade To Music. Steeped in history as well as landscape, these were the musical equivalents of Powell and Pressburger's *A Canterbury Tale* – just as the domestic architecture of Lutyens at the turn of the century was an homage to the Tudor idyll.

More important than what this music sounded like, in some ways, was what it seemed to stand for. Both Astley and Vaughan Williams were reaching for some melancholy rapture of unashamed English romanticism, whose summit was a tonal stillness, and *From Gardens Where We Feel Secure*, despite its Laura Ashley lyricism, can be seen as a whispered coda to the works of those romantic English composers who stand between the late afternoon of the Edwardian summer and the innovative genius of Benjamin Britten. And, fancifully, one can think of Astley's lush, wordless lullabies – both pointless and poignant – as marking pop's acknowledgement that the secret door in the garden wall that used to lead to Arcady is now well and truly locked. The New Arcady, of opulent costume dramas or ironic neo-neo-classicism, is a Virtual Arcady that must stand in for the original.

But if we accept that the English Arcady was always a largely illusory place, which did the bulk of its work by doubling as a state of mind, then we can see how its values will reduce with the shedding of innocence and the gaining of experience – a process mirrored within C. S. Lewis's 'Chronicles' of the fantasy kingdom of Narnia (itself a stylized England), in which worldly cynicism sees the close of the Arcadian–Anglican values of the original realm in an apocalyptic 'Last Battle' prior to the deliverance of the faithful to a new Narnian 'heaven'. And, once again, the role of childhood within the Arcadian formula is pronounced: by the time of *The Last Battle*, Susan, one of the children who has previously visited Narnia and even co-reigned there as a Queen, is no longer able to reach the country with her brothers and sisters because she has lost her faith in what she now calls 'the silly games we used to play as children' and has grown up to be interested in earthly teenage accessories – Jerome K. Jerome's 'poisoned sneers of artificiality', perhaps.

The English equation of Arcady is a struggle with conscience and promise on a par with the American Dream; the Arcadian dream of Englishness could never remain in its idyllic phase, but we cherish the idea of our Arcadian values with all of the ambivalence that we reserve for cultural catalysts. Now, at the end of the twentieth century, the Edenic properties of Arcady are seen as both eccentric and open to manipulation; we have hardened, inevitably, and it is the dark Satanic mills of Experience, rather than the green and pleasant land of Innocence, that seem most relevant to the English condition. Culturally, Modernism has passed a baton down to pop as the best means of articulating this massive retreat from the Arcadian idyll of Englishness.

-▦-

Box Hill, in Surrey, was both admired by John Keats and referred to by John Lydon, in his tribally mesmeric chant, 'The Flowers Of Romance'. The Box Hill district of the Mole valley is best seen in late summer, when the warm air is rich with the scent of pine resin and chalk. Halfway up the hill is the grave of a Surrey eccentric who asked to be buried standing up, and from the top of the hill – a favourite venue for motorcycle clubs – there is a good view of the county that Pevsner, the Anglophile art historian, described as 'serving the needs of urban man'. Nearly visible there is a small country house, built in the soft-core domestic classical of a Greek villa, called Polesden Lacey. The house, finished in 1827, is one of the smaller jewels in the National Trust's crown, but it is low and elegant and commands a spectacular view, to the south, of landscaped meadows and gentle escarpments. In late summer, the perspective of this view is marked by the pale proportions of scattered oaks and chestnut trees, their full silhouettes cross-hatched by shadows and heat haze. The place has a wide and varied selection of the standard Arcadian reference points: there are the statue plinths along the long garden walk which are inscribed with Augustan translations of the *Aeneid*; there is the small, open-air theatre; and, above all, bang on cue, there is the inscription which runs around the statue of a smirking god: 'Traveller, make haste. The sun is sinking low, he shall return, but not thou.' The Queen Mother spent part of her honeymoon here. And here, on a hot gravel path between trimmed and pungent box hedges, we are reminded of mortality: 'Et in Arcadia Ego' – Death's catch-phrase, the Either to Arcady's Or.

Englishness thrives upon such cosmic put-downs, for the English sensibility is based largely on a history of contradiction, perversity and paradox. The entire Arcadian theme, for instance, which stretches back through our conception of ourselves to Chaucer, could be largely discredited by the briefest glimpse at historical reality. But still we cling to it, weaving nymphs and shepherds in one disguise or another into everything from propaganda films to advertising campaigns. And yet it is this paradox within Arcady – death in the midst of beauty – that makes it a vital

component of the English sensibility. Arcady is both our monument to lost innocence and the setting in which we lost our
innocence.

Arcady's first paradox, as a cultural institution within Englishness,
is that it became the province and privilege of the rich. This
confounded the notion of Arcady as a rural democracy, in which
the spirit and beauty of nature took precedence over the values
of greed or cultural materialism. The translation of Arcady from
one mythology to another, by way of an expensive classical education and the Grand Tour, had entwined its sensibility with
landed wealth and intellectual superiority. Pope's pastoral imitations were Arcadian in sentiment but aristocractic in sensibility,
thus marking that particular English rebel poet as a writer who
could use mannered language both for and against the service
of mannered society. And as Pope was a master of the art of
paradox, and thus laid the foundations of English wit as it was
received, by way of Wilde, into the literature of the early twentieth century, it was the Edwardian and Georgian manifestations
of Arcady which were the venues for a new kind of rebellion:
the lashing out against traditions of Englishness by disaffected
bourgeois or aristocratic inheritors of the Arcadian dream. While
English pop would have its roots in working-class or newly suburban dissatisfaction with the conditions of post-war austerity
in the 1950s, this prehistory of the English sensibility of subversion – the English tic of ambivalence towards its own culture –
can be traced back to the sons and daughters of the late
Victorians in their inherited parks or newly acquired domestic
mansions.

This rebellion – the hatred of certain young people for the values
and environments of their privileged families and ancestors –
began at the end of the nineteenth century in the cult of
aesthetics and artifice which grew around Oscar Wilde, and
eventually destroyed him, the first martyr to modern bigotry. In
Nancy Mitford's *The Pursuit of Love* (1945), we find aristocratic

teenagers of the 1920s still fascinated by Wilde as a mythologized demon:

> Linda and I were very much preoccupied with sin, and our great hero was Oscar Wilde.
> 'But what did he do?'
> I asked Fa once and he roared at me – goodness, it was terrifying. He said: 'If you mention that sewer's name again in this house I'll thrash you, do you hear, damn you?' So I asked Sadie and she looked awfully vague and said: 'Oh duck, I never really quite knew, but whatever it was was worse than murder, fearfully bad. And, darling, don't talk about him at meals, will you?'

Having been driven underground for more than a decade of moral purging, the fight against blinkered Englishness had resumed in earnest during World War One. The sentiments of Georgian aesthetics and late Victorian principles – love of country above all else – were hard to maintain after two years of trench warfare, and the modernist spirit, fledgling though it was, began to loathe all of those things which the war claimed to represent. (Typically enough, the arrogance of the Bloomsbury Group, who seemed to believe that they had an intellectual monopoly on opposition to the war, and who were condemned by Wyndham Lewis in his memoir *Blasting and Bombardiering* (1937), for hiding in 'sun bonnets' while others fought, was summed up by one of their members pronouncing, when on trial for not joining up: 'I am the civilization for which you are fighting.' Their self-obsession and petty fine-mindedness had all but blinded the Bloomsberries to their distance from reality.)

The anger and anxiety of British youth from all classes at the murderous insanity of the war was gradually crystallized into the realization that the senior generations were out of control but incapable of admitting their incompetence. And this exposure to a massive flaw running across the very centre of Englishness could be read as a final confirmation that England, socially and culturally, had been running on empty for some years prior to

1914. England as Arcady – the rural democracy of the green and pleasant land, translated into the suffocating fabric of English society – had been a pretty disguise for much that the youth of the twentieth century would refuse to tolerate.

There are some key texts which pinpoint the revolt against Englishness, and which establish a pattern for acts of cultural revolution that will be repeated, throughout the twentieth century, in different media. We should first look to the ultra-Englishness of E. M. Forster – whose literary precursor was the deceptively savage Jane Austen – for the original glimmerings of subversion in suburbia and anarchy in Arcady. Forster wrote five of his six great novels before the outbreak of World War One; it was his homosexuality (painfully concealed from his mother and attendant aunts) that enabled his language to anatomize with such accuracy the hollow edifice of English pomposity and hypocrisy. Forster's heroes and heroines are not universally doomed, but his motto for *Howards End*, 'Only Connect', expresses in two words his conviction that tragedy is born of 'muddle'. It was typical of Forster to use a domestic term such as 'muddle' (a word his mother might use to describe a lost parcel or an unpaid grocer's bill) to signify disasters of cosmic proportions.

Forster's novel *The Longest Journey* (his personal favourite) describes the effects of stifling suburbanism on a young man who is a fully paid-up believer in Arcady – or in his perception of Arcady as created by Cambridge University. On leaving Cambridge, where the undergraduates wear daisy-chain crowns as they stumble through philosophical discussions, our hero Rickie Elliot marries a handsome but unimaginative woman called Agnes Pembroke. Almost immediately, through his own weakness and his love for Agnes, Rickie gives up his dreams of writing Hellenic short stories and becomes a Classics master at a cruel and mediocre public school, where Agnes's brother Herbert is flourishing as an administration-obsessed house-master. It is here, in the suburb of Sawston (which Forster will return to in other stories), that Rickie commences his tragedy of disillusionment, exploitation, lies and despair. And yet he commences life in Sawston with a deep (if obedient) faith in England. 'Thank God I'm English', he says, patting the ruddy Jacobean brickwork of the school chapel as he is shown around the grounds; 'Thank Him indeed,' comes the grave reply from Herbert Pembroke. Given the novel's cumulative tragedy, Rickie's admission of devout, decent patriotism becomes terrible in retrospect.

Forster's scepticism – the scepticism of a gay man in an age of popular jingoism and social division – could not be more pronounced. All that is most seductive about Englishness (the very values, ironically, that Merchant Ivory would emphasize eighty years later) turns out to be rotten at the core. The rage in Forster's vision, however disguised by humour, moral generosity and mannered language, is the rage of the romantic who discovers that his dreams were not only false, but corrupt. In short, as we shall see throughout the century, the love of Englishness which lends wings to eloquence contains a hatred of England, born of reproach, at its centre.

Forster's greatest Arcadian rebel is the hero of *Maurice*, his least convincing book. *Maurice* could be an allegory of the sensibility of English pop: childhood trauma left unaddressed by the forceful workings of English suburbia and an English education; the realization that one is somehow different – in this case homosexual – but powerless to articulate the difference in any tangible manner. For Maurice, his first love with a fellow undergraduate who turns out to be an emotionally immature but intellectual Platonist – which for Forster constitutes a personal dishonesty, one feels – simply adds another bolt to the prison door. Thus Maurice, echoing the outcasts for whom Wilde wrote 'The Ballad of Reading Gaol', sees himself as finally and terminally damned – in his own eyes as well as those of society or God. So what values do society and God actually uphold? This being in an England before pop, Maurice cannot learn to play the guitar and become a legend; rather, he finds himself buying a wedding present for his first male lover, and catches a glimpse of himself in the shop mirror: 'quiet, honourable, prosperous without vulgarity. On such does England rely. Was it conceivable that on Sunday last he had nearly assaulted a boy?'

Maurice dreams, sentimentally, that two men such as himself could become outlaws within the English greenwood, and live there in defiance of orthodoxy or convention, troubling nobody but willing to defend one another to the death. This dream is realized in part, at least, by Alec, who is the game-keeper on the estate of Maurice's first – now married – lover. Alec abandons his passage to Argentina in order to stay with Maurice – with whom he slept on the night before the Park vs Village cricket match. Forster later acknowledged that *Maurice* was unpublishable in Britain for years, largely because it contains no moral in favour of heterosexuality, and doesn't finish up with 'a boy dangling in a noose'. *Maurice* is more interesting, in retrospect, as a study of rebellion than of sexuality. The novel explores the Arcadian theme in relation to defiance and exile, as Maurice both longs for the greenwoods and despises the society that owns them. Most importantly, there emerges a fictional character who no longer believes in the innocence of England and who could embrace experience as an act of rebellion.

Judith Earle, the sensitive heroine of Rosamond Lehmann's first and most successful novel, *Dusty Answer* (1927), follows the trajectory of innocence to experience by way of all the Arcadian detours: the serene idyll of Englishness, the garden where Judith can feel secure, the openness of childhood and the seduction of infantilism. Judith could be a model for a character out of Enid Blyton's children's books, and her story begins with all of the elements of Blyton's definitive version of the English paradise. There is the beautiful old house by the river, there are elegant Mama and remote Papa – dignified, aloof, and as solidly late Victorian as the best chairs in the dining room. And then, crucially, there are the children next door: Charlie, Julian, Roddy, Martin and Mariella – a rag-bag assortment of brothers, sisters, cousins and friends, all of whom are touched with the glamour that being answerable only to a usefully libertarian and doting granny bestows on childhood acquaintances. To Judith, the children-next-door possess the power to bestow success or failure. In the early chapters of the first-person narrative (compellingly written as a minutely observed study in personal embarrassment) she recollects at length her earliest relationship with them. Childhood memory is once again the fulcrum about which Arcadian sensibility is balanced, but for Judith the emergence into Experience occurs with a brutality shaped by war and sharpened by adolescent insecurity. When her childhood friends leave the house next door they are 'cut off sharp in a final group on the hillside, as if horror had in that instant made a night and blotted them out for good' – and Judith must progress into adolescence and young womanhood alone, caught in a time-bubble of domestic English Arcady. World War One happens – England has a nervous breakdown – and the children-next-door (minus Judith's favourite, Charlie, who had married Mariella and then been killed in action) come back to resume their involuntary adjudication of Judith's rites of passage. It is rather as though we are getting to meet the Famous Five after they have all grown up – gay, frigid, brain-damaged or whatever.

Innocence has been lost. Charlie has had a child by the listless Mariella, and dependable Martin is en route to Cambridge, as is Roddy, whom we must take as the boyish charmer of the outfit. Julian, on the other hand, has become a shell-shocked dilettante. He has worked for the Ballets Russes, had a French and a Russian mistress, and likes to think of himself as beyond morality, beyond redemption and certainly beyond the Thames valley, where the bulk of the story is set. Julian is a Prufrockian figure, yet too melodramatic to be credible – wherein lies his self-hatred. ('Sometimes – in moments of clear vision – I see it all, the whole futile sickening farce,' he confesses from the piano stool.) He urges the now sexually attractive Judith to Wildean wickedness, but with less success than he might hope, for it is the boyish Roddy with whom she loses her way beneath the willows. The book explores Judith's failed relationships with all four of the remaining children, and her Sapphic dalliance at Cambridge with what appears to be the last of the pre-Raphaelite pin-ups, Jennifer. The story ends with Judith restored, older and wiser, to the Arcadian garden beside the river. The cherry tree, needless to say, has been felled by the gardener's axe.

Dusty Answer may be mawkish and sentimental, touched by melo-drama and adolescent earnestness, but it reads, now, as a vital account of transition within the English sensibility. Julian, in particular, describes a personal sense of doom that links readers of *The Waste Land* to fans of the Only Ones, but *Dusty Answer* as a whole sees an entire generation taking leave of Arcady. Historically, the characters might live through World War Two (indeed, we meet Judith in a later novel) to see the construction of the first tower blocks. They might even wince to the Who and would remember the civilized values of the Thames valley then reduced to photographs, letters and heirlooms. But Arcady itself, the Arcady behind them, will survive only as a cipher for some lost spirit of nobility which was never that noble in the first place, and could never endure the acceleration of experience that would occur throughout the remainder of the twentieth century.

As the Arcadian theme reinvents itself in the history of the English psyche, we find the Arcadian rebel who becomes essentially a malcontent and a romantic. Julian, from *Dusty Answer*, is developed into the character of Peter Jenkin in Lehmann's later novel, *Invitation to the Waltz* (1932). Peter can be described as a proto-punk, filled with hatred for his contemporaries and enthusiastic only about his one friend, whom we never meet, who publishes an avant-garde review at Oxford called *Attack* –

a clear reference to the vorticist magazine *Blast*. From the beginning, Peter is trouble: 'They approached a youth standing upon the hearthrug, posed in a sombre and defensive attitude. The first thing one noticed was his hair. He wore it over his forehead in a crooked fringe.'

Invitation to the Waltz, as another novel about English society in transition, follows the experience of two sisters as they prepare for their debut at a county ball. The novel is comic and self-aware, but it also dissects with surgical precision the lingering anti-Wildean, heartiness of young men who hunt, and their enduring belief in all of the values which World War One had proved so hollow. The character of Peter – described by one of his Oxford contemporaries as a 'distinctly unappetizing specimen' – is the fly in the ointment that reveals Lehmann's true sympathies. Unbearable he may be, but his eventual tears and his friend who writes poetry are deeply refreshing in a society where love of school equals love of country and love of country equals love of God:

> The buzz, the chattering idiocy . . . If sides must be taken, it was not their side one could take. Of course he was awful, a mass of affectation; and then so cruel; and doing his hair in such a dreadful way. He looked as if he took no exercise. He was an outcast, made for hatred and derision. But – what was it then that made one feel, with just a few more clues provided, one could get to know him, understand his language? I should soon feel at ease with a person like him; receive his confidence. Be sorry for him. Not think him absurd and contemptible at all. There must be something shady in me too, then, something decadent. I'm different from them, though they don't know it. I'm not going to do the things they'll do.

Peter, eventually, is persuaded by his new (and only) supporter not to remain at the party. He leaves the Arcadian mansion to its benighted nymphs and shepherds, no better than them – worse, in some ways – but vitally different:

'These fools,' he said, looking about him.

Why did he go on about them like this? He seemed to have his
knife into them terribly. His manner appeared to imply infinite
disgust and contempt for all this sort of thing – houses, titles,
people like the Spencers – what he called the upper classes.
Whereas oneself, one had always been led to believe they were
very admirable, very desirable.

'Do go.'

'All right, I will.'

He turned and went away, without another word.

Good evening, Johnny Rotten. In their slightly different ways, Peter
and Julian are rehearsing the sensibility of English pop: to pull
a face and walk away when England tells you that you are getting
above yourself. As with the other Peter the Poet, in Powell and
Pressburger's *A Matter of Life and Death*, England would expect
its poets to remain faithful to Arcadian Englishness. But by the
1930s there was a new generation of malcontents who could love
and loathe England in the same breath: they saw the natural
beauty and the cultural richness, they loved the language
and the history – so they used the same language, culture and
natural beauty to tell truths about England that England didn't
necessarily want to hear. These early rebels, re-creating English
literature, were upper-class or bourgeois precursors of the
working-class rebels who would appear in the kitchen-sink
dramas, books and films of the post-war period. Until the 1950s,
the class system was largely intact in England, with its prejudices, injustices and indifference towards all forms of radicalism
and militancy firmly in place. For Lehmann or Forster, addressing Edwardian and Georgian England through their discreetly
subversive fiction, sexuality was the best vehicle for taking the
fight to the enemy.

Homosexuality was the worst crime in the English directory of sins.
Evelyn Waugh's brother had been expelled from Sherborne for
'immorality' in a typical piece of public school policing which

still saw *fin-de-siècle* decadence as an enduring threat. World War One had been greeted as the 'Condy's Fluid' that could purge English blood of Wildean decadence, and there were many supposedly sane men who welcomed the war as a national cleansing agent. This attitude was officialized and defined by the Defence of the Realm Act (abbreviated, like some grotesque nanny, to DORA) which was brought in to ensure national security at a time of war but used, increasingly, to police 'attitude'. A similar outlook affected the arts, when the Masterman Committee recruited artists and writers to interpret the war in a way which would redound to England's greater glory. Needless to say, the sturdy official war art of painters such as Muirhead Bone was quickly proved irrelevant and untruthful when compared to the works of Wyndham Lewis and William Roberts, vorticists both, who had actually fought on the front line and could convey the vertiginous high-speed carnage that reduced men to shell-shocked automata and showed nature, not as an Arcadian or imperial backdrop, but as an indifferent sludge. The war, having been announced as a purge for one form of sickness, had proved itself to be symptomatic of a far deeper malady. As a consequence of this, the revival of 'decadence' in the inter-war years was a powerful weapon against the hypocrisy of the 'old men'.

World War One left England concussed and confused, with ambivalent feelings towards its own identity. There were almost two Englands, the Ancient and the Modern, and young people well-off enough to consider the case could find themselves stranded between them. Illness, it transpired, would remain a suitable metaphor for England's unease. Throughout the 1920s and the 1930s, Arcady was handed over to suburbia and the motor car, the result being that early cultural materialism and democratic consumerism – the twin tenets on which our own period is founded – all fed the spiritual nausea of those young people who saw in this domestication of Arcady a kind of delayed victory for the Victorians. The Victorians, with their Staffordshire pottery dogs and amateur collections of ethnic bric-à-brac, were regarded by the inter-war rebels with an ironic ambivalence; what better way, in terms of decadent wit, to attack the Victorians than to fetishize their culture? This can be seen not only in John Betjeman's camp love affair with Pugin's ecclesiastica (for Betjeman, as we learn from his verse autobiography *Summoned by Bells* (1960), could imagine no fate worse than working for the family firm that had actually provided Victorians with their fancy fittings) but also from Harold Acton's deliberate choice, on arriving at Oxford intent on a career of aesthetic mischief-making, to take rooms in the then hopelessly unfashionable Meadow Buildings at his college of Christ Church. This was attack by ironic appropriation – a form of mockery as protest that would mark the early works of both Waugh and Betjeman.

Evelyn Waugh's first novels, indebted as they are to the surreal logic of *Alice in Wonderland*, satirized England by constantly reversing the status of their characters. In *Decline and Fall* (1928), *Vile Bodies* (1930), and *Scoop* (1938) we are introduced to a succession of sophisticated types who are reduced (or have already been reduced) to near insanity by a world which has gone out of control or bored itself into delirium. Once again, sickness is the principal conceit, both spiritually and morally, as is shown by Agatha Runcible's terminal delirium after entering a motor race, in *Vile Bodies*:

'That's all right, Miss Runcible, that's all right. You mustn't get excited,' said the matron. 'Sister Briggs, run for the ice-pack quickly.'

'All friends here,' said Miss Runcible, smiling radiantly. 'Faster . . . Faster . . . it'll stop all right when the time comes . . .'

That evening Miss Runcible's temperature went rocketing up the chart in a way which aroused great interest throughout the nursing home. Sister Briggs, over her evening cup of cocoa, said she would be sorry to lose that case. Such a nice bright girl – but terribly excitable.

Arcady, for Waugh, was the English country house, which he continued to regard as the definitive statement of civilization: an
organic manifestation of nobility and honour, expressed in the
accumulated art and crystalline architecture of an aristocratic
house and garden. Hence his luxurious description of the young
Charles Ryder's first experience of Brideshead Castle:

> It was an aesthetic education to live within those walls, to wander
> from room to room, from the Soanesque library to the Chinese
> drawing room adazzle with gilt pagodas and nodding mandarins,
> painted paper and Chippendale fret-work, from the Pompeian
> parlour to the great tapestry-hung hall which stood unchanged,
> as it had been designed two hundred and fifty years before; to
> sit, hour by hour, in the shade looking out on the terrace.

In Waugh's earlier works, through to the near-perfect tragedy of *A
Handful of Dust* (1934), he describes the country house as under
attack from ancestral decrepitude within and modernist re-
visionism without. Suburbia, too, has borne down on Waugh's
Arcady. Nina and her hapless fiancé Ginger, in *Vile Bodies*, look
down on suburbia from a party in an airship. Aesthetic repulsion
at the sight of row upon row of neat suburban villas, rather than
her excuse of air-sickness, prompts Nina's one comment on the
view: 'I think I'm going to be sick.'

Certainly, for the young Graham Greene as much as for Betjeman
or Waugh, suburbia – the spiritual home of English pop – held
a morbid, mesmeric fascination which they could neither ignore
nor reject, most probably because they were all suburban sons
themselves. Caught in a dilemma of ambition, these three sub-
urbanites had been educated in the grand Arcady of Oxford (the
perilous sensuality of which Waugh described in the first Book
of *Brideshead Revisited*, 1945, entitled 'Et in Arcadia Ego') but
were really the product of a modern, less opulent sensibility.
They took suburbia with them to the 'dreaming spires', and,
despite longing to be aristocrats, and even pretending to that

role, their rebellion was fuelled by their statelessness. Their lucidity and originality as writers (their wit, most importantly) was the direct result of their being placed in a world where they didn't really belong, at the point of collision between two opposed states of mind: the Arcadian and the suburban. Had Waugh been a real aristocrat, as opposed to a neurotic who tried to play the part, he wouldn't have become a novelist. This statelessness is central to successful articulations of England; the violence of English talent incubates in the frustrations of suburbia or the bland estates on the edges of indifferent conurbations. What turns a spotty Mod into a glorious pop hero is not the glamour of London but the confines of his dismal bedroom in the suburbs.

The allure of infantilism within England's Arcady (the search for lost childhood, lost parents and lost innocence) was a founding principle within the writing of Forster, Lehmann, Waugh and Betjeman, and became articulate as the romantic description of classical education at public schools and Oxbridge. This was typical enough of their class and generation, but it also provided them with perfectly poised venues for their rebellion. In love with the romance of these Arcadian institutions, whose Hellenic ideals had been flattered and underwritten by centuries of arcane tradition, they were at war with the authority that they also represented. Whether Maurice's disdain at what he sees as his College Dean's hypocrisy towards Hellenic friendships, or George Orwell's repudiation of Etonian values, this early class war was very much a matter of Cavaliers and Roundheads, with idealistic (or ideological) romance fighting it out with the forces of unquestioning team spirit. Ultimately, this historic struggle was best described by Lindsay Anderson, in his film *If . . .* (1968) which saw public schoolboys Mick Travis and his Crusaders (English to the backbone) taking on the tyrannical forces of College.

The notion of revolt within a public school had also been rehearsed by Nancy Hayes, in her children's novel of 1947, *The Castle*

School. Hayes, however, reversed the consequences of the rebellion to make a moral point in favour of the school. Neil and Dinah, the heroes of *The Castle School*, are an isolated brother and sister who have made their secret world and their 'enchanted nook' around a romantically ruined tower which stands in the Arcadian countryside which surrounds their home. They can be King and Queen in their private kingdom (the ruins, presumably, of a real seat of power, now overthrown) and they can live unanswerable to the grubby business of communal living and cheerful selflessness that is required by public schools. They are hit by a double blow when their parents, in one of those sudden evaporations which typify children's fiction of the period, decide to go abroad for a year or two and place them in a school for 'sickly children'. The 'sickly' is telling, for although Neil is a bit chesty and Dinah has lost her bloom, the inference is that the Castle School will somehow cure them of their bad attitude. Worse than this is the fact that their new school has bought the very land upon which Neil and Dinah's private Nook of Dreams points its broken finger towards the English sky. Now, far from being their personal kingdom, the nook and all that it represents will become a republic – a coup against which brother and sister pledge all their powers of resistance. When personalized Arcady is placed under threat by all of the imposed jolliness of public school morality, something is bound to snap.

And snap it does. Not content with placing themselves in self-imposed Coventry, Neil and Dinah plot a campaign of terror against their new classmates and teachers. Their greatest moment comes when they drop a sizeable portion of cliff face on the Head Boy, but it is for general surliness that they are locked up in the school gymnasium while awaiting further trial. They escape by swinging on a rope and smashing the gymnasium windows, to face the rage and exile of the romantic who refuses to conform. Which is, of course, a further example of getting above oneself.

In Enid Blyton's *Third Year at Malory Towers* we are shown a similar case of individualism brought down in the tragedy of Mavis, an aspirant opera singer, whose obsession is compared to the level-headedness of another schoolgirl artist, Belinda:

> 'But the worst of Mavis is that she doesn't see that she's only just a schoolgirl, with duties to do and work to get through, and games to play. She's always thinking of that voice of hers – and it's wonderful, we all know that. But what a pity to have a wonderful voice in such a poor sort of person!'

The correct handling of the creative vocation is then put forward.

> Everyone loved Belinda's clever sketches. She really had a gift for drawing, but, unlike Mavis, she was not forever thinking and talking of it, or of her future career. She was a jolly schoolgirl first and foremost, and an artist second.

The case could not be put more clearly: the English Arcadian education demands the subordination of individualism to the demands of team spirit; to withdraw, to question or rebel is a sure sign of illness, vanity and immorality. For Neil and Dinah, in the dramatic climax to *The Castle School*, it takes an earthquake (strange, in Devon, but there you have it) to make them realize their responsibility to the school and all that it stands for. Indeed, the school would not be standing at all were it not for Neil and Dinah's plucky dash from their hideout to warn their teachers of the approaching seismic tremor. Their conversion to collective responsibility stills the hand of God. Surveying the arrested fissure Neil remarks: 'Do you suppose we could have been rotters all along, and never really known?'

We hear an echo of this hard-won enlightenment at the end of *Third Year at Malory Towers*:

> 'I suppose that's what Daddy would call strength of character,' thought Darrell. 'He's always saying that strength of character is one of the greatest things anyone can have, because then they have courage and pluck and determination, no matter what

difficulties come. Bill's got it. I bet she won't dream or gaze out of the window again or not bother with her work. She's going to repay Miss Peters for Saturday night!'

Miss Peters has saved Bill's horse Thunder from crippling indigestion; Mavis, however, is left crushed by her ambition.

Arcadian Englishness would always be entwined with childhood and nostalgia, in terms of its apparent idyllic innocence, and that memory would become more vivid as it was increasingly opposed by the gaining of personal and cultural experience. The Arcadian institutions of Englishness evoked or challenged by the writers, artists and composers who grew up with the century would be seen as gilded theatres in which to act out the rites of passage, and an ambivalence would be derived from the attendant trauma of discovering the childish paradise to be as vulnerable and ambiguous as it was rose-tinted and sacrosanct.

The rebels in England's Arcady, from Maurice and Alec in their greenwood to Mick Travis and his Crusaders firing down on College from the chapel roof, are defending the Arcadian values that they love, passionately, from what they recognize as abuse at the hands of self-serving tyrants and their occupying armies. Despite the overwhelming opposition, they know that England is theirs, and they have dug in for the fight.

wit & warning:
cecil collins, w.h. auden,
the vorticists, derek jarman
& the pet shop boys

Mysticism, in England, has a first function to monitor the spirit of
landscape, Arcadian or otherwise. Even the medieval masons
who carved the tracery and gargoyles at Southwell Minster, near
Nottingham, with an eye to the pagan past and to their own
security, felt obliged to acknowledge the supernatural mysticism
of the woodland deities. In the very heart of the rising Minster,
with a certain audacity, they included some effigies of the pre-
Christian Green Man, tucking them in nooks and crannies in
the circular chamber where the Church Council would meet to
discuss matters of theology and administration. With their carved
mouths extruding foliage and their compressed heads sprouting
leaves, the Green Men have spied on Christian officials for
nearly a thousand years. The masons who carved them, while
probably good Christians themselves, were not quite strong
enough in faith or deficient enough in superstition to deny a
last laugh to the pagan spirits of the woodland whom they

believed had been around since the beginning of time. And, nearly one thousand years later, when artists and propagandists during World War Two were turning to idealized notions of Englishness, the Green Men would pop up again, finally achieving institutional respectability as the cover stars of the British Council's *Sculpture in England* catalogue, published in 1951. Then, as though to redress the mystical balance, their darker, unknowable presence was echoed in the bio-chemical morphing of the astronaut Caroon into a nightmarish piece of living foliage in the English tele-drama of 1953, *Quatermass*. In this version, Caroon's fate can be seen as nature's revenge on unchecked science. Twenty years after that, the young Peter Gabriel would eventually front Genesis wearing a Green Man mask of leaves.

The Green Man is a useful way of understanding England's ambiguous, somewhat covert relationship with non-Christian mysticism. In the twentieth century, from Forster's Hellenism to Richard Long's stone circles, there has always been a need for English culture to acknowledge the workings of a higher erudition. This process of acknowledgement can take the form of visionary poetics and political subversion, more often than not combining the two, and so the mystical, in England, has often lent itself to underground or alternative thinking.

As English culture contains deep strata of mystical feeling, the expression of which is often linked to marginalized political activity, we can find in its theology the romantic idealism of Blake and Shelley. Both of these poets explored numinosity within nature and landscape, their visionary experience giving way to meditations on revolution, republicanism and social justice. In this much, by way of landscape, ecstasy and exile, English romanticism found its way to the mystical through a coded account of the position of the individual to the universe.

From the eighteenth century onwards, mysticism, in England, can be seen to flourish at times of sudden scientific advancement; and this is a trait which it shares with Gothic Romance: as the universe becomes more comprehensible, so we desire the frisson of the unknown or the unknowable. The Industrial Revolution produced, in time, the vogue for Gothic tales of the supernatural; similarly, during the late summer of the Empire, when England was safe in a nannyish relationship with the matriarchal Victoria, there was the cult of Orientalism and the exotic which linked the plumage of the Aesthetic movement to the arcana of European symbolism. Suddenly, owning a peacock screen or some blue and white china was a badge of mystical sympathies. This established, once and for all, the love affair between mysticism and fashionability which would flourish throughout the twentieth century, from the ethnic bric-à-brac fetishized by the Beats and psychedelia, to the corn circle occultism that would be put to brilliant graphical use on the cover of Led Zeppelin's *Re-Masters* anthology.

Mysticism could lend itself to popular protest; hence, in English pop, Marc Bolan's early dedication of his songs to 'Aslan and the Old Narnians', or the colonization of the area around Glastonbury Tor by travellers with a penchant for macrobiotic food and runic sagas. Hence, also, the troubadour mysticism of Donovan at his most idealistic ('Universal Soldier') or the pseudo-Eastern ramblings of Yes at their most extensive (*Tales From Topographic Oceans*). The mystical impulse which doubled as political subversion was sub-contracted to the enduring needs of pop fashionability throughout the late 1960s and early 1970s – and eventually betrayed by the conversion of ideals into sophistry or apathy.

Despite the tribalism associated with mysticism in English popular culture, from Psychik TV's worshippers with their Temple Ov Psychik Youth to the eco-activism of New Age travellers, the principal seers of English mysticism have travelled alone – in keeping with their role. Robert Graves, writing his Preface to *The White Goddess* in 1946, a vital repositioning of the history of myth and mysticism on the reading and writing of poetry in the twentieth century, describes his self-imposed exile in Mallorca as making him 'the fox who has lost his brush':

> I am nobody's servant and have chosen to live on the outskirts of a Majorcan mountain village, Catholic but anti-ecclesiastical, where life is still ruled by the old agricultural cycle. Without my brush, namely my contact with urban civilization, all that I write must read perversely and irrelevantly to such of you as are still geared to the industrial machine.

Further evidence of such disconnection can be found in the writings and paintings of Cecil Collins and, to a lesser extent, the work of E. M. Forster. Both were inspired by the mythology and prehistory of the English landscape, and both evolved a personal mysticism which was at odds with the technological future and the effect of that future on nature. This positions them as artists who serve as mediators between the known and the mysteries of the unknowable – a kind of English shamanism in which the artist could be wounded or exiled by a foreknowledge of our collective folly. This is something of a rehearsal of the hippie values imported from America during the 1960s (and the subsequent rediscovery of those values in the 1990s) but by the time of the Hippie Utopia there was little chance that chemically-enhanced alternative lifestyles, despite their espousal of mystical idealism, could survive unscathed in the face of total capitalism. As fed into the Arcadian formula, the development of English mysticism in the twentieth century can be seen as an attempt to balance the spiritual gravity of Innocence and Experience, with technological progress adding weight to the latter.

Forster, more than Collins, acknowledged the deposition of his Anglo-Hellenic mysticism by the forces of progress and technology. Writing in the Introduction to his collected short stories, in 1947, he gloomily remarked:

> Much has happened since; transport has been disorganized, frontiers rectified on the map and in the spirit, there has been a

second world war, there are preparations for a third, and Fantasy today tends to retreat or to dig herself in or to become apocalyptic out of deference to the atom bomb.

Concluding, he mixes the sagacity of a Cambridge Fellow with the despair of an out-of-work prophet.

Now that the stories are gathered together into a single cover, and are sailing into a world they never foresaw, should they be dedicated anew? Hermes Psychopompous suggests himself, who came to my mind at the beginning of this introduction. He can anyhow stand in the prow and watch the disintegrating sea.

Forster, on the side of nature and free thought, thought more highly of love than he did of books, bookishness or intellectual rationalism. His most convincing characters are those who exchange (not, usually, without a struggle) their spiritual and intellectual claustrophobia for a sudden inhalation of brutally fresh air. This inhalation, which brings with it either rebirth or tragedy, according to the cruelty of the gods, is often prompted in Forster's fiction by some *genius loci* – a challenge from a higher or parallel force which is transmitted through nature and a deeper sense of place to find its way into every crease of suburban complacency. Such a dialogue with unseen forces, which are neither wholly supernatural nor merely literary shorthand for fate, can constitute an English mysticism which accepts that the mystical will touch our daily lives. Released from its natural habitat of poetry, where mysticism was considered acceptable – even compulsory – and seen at work as a force in the polite drawing rooms of Surrey villas, set loose from its aesthetic containers, this mysticism becomes threatening to the blinkered, the muddled or the despotic. Hence the destruction of the local intellectual in Forster's story 'The Celestial Omnibus', or the influence of the Avon stone circles in *The Longest Journey*. Mysticism, for Forster, is the secret weapon of the Arcadian Rebels.

This partially politicized use of mystical consciousness will link the artistic projects of Robert Graves and Cecil Collins, both of whom opposed the eclipse of ancient codes by modernity. Graves puts the case in his Preface to *The White Goddess*:

> The function of poetry is religious invocation of the Muse; its use is the experience of mixed exaltation and horror that her presence excites. But 'nowadays'? Function and use remain the same; only the application has changed. This was once a warning to man that he must keep in harmony with the family of living creatures among which he was born, by obedience to the wishes of the lady of the house; it is now a reminder that he has disregarded the warning, turned the house upside down by capricious experiments in philosophy, science and industry, and brought ruin on himself and his family.

Cecil Collins, whose paintings can be seen as a representation of Graves's argument and Forster's notion of destiny in fiction, was born in Portsmouth in 1908 – the year that the young E. M. Forster published his short story, 'The Machine Stops'. He studied painting at Plymouth School of Art and then at the Royal College of Art, developing a style which was at once luxurious and naïve, vibrant and enigmatic. His colours are rich yet natural, and his subjects – focusing on the Angel and the Fool – are mystical and sacred within the natural landscape. In this much, Collins is an English Chagall, concerned with bringing joy and sorrow to the surface of his paintings and communicating the numinous and the mystical through seemingly simple yet vivid images. Like Forster, his theme is honesty, but he is first and foremost the natural successor to Blake, an artist dealing with Innocence and Experience – the mathematics of being – on his own terms. In his line and watercolour painting of 1940, 'Fool Picking His Nose in Front of a Bishop', Collins expressed a playful irreverence for organized religion which Forster's Mr Emerson – the Pantheist Socialist in *A Room with a View* – would have enjoyed immensely.

In his writings, which match Robert Graves's distrust of 'nowadays' almost point for point, Collins defined a personal credo which rehearsed much of the thinking that would find its way into the mysticism of pop. It is worth remembering that the Fool, within the Tarot, is a subversive figure of wisdom and enlightenment; the gurning grimace of the young John Lennon or John Lydon – part clown and part anarchist – was a continuation of the tradition. Collins describes the artist as an outsider and then as a rebel thinker:

> There was a time when artists were employed to set up altars to the gods of Life in civilizations that were temples, and deep within us we artists must endeavour to remember the services we were once able to give to humanity and to man's deepest experience of reality. To understand this, is to understand why we feel exiles. Beneath our technological civilization, there still flows a living river of human consciousness within which is concentrated in continuity the life of the kingdoms of animals, plants, stars, the earth and the sea, and the life of our ancestors, the flowing generations of men and women: the sensitive and solitary ones, the secret inarticulate longing before the mystery of life. The artist is a vehicle of the continuity of that life and his instrument is the myth and the archetypal image.

> There is a growing awareness that modern culture is approaching a severe crisis and that sooner or later it will have to undergo a ruthless revaluation. That revaluation must reveal the cause of the disorientation of contemporary culture which for so long now has been made a virtue of, or has been accepted without intelligent criticism or questioning.

As the century progressed, and mysticism of this sort was translated into a new language of protest, the mystical impulse within English culture would exchange its Arcadian font for a new urban relevance. The baton of rebellion was handed on.

The history of art in the twentieth century is also the history of psychoanalysis. The sense that one notion of civilization had reached critical mass (a Vortex) with World War One, was matched in art by a need to describe states of mind as opposed to things. This brought modernist art to a dialogue with anxiety and uncertainty, rejecting Arcadian imperialism as either redundant or a dream in poor taste. The vorticist movement, which took root in London just prior to World War One, advocated a manifesto which married aesthetic revolution to the history of ideas. Overseen by Ezra Pound and Wyndham Lewis (an American and a Canadian come to re-energize English art and letters), the vorticists were as significant for their strident opposition to the cultural despotism of the Bloomsbury Group as they were, individually, for their paintings, sculpture and writing. Like most movements, they swiftly reduced to their principal architects – Pound and Lewis – whose mutually prolific output included establishing a blueprint for self-advertisement which would do credit to the most accomplished of the contemporary PR companies.

The Great London Vortex, as defined in what could legitimately be described as the first (and most successful) punk samizdat, *Blast*, was both an attitude towards cultural opposition and a technical proposition for writing, painting and sculpture. Indeed, its two functions were wholly interwoven in the simple listings of those people and phenomena who were to be blasted or blessed (as would be echoed by the early Westwood and McLaren 'list' T-shirt in the late 1970s) and sometimes both, in *Blast*'s editorial. Lewis's later journal, *The Enemy*, which he more or less produced and wrote single-handed, would continue the defiant campaign of the Vortex as both a philosophical enterprise and an act of revolt. Former punks will remember the Vortex as a club contemporary to the Roxy, when English punk rock was similarly taken with the end of history and opposition towards the past; similarly, in English pre-war culture, the term 'vortex' in its

Yeatsian (apocalyptic), vorticist (mystical and aesthetic), and Cowardian (psychological) usage would have the same many-levelled and ambiguous function as the term 'punk' possessed towards the end of the 1970s. It broke cultural boundaries, and existed as a metaphor, a rallying cry and a cultural stance.

Lewis's Vortex, as defined by Pound, was a whirlwind system of 'bringing out all the positive ideas in innovative theories and putting them into a new synthesis'. Addressing such issues as industrialization, speed, and the movement of sculptural planes as energized forces of matter, vorticism had at its heart an urban mysticism which recognized a geometry of modern perceptions but no gods. The idea was to declare war on more or less everyone, from the seemingly sympathetic Italian Futurists (led by the bombastic Marinetti) to Roger Fry and the Omega Workshop. Lewis's novels, such as *Rotting Hill*, *The Apes of God* and *Self-Condemned*, continued the project as vicious satires on cultivated metropolitan life during the inter-war years.

As both a blueprint for punk rock – right down to the celebration of primitive printing, enforced by poverty, that lent *Blast* its brattish immediacy – and as an important development in the history of art, Vorticism derived its power and notoriety from changing Arcadian sadness and speculation for urban anger and obstinacy. The right-wing sympathies of Pound and Lewis (Pound would support Il Duce, with drastic results for his reputation in cultural history) have done much to discredit their radicalism and achievements, but the justifiable squeamishness with which we react to crypto-fascism should be adjusted by remembering the political ugliness with which many cultural figures could be charged. Were the decent Left of the 1920s and 1930s actively supporting Stalin? And, if so, does that erase their writing from the civilized canon? This leads us, by extension, to the punk appropriation of serial killers and Nazism as a part of its founding imagery. To write off such shock tactics as mere irony or publicity-gathering is disingenuous and would not hold up in the courts of political correctitude. Part of the problem is an historical shift away from the reality of content in favour of mere surface – the old chestnut of post-modern 'intentionality'. But while the ramifications of that particular conundrum suggest a devastating erosion of subjectivity, the actual politics of either individual punk rock stars or Ezra Pound and Wyndham Lewis remain embedded in the facts of their biographies, indurate to any 'sign' massaging that cultural theorists might care to employ. Pound's contemptible attitude towards Jews was unfortunately popular, as was Lewis's admiration for Black Shirt rallies. But to separate the art from the man, and the personal opinions from their contemporary index of prejudices, in an attempt to find solid ground upon which to deliver aesthetic judgements, is a cul-de-sac within the practice of criticism. In the case of Pound and Lewis, their ugly politics were stirred into the chemistry of their art to the benefit of its vigour and vision. The complexity of that chemistry cannot be broken down, because it is held together by the internal contradictions within its psychology, which push and pull with equal strength. Hence the simultaneous Blasting and Blessing of various items in *Blast*; hence the double role of twentieth-century art as a history of psychoanalysis.

Vorticism, as an aesthetic response to an accelerating and increasingly technological society, met violence with violence in its description of the new world of mechanized warfare and vertiginous perception. As such, it accepted the loss of Arcadian Innocence as given, and served as the armed advance party of a modernist acknowledgement, even celebration, of Experience. England, compromised by the tragedy of World War One and the lingering shadows cast by the trial of Oscar Wilde, was demanding complex articulations which could be voiced only through an ambivalence towards the institutions and icons of Englishness itself.

This ambivalence, translated into personal politics, was central to the early writings of W. H. Auden. His mysticism, derived from the collision of the Arcadian and urban modernist experience, saw the souring of the European political situation to be as portentous of disaster and the loss of spiritual integrity, as Graves or Collins would see the advance of technology over sacred myth. Auden arrived at Oxford University just as the Arcadian rebels (Waugh, Betjeman, Howard et al.) were going down, and his position as an undergraduate bent on forging a literary reputation for himself was precisely the reverse, in terms of image and social prominence, of the kamikaze dandyism of the previous generation. Auden, in comparison to the pseudo-aristocratic bright young things, was shambolic and nocturnal, with a different index of affectations. Chain-smoking, shunning natural light and wearing a celluloid eye-shade in his rooms, he must have seemed more like an eccentric office worker, busying himself with a kind of psychic Mass Observation, than a typical Oxbridge personality. His image, however, was as realized as those of his more flamboyant predecessors, and one can see a rehearsal of the style directory created in the early 1980s, when suits and a fetishizing of techno-European elegance vied with the trash rococo of New Romanticism – Auden as Neil Tennant to Brian Howard's Boy George.

But, with the standard mixture of contradictions that marks out a key player in the etymology of modern Englishness, Auden was going straight to the heart of a new seriousness – delivered, initially, in the Trojan horse of wit – that would distinguish the writers of the 1930s from those of the 1920s. His growing awareness of the rise of international fascism, and his analysis of what he believed to be a run-down and morally overdrawn England, turned him into a high priest of disenchantment, a role compounded by his upper-middle-class background and his homosexuality. When ordered from the family home, by his uncle, for supporting the General Strike, he replied with disarming charm: 'Mayn't I have my lunch first?', thus rehearsing the fractured relationship between the elder generation and the younger that would lead Billy Fisher's father, in *Billy Liar*, to accuse him of decadence and immaturity because of his 'suede shoes and fountain pens'.

Auden's loaded ambivalence towards England and Englishness found eloquence through his gifts as a mimic and his eye for English detail. In his prose poem *The Orators: An English Study* (1932), he impersonates a speaker invited to address a public school on prize day. Once again, the central conceit is that of illness – shades of Neil and Dinah – and Auden loads irony upon irony in his orator's address: 'Take a look around this hall, for instance. What do you think? What do you think about England, this country of ours where nobody is well?' By evoking Dante's Purgatory, the orator asks the boys to locate the three main groups of sinners in their midst, and to flush out their unhealthy influence. (The programme of moral cleansing that did for Evelyn Waugh's brother at Sherborne.) He concludes with a call to arms that suggests the establishment of a police state:

Now, boys, I want you all to promise me that you'll never be like that. Are you just drifting or thinking of flight? You'd better not. No use saying 'The mater wouldn't like it', or 'For my part I prefer to read Charles Lamb'. Need I remind you that you are no longer living in Ancient Egypt? Time's getting on and I must hurry or I shall miss my train. You've got some pretty stiff changes to make. We simply can't afford any passengers or shrimshankers. I should like to see you make a beginning before I go, now, here. Draw up a list of rotters and slackers, of proscribed persons under headings like this. Committees for municipal or racial improvement – the headmaster. Disbelievers in the occult – the school chaplain. The bogusly cheerful – the games master. The really disgusted – the teacher of modern languages. All these have got to die without issue. Unless my memory fails me there's a stoke hole under the floor of this hall, the Black Hole we called it in my day. New boys were always put in it. Ah, I see I am right. Well, look to it. Quick, guard that door. Stop that man. Good. Now, boys, hustle them, ready, steady – go.

The purge of the Peter Jenkin types is well under way. The orator's speech, with its bluff tone of patriarchal incitement (shades of Baden Powell), can be compared to the speech given by General Denson, in the closing scenes of Lindsay Anderson's film *If . . .*, to the assembled College who are about to be under attack from the Crusaders. The tone and sentiment of Auden's orator find echoes point for point, even the stoke hole reappears – an oubliette for the orator's unclean victims, a means of smoking out College for the Crusaders. General Denson, in fact, could be the orator, sermonizing on the corruption of England:

You're lucky. Yes – a lot of men would give their eyeteeth to be sitting where you are sitting now. You are privileged. Now, for heaven's sake, don't get me wrong. There's nothing the matter with privilege as long as we're ready to pay for it. It's a very sad thing, but today it is fashionable to belittle tradition. The old order that made our nation a living force are for the most part scorned by modern psychiatrists, priests and pundits of all sorts. But what have they got to put in its place? Oh, politicians talk a lot about freedom. Well, freedom is the heritage of every Englishman who speaks with the tongue that Shakespeare spoke. But, you know, we won't stay free unless we are ready to fight.

Five minutes later, needless to say, General Denson is ordering College to break open the armoury to establish bren guns on his right flank, trained on the Crusaders. But, as Lindsay Anderson pointed out in his director's notes to *If . . .*, the Crusaders, as much if not more than the College they rebel against, are English romantics defending the very right to freedom that General Denson describes – but in fact denies – as their 'privilege'. The anarchists and the forces of authority, paradoxically, share the same language.

Auden's gift for mimicry, and the metrical dexterity that allowed

him to make rag-time metre serve poetry, empowered his early
verse with a virtually Cowardian wit. Using the nimble rhythms
of jazz, and a tone of high camp, he could articulate his protest
and disaffection in the 'more-English-than-English' sophistication of a cabaret entertainer. As Betjeman could woo the
bourgeois subjects of his lighter verse by adopting the rhyme
schemes of witty near-doggerel, so Auden could advance masked
behind what Coward sang of as 'a talent to amuse'. For Auden,
anatomizing England as he found it, this style achieves its
apotheosis in his 'Letter to Lord Byron' (1936):

> England, my England – you have been my tutrix –
>   The Mater, on occasions, of the free,
> Or, if you'd rather, Dura Virum Nutrix,
>   Whatever happens I am born of thee;
>   And Englishmen, all foreigners agree,
> Taking them by and large, and as a nation,
> All suffer from an Oedipus fixation.
>
> With all thy faults, of course we love thee still;
>   We'd better for we have to live with you,
> From Rhondda Valley or from Bredon Hill,
>   From Rotherhithe, or Regent Street or Kew,
>   We look you up and down and whistle 'Phew!'
> Mother looks odd today dressed up in peers,
> Slums, aspidistras, shooting-sticks and queers.

Such verses could be intoned with dead-pan, pseudo-scholastic self-
assurance, or lightly sung to a jaunty piano accompaniment in
the style of Cole Porter. There is an ironic detachment in the
language which lends greater emphasis to certain statements,
and underlines the 'England versus England' technique to hone
its sharper points. With its mannered wit and alliteration, this
language could be borrowed straight from Pope's 'Moral Essays',
courting the cartoon-like to deliver its ambiguously magisterial
comments. For instance (from Pope's Epistle II):

> Papillia, wedded to her amorous spark,
> Sighs for the shades – 'How charming is a park!'
> A park is purchased, but the fair he sees
> All bathed in tears – 'Oh odious, odious trees!'
> Ladies, like variegated tulips, show,
> 'Tis to their changes half their charms we owe;

Pope was the godfather of mannered English against mannered Englishness, searching, like Forster, for a resolution of the 'muddle' of the national temperament.

But as a love poet, too, Auden combined quiet lyricism with an acute understanding of loneliness, self-doubt and longing – dropping a level into elegant crooning with an under-current of world-weariness and alienation. Love, like nationhood, is a struggle for clarity against duplicity, sophistry or lies, as here, in 'Dear, Though the Night is Gone' (1936):

> O but what worm of guilt
> Or what malignant doubt
> Am I the victim of;
> That you then, unabashed,
> Did what I never wished,
> And I, submissive, felt
> Unwanted and went out?

By way of their sexuality, their political conscience, their urbane romanticism and their wit, the young Auden and Noël Coward with his pre-war cocktail of wit and emotional intensity, as defined by *The Vortex*, *Hay Fever* and *Design for Living*, are rehearsing much of the melancholy, humour and satire that the Pet Shop Boys were to bring to their own brand of 'pop rush' disco music in the 1980s. Similarly, as authorized by their position as pop stars whose 'talent to amuse' was underwritten by a harder, political agenda of social commentary, the Pet Shop Boys would come to represent their own independent position as ambassadors for an attitude towards their times – as anatomized with flawless perspicacity by Chris Heath in his two books,

Pet Shop Boys, Literally and *Pet Shop Boys versus America*, in which he allows a near-mimetic transcription of their conversation and working schedule to do the work of prolonged analysis and critque.

The Englishness of the Pet Shop Boys manipulates mannered language (the undefended argot of the urban bourgeoisie) and forces it to comment on itself. This, in turn, is emphasized with the sincerity beneath the wit that they share with Auden or Coward. If we look at a disco-stomper like 'I Wouldn't Normally Do That Kind Of Thing', from the *Very* LP, we are more or less in the language of 'Letter to Lord Byron' or 'Mad Dogs and Englishmen':

> I feel like taking all my clothes off
> And dancing to The Rite of Spring,
> And I wouldn't normally do that kind of thing.

or such a couplet as:

> I'm always hoping you'll be faithful,
> But you're not, I suppose,
> We've both given up smoking, 'cos it's fatal,
> so whose matches are those?

from 'So Hard', Drifting between the opulent and the eccentric, in an Englishness peopled with disco divas, self-important celebrities, doomed lovers and funny uncles, the Pet Shop Boys assume, with the least self-consciousness, a combination of melancholy humour and urbane sagacity, thus leading them to flippant resignation in the face of an imagined apocalypse:

> And if it all came to pass now,
> You feel we'd all deserve it somehow.

This ability to turn observations into neatly handled aphorisms has often been employed by English poets to record their witnessing of some quality of Englishness passing for ever. The doomed lover and the despairing social commentator are never far apart in this particular English voice, prompting, for Pet Shop

Boys, the Cowardian internal rhymes and wide-reaching wit of 'Decadence':

> You better change for the better,
> It may be rather intense;
> Stop this caprice, you've got to cease this
> fin-de-siècle pretence.

or the soulfully detached self-awareness of their brilliant elegy to the rites of passage, 'Being Boring'. The opacity of this title sums up the sentimentality of nostalgia as it confronts the maturity of hindsight – an assessment of youth from the fulcrum of early middle age. Small wonder that Pet Shop Boys should record a version of Noël Coward's equivalently poised 'If Love Was All'. But for Auden, Betjeman and Larkin (to say nothing of Coward in his 'London Pride' mood), the treatment of memory and speculation had brought their language of loss and mourning, inevitably, into the orbit of sentimental nationalism. If we regard Auden as left-wing, Larkin as right-wing and Betjeman as apolitical, it is remarkable how similar their feelings about English decline and compromise come across in their poems. For Auden, the tone was striking and embittered, as we see in this untitled poem from 1930:

> Get there if you can and see the land you once were proud
> to own
> Though the roads have almost vanished and the expresses
> never run:
> Smokeless chimneys, damaged bridges, rotting wharves and
> chocked canals,

Such an opening reads like a call to arms – which it is, but not in the expected sense. He continues with this timeless meditation on English inertia:

> On the sopping esplanade or from our dingy lodgings we
> Stare out dully at the rain which falls for miles into the sea.

which rehearses the language and sentiment of Morrissey's pop classic, 'Every Day Is Like Sunday', with its bereft and angry plea:

> This is the coastal town that they forgot to close down,
> Come Armageddon, come Armageddon, come!

Auden, too, concludes with a warning – addressed perhaps to the metropolitan or Oxbridge sophists:

> Shut up talking, charming in the best suits to be had in town,
> Lecturing on navigation while the ship is going down.

Now compare Auden's despair at the fate of the nation with Larkin's poem of 1972 (a world war and a world away from Auden's experience), 'Going, Going':

> And that will be England gone,
> The shadows, the meadows, the lanes,
> The guildhalls, the carved choirs.
> There'll be books; it will linger on
> In galleries; but all that remains
> For us will be concrete and tyres.
>
> Most things are never meant.
> This won't be, most likely: but greeds
> And garbage are too thick-strewn
> To be swept up now, or invent
> Excuses that make them all needs.
> I just think it will happen, soon.

Both Larkin and Auden (and Morrissey), with a mixture of bitterness, resignation and hatred, are mourning some evaluation of Arcady which has been destroyed by its modernizing host culture. And yet none of them is a sentimentalist, or even a convincing patriot. They are – like Neil and Dinah in their private kingdom – reasonably certain that the English have become poor caretakers of Englishness itself, but the precise identity of that Englishness (Democracy? Beauty? Civilization?) is unclear. The real enemy, most probably, was embodied in the likes of Sir Arthur Bryant and his prescriptive notions of what makes the English happy. Interestingly, neither Auden's soft socialism nor Larkin's stage Toryism did much to separate their eventual conclusions on the subject of Nation. In both of them, their ambivalence towards England – their simultaneous love and hatred for the country and its culture – was the refining element of their lucidity.

Auden, however, rehearses the English artist as the exiled prophet, sent off, eventually, on his own flight to America. In a letter to a friend in 1939 he wrote: 'I never wish to see England again. All I want is when this war is over, for all of you to come here.' Auden's self-imposed exile would match that of Graham Greene and Noël Coward. The likes of Larkin would find deeper exile in their own despair.

Bonding, in terms of cultural history, ambivalence and political mysticism as a means of hymning Englishness, and the passing of England from the Arcadian to the atomic age, was the painter, writer, gardener and film-maker, Derek Jarman. All of Jarman's work had one foot in Arcady and the other in the ruins of the atomic age. Later, as a gay man dying of AIDS, illness would enter his work as both metaphor and reality, finding final expression in his last great sequence of paintings, directed to an assistant before he died. Like Collins and Forster, Jarman recognized the symbolic and magical power of nature and his Super-8 footage of the Avebury stone circles, with their sense of psychic witness and flickering impressionism, as well as his garden – the shades of a nuclear winter – at his cottage in the shadow of Dungeness power station, show a continuation of their mysticism. As with Forster and Collins, his mysticism was political in its demand for both honesty and intelligent conservation.

As an artist of contemporary London, Jarman chronicled (in a visual counterpart to 'Being Boring') the social life of a generation; and this had a deep influence on both his aesthetic and his position as an overtly political artist. He had deeply mixed feelings about Ezra Pound (in his notebooks for his film, *The Last of England*, Jarman records: 'I'm fascinated and repelled by him: mad, bad Ez and the usury business. Declared insane by doctors and politicians perjuring themselves to save the SOB from the firing squad. 11 years in the St Elizabeth's asylum until back in Italy he gives the fascist salute as he docks at Naples; up yours!!') but he shared with the vorticists their aesthetic commitment, and, as importantly, their urban vision and rebel art status. Jarman was one of the few artists actually to bring fine art to punk rock – seemingly an anathema – and this was compounded by his making an artistic virtue out of the comparatively low technology that his position, as an initially unfunded radical film-maker, forced him to use. Borrowing from home movies as much as from the style of Warhol's early 'screen tests', Jarman used Super 8 with the dexterity that other artists used oil and turps.

But Jarman was a painter first and foremost, whose obsession with light and colour gave his films their depth of surface and masterly composition. He was a child of World War Two, and his father, an RAF pilot, was a keen amateur film-maker. The English Arcadia in Jarman's own films is sometimes expressed in his use of his father's home-movie footage, thus prompting one of his actresses, Tilda Swinton, to remark: 'They don't make summers like that any more.' And this, in some ways, is precisely the effect, aesthetically and intellectually, that Jarman was hoping to achieve. Collaged into the frequently confrontational and violent substance of his own films, this amateur 'innocent' footage creates a poignancy born of ambiguous mourning, once again, for a lost England.

Rehearsed in his uneasy punk fantasy *Jubilee* (1976), Jarman's lament for England was realized at feature length in *The Last of England* (1987). Punning on the subject and title of Ford Madox Brown's grim portrait of emigrating Englanders, Jarman created a loose narrative of urban survival to describe a national state in which boredom, violence and despair were matched by jingoism, martial law and decay. At once deeply English and viciously anti-English, *The Last of England* is shot through with a mysticism which addresses the dark side of the pop age, its prehistory and drifting psychology. 'The oaks died this year', announces the Tiresian narrator at the beginning of the film, thus marking its Englishness as clearly as the appearance of Elizabeth I's magician, John Dee, in the opening scenes of *Jubilee*.

Parts of *The Last of England* (prophetically, some might argue) were shot in London's Docklands, politically charging the scenes of desolation. As Jarman said in one of the interviews in his film diary:

> After this there are miles of desolation with the odd post-modern office building. Beckton, with its ruined industrial complexes is one of the eeriest places, like a mammoth silent movie set, its buildings dynamited into the craziest angles. Much of the film was shot on these locations: the old Spillers building at Millennium Wharf, the Royal Victoria docks and of course Liverpool – where the 60s housing developments have proved so hostile to the inhabitants. I gave the desolation continuity in the film by relating it to the camouflaged married quarters at RAF Abingdon with their garden fences topped with barbed wire, and RAF Lossiemouth with its H-Blocks.

Such a collage allowed Jarman to capture an urban numinosity which echoes Eliot's symbolic use of the Thames as a river of conscience and consciousness. Within the clichés of advertising and innocuous pop videos, urban detritus is often used to convey street-wise glamour or a one-dimensional morality, thus cheating the scenes of their legibility and mutating them into stylish backdrops for product shots and inane abbreviated narratives. Jarman, however, peopled his wasteland with heroin addicts, aimless wanderers and a sadistic, masked militia who round up the homeless or the disaffected for random execution. Jarman's handling of Docklands was closer to Pasolini than adverts for

building societies and fizzy drinks. Interestingly, Jarman seems
to refer to Powell and Pressburger's *A Matter of Life and Death*
in the sequence in *The Last of England* where a young punk is
found sitting on a dune of rubble playing the Pan Pipes. Lacking
any formal narrative, the film describes the actual and spiritual
wasteland between Innocence and Experience, portraying an
apocalyptic landscape which is real enough to be recognizable,
yet stylized by Jarman's imagery it assumes the fractured logic
and lurid colouring of a dream.

This ambivalence towards England, and the cultural history from
which it stems, was central to the sensibility of English pop.
Jarman's cultural inheritance linked him to punk rock and the
Pet Shop Boys (with whom he worked as a film-maker and
artistic director) as well as to the older tradition of mysticism
defined by Forster and Collins. But Jarman's proximity to his
artistic precursors was possibly shown best in his film of Benjamin Britten's *War Requiem* (1988). A homosexual, like Jarman
(whose gay circle in the 1970s and 1980s could be likened to a
politically active version of the pre-war 'Uranians'), Britten was
within the circle that linked Forster and Auden to John and
Myfanwy Piper and Eric Crozier, with their shared interest in
liberal humanism, English heritage and the coming of the atomic
age. Like painters such as Michael Ayrton, John Craxton and
Leslie Hurrey, whose alternate Arcadian lyricism and modernist
morbidity described the psychology of a national identity *in
extremis*, Britten, as a composer, was both progressively modern
and steeped in the pastoral fables of Englishness – as exemplified
by his Serenade for Tenor, Horn and Strings, with its settings
of Keats, Blake and Tennyson. His *War Requiem* was premiered
at the consecration of Coventry Cathedral (in Philip Larkin's
detested home city) and the work marks a point at which his
music was addressing England's past and future with equal sanc-
tity and gravitas. As such, *War Requiem* was Britten's *Last of
England*, and the notion of a doomed youth inheriting a bankrupt

future was a baton passed on to Jarman which was deftly
received.

Throughout the first five decades of the twentieth century we can
see in the bitter retreat from Arcady the development of an index
of new concerns about what it meant to live and work in England.
The Tudorbethan domestic architecture of Lutyens (described
by the architectural historian Pevsner as an Englishness which
'led the world in 1900') for instance, and all that it stood for,
would be eccentric by 1950. But up until the end of World War
Two, however, nearly all the articulations about the English
condition, as expressed in culture, were from bourgeois or upper-
class artists and writers whose knowledge of reality beyond their
gardens, clubs and diaries was limited at best and affected at
worst. The working classes were much discussed and fashionably
championed, but they were ultimately either denied a voice or
seldom in a position to speak for themselves – a situation which
Edward Upward's crucial trilogy *The Spiral Ascent* (1962–77),
anatomized so well in its account of a literary intellectual of the
1930s attempting to find his political conscience.

As a direct reaction against the Arcadian notion of romantic English
rebellion, with its pitting of upper-class or pseudo-aristocratic
values against themselves, George Orwell's novel *Coming Up for
Air* was supremely radical in both its language – the first-person
narration of a lower-middle-class insurance salesman, George
Bowling – and its cleverly personalized, yet virtually apolitical,
messages of rage, sadness, nostalgia and apathy. Appearing in
1939, the year after Graham Greene's *Brighton Rock* was published, *Coming Up for Air* shares with *Brighton Rock* a vision of
English dissaffection that seems to have more in common with
the concerns of the late 1950s than the late 1930s. And, while
Greene's Catholic interpretation of Brighton's teenage gangland
anticipates the 'delinquency' fables of the 1950s (and would find
success as a film in 1947), so Orwell's George Bowling, a suburban 'five to ten quid a week Fatty', articulates a massive shift

in Englishness which rehearses the postwar voice of the 'little man' from Ealing comedy to *The Rise and Fall of Reginald Perrin*. Bowling's only form of revolt (like that of the insurance clerk Leonard Bast in Forster's *Howards End*) is to steal a brief holiday – in the shape of a covert, mystical pilgrimage – from the commuter train and the office to revisit the countryside of his childhood, in this case a suburbanized village near Reading called Little Binfield. Recalling his boyhood and youth, his experience of war as first horrific and then quite pointless, then recounting his passion for fishing, Bowling, while never swaying into unbeliev-able idealism, puts forward a plea for humanism and common sense in the face of both patriotism and the political sophistry of the Left and Right. Discovering that the woodland around his favourite fishing pool in the grounds of a small county man-sion (now turned into a mental hospital) had been taken over by a progressively soft leftist 'ideal suburb', and that the rest of his village has been expanded by manufacturing industry, Bowling finally gives way to his rage:

> And they'd filled my pool up with tin cans. God rot them and bust them! Say what you like – call it silly, childish, anything – but doesn't it make you puke sometimes to see what they're doing to England, with their bird-baths and their plaster gnomes, and their pixies and tin cans, where the beech woods used to be?
> Sentimental, you say? Anti-social? Oughtn't to prefer trees to men? I say it depends what trees and what men. Not that there's anything one can do about it, except to wish them the pox in their guts.

Orwell, as the literary alter-ego of the Old Etonian Eric Blair, could be argued to belong more to the gilded Arcadians, by way of his education, than to exist alone as a classless voice of prophecy and protest, despite his political drive to fight in Spain and wash dishes in a Parisian hotel. The argument could be made that he 'chose' to write about Wigan (for example) rather than being a genuine product of the working classes. But, like Betjeman,

Waugh and Greene, who also shared a background in either public schooling or Oxbridge, or both, Orwell's articulation of Englishness pursues the ambivalence that Auden pronounced in 'Get there if you can and see the land you once were proud to own'. 'Fatty' Bowling, however, is a wholly credible suburban character, whose voice carries the conviction of the dispossessed Everyman, and his vision of England in 1939 retains a lucidity and honesty that the well-paid, fashionable Left of the post-war period would fail to achieve primarily because of their safe tenure within the university system.

Pop, when it took off in the late 1950s, was a largely working-class response, through the new mass media, to the society and culture which had been inherited from a deliquescing and class-based English society. That class system was still largely intact, despite the rapid progress of democratic consumerism and cultural materialism, but the daily acknowledgement of class as the donor of certain unquestionable rights had been wholly rearranged. Class, held in place by monarchy, would become an issue of central ambivalence within English society – denied by the new Britons in their consumer republic, but slavishly upheld as an idea of traditional Englishness. English pop, however, was empowered with an unstoppable exuberance which was wholly modern. This would lend glamour to protest, new passion to new feelings, and deliver a revolutionary means of communication to a vast section of English society which had been nannied or bullied into obedient silence.

εt in arcadia jocunt

'The working man begins to lose faith,' went on Lofty.
'He loses faith in his boss, he loses faith in the top
dogs who are running the country, and he gets as he
don't want to know.'
'I blame the newspapers,' said Perce.

BILL NAUGHTON, *Alfie* (1966)

In one of those colourful appropriations of a folk hero from one era
to another, Sherlock Holmes found a place in a sequence of
British propaganda films as a Nazi-hunter on the Home Front
during World War Two. In *Sherlock Holmes and the Voice of
Terror* (1942), Holmes, played with sinister elegance by Basil
Rathbone, is accompanied by the Pooh-like Watson to an underworld pub in the East End. Their mission is to persuade Kitty
(a recently bereaved moll) to get her criminal friends to flush
out a traitor who has been giving military secrets to 'The Voice
of Terror' – a Lord Haw-Haw figure who drawls abuse at the
British on his nightly wireless broadcast.
In the pub, which is Dickensian, dank and dangerous for detectives,
there is a dialogue between Holmes and Kitty in which the
former explains that grassing for Britain is both noble and necessary. Police and thieves, urges Holmes, must be united in their
stalking and apprehending of the common Nazi enemy. Roused

by his fervour (the glassy-eyed conviction of a gentleman sleuth) Kitty turns to the crowd of darkly muttering burglars and cut-throats and relays the message of 'England unite!' to them in their own language, as Holmes looks on with quiet paternal pride. She appeals to the hardened element as both a woman and one of their own; she calls the villains to conscience by their first names and nicknames, exhorting them to understand that the traditional hostilities between Scotland Yard and the criminal fraternity must be suspended in the defence of England. 'Udderwise,' she argues, 'yew's all as good as Nazis – everywanna-yew!' Not even her broad Brooklyn accent can dissuade the assembled low-life that this is anything but a cry for help from a regular Cockney sparrer, and, eventually, with shouts of agreement and sudden recollections of vital clues, the mob disperses into the night to carry out Sherlock's demand for information.

The scene is telling, not just in its romantic depiction of an England united in the name of patriotism, but also as a portrait of a class-system that accepts itself as active and distinct. But World War Two, ironically, would complete the erosion of faith in the English class system that had begun with the national nervous breakdown of World War One, when England had discovered that the officer class was neither immune to incompetence nor morally invulnerable. The patrician certainty with which Holmes and Watson could descend on the East End, armoured by their rank as much as by their revolvers, would be lessened by 1949 and wholly rearranged, as an accepted right, by 1959. Interestingly, in 1967, the television documentary based on G. Fletcher's book *The London Nobody Knows* saw James Mason descending on the still Victorian remains of the East End, this time armed with a tweed cap and a tightly rolled umbrella as well as his patrician self-assurance. By then, the gentleman's role as a tourist to a working-class district had changed, in as much as Mason neither judges nor sentimentalizes the lives and landscape of London's less fortunate but leaves the viewer with a collage of naturalistic scenes. As a narrator and as a 'star' Mason's outlandishly aristocratic accent is at odds with his subject, but there is an honesty in both which builds a bridge beyond class. The swinging young people window-shopping outside Kings Road boutiques are described in the same visual language as street callers on East Lane market, and there is a democracy of mediation which makes the film strangely timeless. Such examples of popular naturalism are extremely rare, and *The London Nobody Knows* (with its fascinating visit to Fournier Street, where the artists Gilbert & George would set up a residence, to make their sexually charged self-portraits with attendant contemporary Lambeth Boys) is something of a neglected treasure.

But as informants of English pop music, the new perception of class, 'generation gap', and the technologically accelerated rise of consumerism would be vital. Until 1950, it could be argued, Victoria had never really been off the throne, thus making the immediate postwar decade do the cultural work of half a century. This historical leap, in which Utility furniture and sub-Dickensian lodgings could briefly co-exist as a norm, thus underlining an uneasy relationship between new youth and cultural infirmity, took its preparatory run through the blitzed inner cities and ports left behind by the war in 1946. The prominence of scorched and pitted bomb-sites, in films such as *The Blue Lamp* (1949), do much to remind us that George Dixon's London, as well as Harry Lime's Vienna, was a landscape of stripped and blackened wasteland, with entire postal districts turned into ghost towns. The surviving architecture, with its Victorian confidence subdued and eclipsed by bomb damage, looks deadened and irrelevant, as though the world that it stood for is finished and its only future purpose will be as a picturesque shell. Films and photographs of the blitzed English cities have the jagged and eerie other-worldliness of Graham Sutherland's jarring landscapes, while the melancholy return of nature to the ruins was captured in C. Eliot Hodgkin's rust and leaf-green painting of 'The Haberdashers' Hall' (1945) with its tendrils of twisted metal vying with the flowering weeds beneath an early summer sky. It is as though the sense of 'something passing', which Henry James had noted of the eve of World War One, had finally been realized by the effects of World War Two. What that 'something' might have been seems crucial to the partial vacuum that took up residence in Englishness in the late 1940s and early 1950s.

Evelyn Waugh, who had evoked Arcadian England so luxuriously in the opening book of *Brideshead Revisited*, was no less precise in describing the England embedded in the routine and privations of total war. In his 'Sword of Honour' trilogy, Waugh describes the dawn of a new condition of Englishness, in which his old notions of class, honour and civilization itself have been swept aside. Waugh, rigid with neurotic snobbery, has an instinctive loathing for the new class of Britons who will emerge from the ruins and the fighting. He loathes their cheerfulness and their resignation, their comparative classlessness and their complicity with what will become, over the following two decades, the triumph of cultural materialism. As Waugh predicted this triumph, and its assault on his index of values, there is more than a sense that he felt, as a novelist and a British subject, that the world to which he belonged – with all of its faults and looking-glass reversals of sanity – had had its day. For both the middle-aged Charles Ryder in *Brideshead Revisited*, and the weary Guy Crouchback in the 'Sword of Honour', there is little left save withdrawal and despair; their time and their values have ended, the ejection from Arcady is complete.

Describing the London of 1943 in the final volume of the 'Sword of Honour', *Unconditional Surrender* (who, one wonders, is surrendering to whom on Waugh's particular battlefield – the Germans to the Allies or the upper classes to the workers?), Waugh depicts a greyness of climate and spirit which highlights the tedium of war as well as its terror:

> The day was overcast, damp, misty and still. Winter overcoats had not yet appeared. Each member of the crowd carried a respirator – valuelessness, now, the experts secretly admitted, against any gas the enemy was likely to employ, but still the badge of a people in arms. Women predominated; here and there a serviceman – British, American, Polish, Dutch, French – displayed some pride of appearance; the civilians were shabby and grubby. Some, for it was their lunch hour, munched Woolton pies; others sucked cigarettes made of sweepings from canteen floors. Bombing had ceased for the time being but the livery of air-raid shelter remained the national dress.

The war had not only made the proletariat visible to the officer class, it had also given them certain rights according to its levelling of British society as a whole. And this is more than Waugh can countenance. While he can anatomize the blunders of his own adopted class, who were running the war, he cannot face the working men and women who were actually fighting it. Thus, when Waugh describes the hitherto invisible lower order, it is with reflexive distaste and despair. The ordinary people 'suck' cigarettes, 'munch' their meagre lunches and look 'shabby and grubby'. There is little compassion in Waugh's choice of words and images – he simply doesn't like the drab working Londoners, who, a decade earlier, would have been remote or comic as the servant class to the high society of Belgravia or Oxford.

Waugh localizes his loathing and focuses his premonition of disastrous classlessness on the character of Captain Hooper in *Brideshead Revisited*. Hooper, in Waugh's world-view, lacks the gentlemanly ideals and education to be a real British officer. Hooper is slap-dash and ineffectual; he was not born to rule (as Ryder was, albeit with little enthusiasm, save the sense of superiority born of grim misanthropy) and he represents the new, modern Briton for whom all of the values of civilization which are defined by the house and park of Brideshead Castle are either pointless or comically eccentric. In this much, the conversations between Hooper and Ryder at Brideshead itself (requisitioned, now, as army quarters) are central to Waugh's notion of an old and better world being handed over to a new society which cannot begin to understand its codes of honour, and, by implication, are not entitled by rank to understand them. This, then, is an Arcadian ghost talking to the new council tenant of a haunted house, and communication is lost in a middle mist: 'Hooper had no illusions about the Army – or rather no special illusions distinguishable from the general, enveloping fog from which he observed the universe.'

The modern age, for Waugh, obscuring the sense of Englishness which his work had defined, is this 'enveloping fog' – a malign version of Forster's 'muddle' because there is little or no chance of redemption. Hooper's education has been deficient in the character-building lessons which can be learned only at a public school and Oxford: 'The history they taught him had few battles in it but, instead, a profusion of detail about humane legislation and recent industrial change.' It is almost as though, locked in the loaded and specific reference to 'humane legislation and recent industrial change', Waugh is preparing his coda for the Arcadian symphony – the modern world starts here, with its revisionist history and (for Waugh, one suspects) the dubious application of socialism to education. In Hooper, the meek, who will stride like a colossus across the post-war landscape of council houses, tower blocks, the Welfare State and pop music, there is embodied an entire shift in values and perception, thus setting the new world in concrete:

In the weeks that we were together Hooper became a symbol to me of Young England, so that whenever I read some public utterance proclaiming what Youth demanded in the Future and what the world owed to Youth, I would test these general statements by substituting 'Hooper' and seeing if they still

seemed plausible. Thus in the dark hour before reveille I sometimes pondered: 'Hooper Rallies', 'Hooper Hostels', 'International Hooper Cooperation', and 'the Religion of Hooper'. He
was the acid test of all these alloys.

Waugh's brilliance as a novelist in depicting the twilight of one age
and the dawn of another is matched by his perspicacity as a
prophet and social historian. Distasteful though his snobbishness
might be, there is an accuracy in his speculations which predicts
the mute momentum of post-war Britain's rush towards total
consumerism and rampant bureaucracy. Ultimately, neither
Hooper nor Ryder (as cyphers) are 'right'; they stand on opposite
sides of an historic membrane which has been created by the
war and the collision of the past into the future: 'until, in sudden
frost, came the age of Hooper.' Teenagers, too, as a new social
group with its own language, rights and philosophy, would be
born of this collision and 'the age of Hooper'.

For Betjeman, the passing of the pre-war world was experienced,
primarily, through an experience of place and architecture. As
a young reporter on the *Architectural Review*, Betjeman had
expanded his amateur enthusiasm about English buildings into a
professional awareness of new developments and town planning.
Hence, in many ways, the tender sentimentality of his poem
'Margate, 1940', with its conclusion:

> And I think as the fairy-lit sights I recall,
> It is these we are fighting for, foremost of all.

Betjeman – unfairly doomed to become the nation's teddy bear Poet
Laureate, despite the bitter realism of much of his verse – was,
however, level-headed in his melancholy at 'something passing'
in comparison to Waugh's poisonous mixture of bitterness and
despair. It was maybe telling of Waugh's post-war depression
(and decline into neurasthenic paranoia) that his first book after
the war, *The Loved One* (1948) (*Brideshead Revisited* having been
published in 1945), should have been a deeply morbid satire on

the Californian death industry and, by extension, on modern consumerism in general. *The Loved One* is another excursion into *Alice in Wonderland* illogicality, only more nightmarish than funny and peopled, in effect, by a cast of literal and symbolic corpses. Waugh is virtually dancing on his own grave, as though caught up in a gleeful wake of hate and self-hatred for everything that has passed and everything that the New World (and the new world) will deliver. This new world, in England, was all that Waugh had foreseen and rejected in the character of Hooper and the spiritual retreat of Captains Ryder and Crouchback; it would also be the England that Larkin would inherit as his subject matter, as a poet for whom deprivation was the equivalent of Wordsworth's daffodils. The post-war credo of 'Making do and getting by', the Festival of Britain and the successful importation of rock-'n'-roll were a civilization away from either Brideshead Castle (Larkin could have written a vicious description, doubtless, of day-trippers parking their cars in the grounds of Brideshead) or Betjeman's 'fairy-lit sights'. The 'something' which had passed for ever was a spiritual and national centrality, bound in iron by class, that kept all things in their traditional English order regardless of fairness or reason.

⊞

A strong case could be made for the proposition that the English novel as a naturalistic art form, rooted in Fielding and the traditions of mannered comedy, came to an end with Waugh's 'Sword of Honour' trilogy, published in three volumes between 1952 and 1961. The concerns of naturalistic fiction (although not the sympathies) can be seen to have passed into a new form of cinema, in which the business of telling straightforward stories about the new modern world became the principal mirror of a changed and changing England. The establishment, in 1956, of 'Free Cinema', by film-makers Lindsay Anderson, Karel Reisz and Tony Richardson, would have this agenda at its heart. This undertaking was neatly encapsulated by the scriptwriter Ted Willis, who wrote, among others, *Woman in a Dressing Gown*, and created the character of George Dixon: 'They [both] deal with the mundane, the ordinary and the untheatrical. The main characters are typical rather than exceptional: the situations are easily identifiable by the audience; and the relationships are as common as people . . . I am just now becoming aware of this area, this marvellous world of the ordinary.'

Written in 1959, this statement, to Waugh, Old Bloomsbury or the self-elected praetorian guard of English belles lettres, would have seemed like the Red Flag being hoisted over England; it was all summed up in that phrase: 'the relationships are as common as people'. But the common had been well-rehearsed, from Flaubert to Chekhov – if differing from 'Free Cinema' as empowered by their rejection of political judgement in favour of artistic purity; the importation to England of nineteenth-century naturalism, however, would require cinema to harness its potential, in or out of political service. The 'greyness' which Waugh had recoiled from in *Unconditional Surrender* would assume relevance and meaning in the kitchen sink school of film-making, and the stories which emerged would be among the first fictions of the pop age. The baton of story-telling in the new age had been taken by Britain's young cinema, and the concerns of that cinema were the ordinary problems or perks of being young in a modern society. The Age of Hooper had arrived, but it was neither the cultural desert nor social graveyard that Waugh had supposed.

Throughout the 1950s and early 1960s, realist films such as *Saturday Night and Sunday Morning*, *A Taste of Honey*, *A Kind of Loving* and *The Loneliness of the Long Distance Runner* would manage to blend the bleakness of Chekhovian story-telling with a new vernacular humour to show life as it really was for the reinvented working and suburban classes of post-war England. *Billy Liar* would be the *Hamlet* of this new theatre, agonizing beneath the clay-white skies of Stradhoughton.

These excursions into realism would be matched by the so-called 'problem' films that explored and exploited the pop phenomenon of teenagers and delinquency. With irresistible titles such as *Violent Playground*, *I Believe in You*, *The Leather Boys* and *No Trees in the Street*, the problem films were the best possible propaganda, ironically, for delinquency itself. Mingling the charged sparseness of a documentary with the super-cool styling of early teenage and rocker fashions, they described a rebellion which was as English as *The Wild One* or *Rebel Without a Cause* were richly American. These films ooze the English pop sensibility from every frame: confrontational, brattish, tense, erotic, moody, harsh and funny. In the filmed faces of these first, ordinary British teenagers, with their poor skin, heavy lidded eyes and gawky youthfulness, one can almost see the proximity of Dickens to early British Beat music; there is none of the glamorous tan and smooth-complexioned allure that one associates with the wholly modern teenagers of American popular culture of the same era.

As popular entertainment, the new cinema rejected the baggage of self-conscious intellectualization; as the response of youth to the post-war austerity, they picked up on the dissatisfaction of hitherto silenced age-groups and classes. It was as though an entire area of the English experience had suddenly been opened up. The war had authorized the right to be heard, and the sudden rush of pop culture towards the end of the 1950s was certain evidence that too much feeling had been dammed up for too long, and was simply waiting for the right formula of feeling and technology to release it. And, as usual in England, there was both an official and an unofficial announcement of this feeling.

The Festival of Britain, in 1951, was created and staged as a tonic for the nation on London's South Bank. The festival was both a throw-back to the Victorian practice of celebrating the

63

treasures and triumphs of Empire by way of a popular public exhibition (part fun fair, part museum) and a means of introducing the survivors of total war to the potential of the modern age. The festival's logo – a stylized Britannia – was designed by Abram Games and described the spirit of the projected new age in its clear, geometric design of four shaded compass points with the head of Britannia in profile. The axes of the points were linked by a line of bunting, and the year, 1951, was printed as two groups of italicized digits on either side of the southernmost compass point. Initially, this symbol (as it appears on the cover of the festival's souvenir brochure) seems so simple as to be banal, but there is a lightness of touch and clarity of line to the design which belies its eloquence as a wholly new statement. It should be considered in comparison to all of the clutter and bombast with which such an image would have been weighed down before the war. Here, in 1951, light, space, straight lines and openness are the basis of contemporary design, to be picked up in every area from graphics to kitchenware. This revolution in design represented a massive unclogging of English taste, and an unprecedented dialogue with what Betjeman had described as 'beastly abroad'. Indeed, the openness and modernity of British design in the 1950s was not only heliotropic and progressive but, vitally, commercial and democratic. It invited usage and participation from everyone, to make the new suburbs (replacing the old slums) sunnier, sophistication less formal and the daily business of living a largely classless activity. This is not to say that design in the 1950s lacked artistry, craft or subtlety; rather, products (as opposed to class-bound ornaments or functional items) were being created and manufactured which were audacious in their colour and bold use of new materials. Exquisite ceramics from, for instance, Beswick or Midwinter, showed an elegant use of primary colour as a complement to a near graphical style, in which organic forms reminiscent of sculpture by Hepworth or Moore were tempered with domestic prettiness while retaining a scientific strangeness that was utterly modern. 'Atomic' modular designs would follow, anticipating a benign scientific future which said more about Robbie the Robot than the Campaign for Nuclear Disarmament. Above all, the consumer revolution that took off from the Festival of Britain was designed to be open and exuberant, offering better living for everyone at a time of austerity and rebuilding, as well as a distant horizon of new opportunities. Most important of all, as the corner-stone of the pop age, a thing called 'lifestyle' was being actively marketed as a product available for cash down or on HP. With designs called 'Beautility' or 'HomeMaker', the 1950s saw the new Trinity of 'Lifestyle', 'Marketing' and 'Credit' (in a primitive form) taking their guiding place as the three faces of the new god: democratic consumerism. The dark side of this deity, cultural materialism, was what Waugh had perhaps feared in his own weird way, and what the new pop rebels would eventually discover as the retooled, plastic Arcady – another false democracy supported by its own controlling culture, at once despotic and desirable.

The 1950s began by urging a brighter, healthier lifestyle from official heights. The new designs, for instance, suggested a conformity that would be for everyone's benefit. The adverts carried in the official brochure to the Festival of Britain (price 2/6d) were a blueprint for all the new England would stand for, and they were utterly prophetic in their enduring sentiments.

For Shell we have: 'In Festival Year our windows frame a new horizon – a signal of Britain's recovery in which Shell-Mex and B.P. are proudly playing their part.'

And for Cow & Gate:

Royal Babies: we all know that a Royal Baby is bound to be given the best that is obtainable. Twelve Royal Babies to date have been fed on Cow & Gate. Can you do better for your baby? Have the lifelong happiness and satisfaction of knowing that your baby also had the best that money could buy, and the best possible start in life. Get a tin from your chemist today.

And for Creda and Simplex: 'Ours is a nice house, ours is Creda and Simplex – products from one House.'

All the ingredients of contemporary advertising and consumerism are being rehearsed, from benign corporations to caring companies that unite society (it will become 'the planet') as a nuclear family whose purchases and purchased lifestyle make *moral* sense. Also, Arcady has signed up in the service of advertising (that will also become 'the planet' or 'the environment') with a leg-up from Heritage, as can be seen in this advert for Bass & Worthington, with its stirring neo-Georgian sentiment:

This England . . . He who plants an avenue of trees, cannot, in the nature of things, hope to enjoy them in their grandeur – he plants them for England. Much that we have and prize today comes of that attitude in our fathers. They did not make or build to 'last their time', but rather that something worthy should mark their passage – their good lives after them. We, too, must keep this tradition of the thing well made, that our children's children may be beholden unto us. Even in simple matters it can be done; are we not beholden to some centuries of careful craft-proud men, that such a daily need as Bass (or is yours Worthington?) is so superbly filled?

Subjecting the complex syntax of this copy to a brief practical criticism (even allowing for the copy-writer's tongue being slightly in his cheek) we can see how the moral imperatives are built up in a crescendo of edification prior to the cheeky wasp-sting of the product line: 'such a daily need as Bass'. Having established its high-blown tone and language, the advert attempts to include its product in the orbit of that philosophy, however incongruously it may fit. With its stretched associations between national pride, English heritage and brand-profiling, this is the moral universe inhabited by Powell and Pressburger being harnessed to sell beer. It is a formula that will be honed to perfection in the 1980s, on a global canvas, when plaintive dolphins and vanishing rainforests can be used to sell bank accounts and casual clothing.

The new consumerism took all of these moral imperatives – national pride, collective responsibility, pioneering vision, family values and stylized heritage – as the common language for its advertising. In this much, the Festival of Britain was a sorely needed advert for a bright new Britain; but contemporary cynics remarked (famously) that the near invisible means of support which tethered the festival's giant sculpture, the Skylon, was symbolic also of the state of the nation. The Festival of Britain promised much to a nation worn out by rationing, bad housing, disrupted lives and bereavement, but how much of this desperately required comfort and security in the Peace could actually be delivered?

The whole public image was based, understandably, on positivity, pleasantness and pride; pop, while fetishizing the modern as its only known condition, would also take these values but subject them to ruthless and impatient questioning. Where and what was this bright new Britain that youth were being prepared to inherit? What was so good about it, anyway? The first pop outlaws of 1959, the Edwardians and Rockers, didn't want to be told that 'they'd never had it so good' – primarily because they'd never had anything in the first place. Hence the social problem films and the styling of delinquency; hence the development in English pop away from mere Americanized entertainment towards something which, received as sound and sensibility, was far more threatening to English society. The question being asked (with the unfairness of youth) was what did Britain fail to deliver between the Festival of Britain and the Bill Haley riots? The pattern of English subversion, as a side-line of youth, had been rehearsed throughout the twentieth century, as decadence or satire, but the latest version – the pop version – was far wider spread and being carried by a generation for whom class was less important than cash in hand.

An unexpected response to the Festival of Britain was given by Noël Coward in his controversial song, 'Don't Make Fun Of The Fair'. Coward had served on the advisory board of the festival, only to resign in despair at the bureaucracy by which the plans were hampered. Coward's viciously funny lyric makes painfully public the gaping discrepancy between the festival's national drive and the temper of post-war Britain:

We down-trodden British must learn to be skittish
and give an impression of devil may care
to the wide wide world, we'll sing God for Harry
– and if it all turns out all right, knight Gerald Barry.
Peace and dignity we may lack, but wave the jolly
Trade Union Jack and don't make fun of the Fair.
We've never been exactly keen on showing off or swank,
but as they say the gay display means money in the bank;
so we'll make the wretched welkin ring from Penge
to John O'Groats, and cheer and shout and laugh
and sing before we cut our throats.
We know we're caught but we must support this
patriotic prank, and though we'd rather have shot ourselves
we've got ourselves to thank;
Even if nobody comes, don't be conscience-smitten,
If no overseas trade appears we'll have to work for a thousand
years to pay for the Festival of Britain!

On the axis of politically charged English camp, with W. H. Auden and Gilbert and Sullivan as its principal co-ordinates, Coward's point that the patriotic bluster of the Festival of Britain was somewhat out of line with the spirit of the people marks the beginnings of a post-war satire that would be central to early Ealing comedy. While the national standing order was for the whole country to pull together to rebuild, the reality (comic or not) was a sense of resignation among ordinary people in the face of new monoliths, be they government ministries or trades unions. It was as though the old notion of masters and servants had been replaced by a new concept of 'us and them' fatalism – 'them' being everyone in a position of authority from park keepers to the Prime Minister. Ealing comedies such as *The Titfield Thunderbolt* and *Passport to Pimlico*, to say nothing of *I'm All Right Jack*, *The Man in the White Suit* and the early 'Carry Ons', were all concerned in one way or another with the 'little man' fighting back against the power of committees and men in bowler hats – usually summed up in the worried features of Richard Wattis. Often sentimental, these comedies described a new concept of Englishness which was sympathetic, nationally, to the grimmer fables of social realism being told in the kitchen-sink films of the same period. In 1960, the two faces of modern England – one comic, one tragic – would appear to be combined in Anthony Newley's brilliant creation of Gurney Slade, in the radical TV comedy, *The Strange World of Gurney Slade*. Rehearsing the fabulism of Lindsay Anderson's *O Lucky Man!* – in which the anarchist hero Mick Travis is revived as a coffee salesman, trapped in a perilous journey around a corrupt and meaningless England – and mixing it with the pessimism of *Billy Liar*, Newley made Gurney Slade a kind of proto-Mod Norman Wisdom. 'I'm just a walking TV show,' he complains to the camera at the end of the pilot episode. 'Just leave me alone! I've got Big Brother watching me, and Big Sister, and Big Mum. Clear off out of it; I'll have the law on you . . .' The camera relentlessly follows Gurney down a quiet London street until he is out of shot – still complaining.

Noël Coward's satire hinted at the point that many people in Britain could see little for themselves in the new spirit of enterprise, and that the supposed benefits they would enjoy brought with them a whole new set of problems. And this would be particularly acute in young people and teenagers. The gradual move towards better housing, more leisure time and better pay were all enablers of the pop sensibility, from the invention of cheap radios and record players to income for hairstyling and clothes, but these benefits in themselves could not address some deeper, half-formed mood that the pop generation was born with. Despite the advances of the new Britain, many young people still felt trapped and marginalized; they weren't exactly angry, but they were bored and confused and they wanted something to happen.

As a black American musical form, laundered for a white audience first by Sinatra and then by Elvis, pop music (by which we mean rock-'n'-roll as derived from gospel and swing) and popular culture had grown up, organically, in a continent that was young, wealthy and warm. In Britain – which was old, poor and cold – pop was both incongruous and intensified by the host culture into whose arms it had crashed so dramatically. England in the 1950s was low on diners, palm trees, rocket-finned automobiles and semi-tropical High School society. Thus, a black phenomenon which had turned white in the desperate rural poverty of southern America was suddenly transported, by way of GIs posted to the UK (American air bases such as Burtonwood, in Liverpool, served as cultural ports) like an exotic animal to a country which was wholly the reverse of its natural habitat. Post-war England, to say nothing of post-war London (as we can see from films as different as *Sapphire*, 1959, and *We are the Lambeth Boys*, 1958) was still Victorian and institutional in appearance, with its bombed and shabby buildings, narrow shop fronts, neo-Gothic city centre and archaic street furniture. And pop stood out like a sore thumb to be sucked.

But pop's firm domination of English youth did not happen with the release of one record (although 'Heartbreak Hotel' and 'Rock Around The Clock' can be considered fair contenders for that honourable role) or the revolution of one hairstyle. Pop, in England, was a burning fuse of imported ideas and entertainment; there could be no easy delivery of a phenomenon which would affect the younger generation in every aspect of modern urban

70

living from race relations to sexual politics. England's conception of itself as a nation of moderates, however, was placed under threat by a mass-media movement in which the younger generation recognized its one ally, made real by discs, clothes and coffee-bars. And pop, a youngster itself, would accelerate with the speed of youth in the early 1960s, having required a few guinea pigs upon which to test its potency. British rock-'n'-roll in the 1950s, however, had a colossal impact in the laboratory of popular culture. 'Don't You Rock Me Daddy Oh', in 1957, would sound like 'Anarchy In The UK'.

Turning once again to English cinema, we can see that a generation of pallid and socially harnessed young people did not become rebels without causes overnight; there was an endearing mezzanine of awkwardness to be overcome (as we see in the lonely progress of Geoffrey in Shelagh Delaney's *A Taste of Honey*, with his child-like sexuality placed at odds with the emotional turmoil of a pregnant teenager), and this mezzanine, more often than not, revealed the pop age's first dialogue with 'issues': race (*Sapphire*), homosexuality (*Victim*), sexual freedom (*A Kind of Loving*), and the workplace (*Saturday Night and Sunday Morning*). Many of the social problem films in the 1950s and early 1960s showed one generation's anger and frustration at being caught between the old world and the new. Delinquency itself (if delinquency can mean civil disobedience as a necessary response to an unlivable situation) was almost a rallying cry for all young people to discover their delinquent selves, as though a collective rite of passage had to be endured if pop was to grow up and take hold.

Pop's first real villains were perceived to be the Edwardians (or Teddy Boys) who always represented the thuggish and bigoted element of the new youth. More often than not, however, in the social problem films, Teddy Boys are merely 'folk devils' to whom a much broader violence or prejudice is attributed as though to remove the blame from society in general. In *Sapphire*, for instance, where racial prejudice and small-mindedness are the actual villains of the piece, we see Johnny, a black man, being chased through the deserted streets of Shepherd's Bush and denied sanctuary by a newsagent who 'dursn't crorse the Teds!' With their 'Edwardian suits, dance music and a dagger!', the Teds were the first inkling that pop as a social force could turn nasty, but their violence was symptomatic of the deeper national neurosis brought on by enforced growing pains.

The late 1950s and early 1960s, despite the undergraduate fad for 'trad jazz', saw a stream of British pop records that were unstoppable in their sheer exuberance. The first wave of British pop stars, from Alma Cogan to Billy Fury, Dickie Pride, Vince Eager, Cliff Richard and a host of lesser names, made records that were joyous, dramatic and wholly unself-conscious. It was music to dance to, fall in love to and dream to; and despite its comparative innocence it authorized a new attitude and a new language which was breathlessly glamorous and volatile when placed beside all that had gone before. Billy Fury's gold lamé suit marked the zenith of this epoch: a working-class boy from Liverpool with a clumsy surname (Ronnie Wycherley) who was moulded by Larry Parnes and Jack Good into Birkenhead's answer to Elvis. A star like Fury embodied sex, danger and romance simultaneously, while singing with a melodramatic croon or snarl that lifted him way above the run-of-the-mill cheeky rockers like Tommy Steele or Jim Dale. Also, he inaugurated pop's alchemical promise to turn nobodys into big stars.

Pop stars such as Billy Fury did much to suggest that all pop, *per se*, was a form of protest art. Most of all, pop described its own world, and its message leaked in and out, as though osmotically, through the humdrum lives of its audience. From old rocking standards that had been Anglicized, like 'School Days (Ring Ring Goes The Bell)' (covered in Britain by Don Lang and His Frantic Five) through to the teenage romanticism of numbers like 'Teen-age Love' (by the Five Chesternuts), pop was creating a language which authorized a new way of life. Hitherto, particularly for the young working classes, there had been no way of expressing one's life (let alone one's sense of difference) either individually or collectively. (Imagine the usefulness of rock-'n'-roll to decadents like Neil and Dinah.) But, as English pop gathered momentum, and consumerism became complicit with its potential market value, pop could either be domesticated or extrapolated as a threat to English society. Yet for most teenagers of the period (as we can see from a documentary like *We are the Lambeth Boys* with its study of working-class teenagers in Alford House – a south London council estate youth club) pop was not there to be analysed or even thought about. Pop's first audience still had to contend with an England that was 'making do and getting by', and the business of 'business as usual' could be the ultimate frustration for young people. In *We are the Lambeth Boys*, for instance, we hear that: 'Beryl sits on a bench in a factory, making food. She'll probably stay there until she gets married.' Time and again in films of the period, we see the struggle of ordinary young men and women (not the hardened, multi-culturally aware proto-beats, who were pretty thin on the ground at this time) as they try to come to terms with the archaic values of the older generation on the one hand (for whom duty was the basis of pride, family and prosperity) and the increasingly facile notions of a new Utopia being offered on the other. Thus, a walk down the High Street with one's parents, in 1960, could present the disaffected teenager with little choice other than 'rebel or conform'. But rebellion, in England, was never easy. It was hard to be the Wild One or Jim Stark in Surbiton or Stoke. But this didn't stop people trying.

The first pop fashions in England – Edwardians, Rockers, Beats – offered escape from and protest against the orthodoxy of English culture. But England either feared or ridiculed what was happening in the seismic shock of the 'youthquake', and, taking its lead from the moral code of suburban America, set about denying that pop could mean anything but decadence and trouble. What was required was clean pop (like Russia needed a communist Elvis) and this was supplied first by Cliff Richard, whose *Summer Holiday* did as good a moral face-lift on teenagers (by way of a squeaky clean Beat cellar in Paris and a miniature operetta in a *bier keller* with the lyric: 'I have the urge to wear short leather trousers and dance with a fraulein to waltzes by Strausses') as could be expected for the money. The Beatles, too, once they had been shoe-horned into matching suits and put in the Royal Variety show, would briefly be the 'Condy's Fluid' for teenage decadence, flushing out potential moral sickness like a lovable brand of disinfectant. But the Beatles would turn weird and Cliff would settle for his own spiritual path, and pop could live quite happily with its burgeoning reputation for leading decent young people astray. By 1964, with Number One hits from the Rolling Stones, the Kinks and the mutating Beatles, pop had developed its own reflex against bland entertainment to keep in step with the quickening curiosity of English youth. Add to this the first Art Mod rumbling that would come from groups like the Action, the Creation and the Eyes and you had the beginnings of a pop underground that was more effective and more engaging than the main line of commercial pop entertainment. It was a short step in time from Cliff to Cream, but a massive leap for the pop sensibility.

Pop, in fact, was eating itself, in a vertiginous series of reinventions that would make Malcolm McDowell's gold lamé suit – which he wore in his allegorical journey around England in Lindsay Anderson's *O Lucky Man!* in 1971 – acquire an almost mystical significance as the mantle inherited from Billy Fury's pop rebel image of 1960. The pop entertainer would become – gold lamé suit and all – the cheated Pilgrim trying to make sense of his Progress, echoing, perhaps, Jack Good's astute choice of quotation from *Macbeth* in his naming of Billy Fury's first LP: 'It is a tale told by an idiot, full of sound and fury, signifying nothing.' Jack Good's Billy Fury and Lindsay Anderson's Mick Travis –

twin rebels in gold lamé suits – would turn out to have been on the same spiritual journey through England all along. They simply took different routes.

method acting in Birmingham, London & coventry

> I won't dance, in a club like this,
> All the girls are slags
> And the beer tastes just like piss.

'NITE KLUB' *The Specials* (1979)

It is tempting to imagine the career of Waugh's Captain Hooper after the novel and the war have ended. He might have returned to his old job – held open by an indulgent boss – and enjoyed a feather's weight more respect in the office because of his respectable service record. Away from the hostile and bewildering atmosphere of an officers' mess, which he could never see the point of and never felt at ease in, he could resume civilian life with the comforting sensation that it was easier to be affable and informal – one of the boys at work and at play, in the pub, the staff canteen and the golf club. He had never worked out the rarefied stratifications of class, anyway. With a new suit, a company car and a bit more in the wage packet, he might settle down with a girl who was a good sport (met at a dance hall one Friday night) and with her raise a family. 'Yes. I've got two of my own now,' he might say with an indulgent chuckle in 1950, producing a crinkle-edged snapshot from his wallet towards the end of a pub lunch in Staines. The two children ('the little terrors!') would answer the official prayer of central government for a boy and a girl; and affable, classless Hooper, surrounded by thousands of other Hoopers, would be the slightly ineffectual patriarch to a pair of teenagers in the making. These were the new suburban classes. Hooper's children would maybe grow up with memories of Joe Brown and the Bruvvers or Tommy Steele. In the early pop of their childhood, where endless lonesome Johnnies were being pined for by a legion of Little Sues, the power struggles of rock-'n'-roll courtly love made quaint fables. Boys were boys and girls were most definitely girls – havin' crushes, breakin' hearts and longin' for nothing but love.

Innocent and charming, early British pop could describe a world of romance that was defined in the pretty colours of a John Hinde picture postcard by Cliff Richard and Una Stubbs in *Summer Holiday*. Indeed, John Hinde's description of his postcard art could double as a description of *Summer Holiday*'s notion of teenage love: 'Using the medium of colour photography I wish to emphasize the beautiful aspects of the world in which we live and to present these images in a style which would enable them to be instantly understood and appreciated by a mass audience.' This is the graphical equivalent of Cliff singing 'Bachelor Boy' (with the wonderful dance routine by the Shadows) or Una and the girls pairing off, inevitably, with the other three boys on the bus. This was a long way from the last gurglings of the monochrome kitchen sink. It was, in fact, as though the kitchen sink had never existed.

But as English pop matured, so too did its exploration of the self, requiring more than love and marriage as the end result of its inquiries. Pop, so adept at describing modern romance, could turn to the grimmer business of describing modernity itself. This would have particular ramifications for those pop boys who, having inherited a damply British version of Jimmy Dean's troubled psyche, might want to sing about being male in the modern world. Suddenly (by the time the Who hit Shepherd's Bush) just having a girlfriend wasn't enough. If English Mods were attracted to the style, if not the small print, of Left Bank Parisian cool, then perhaps they would tune in, vicariously, to the existential crisis of their teenage sexuality? More likely, they would either grow out of it or take a load of acid three years later, but Mod, with its pursuit of originality above all else, opened up a Pandora's Box of new perceptions that brought with them new responsibilities to feeling. The old world wasn't in place any longer: there were drugs which made life faster or slower, more real or less real; there was an expanding underworld of clubs, music and fashion in which one could get lost for ever. There were black teenagers in your class. And if the boys were allowed to be as vain and fashion-conscious as the girls, there was also the realization that gender, presumed robust and inviolable, was open to investigation.

Mod's experiments with the concepts of self, sexuality and identity (need we look further than 'Substitute', 'I'm A Boy' and 'My Generation'?) brought up every issue in the psychoanalyst's handbook, from primal rage to hypersensitivity, and out of these experiences, vividly articulated by rhythm and blues, soul or early psychedelia, came a version of manhood which blended melancholy, anger and a quest for sincerity with what it actually meant to be young and male in modern Britain. In short, Mod brought Method Acting to English pop, and with it the ability to express pain and isolation as well as teenage camaraderie and the kisses of for-ever.

The idea that bad boys (teenage delinquents as thugs with feelings) could see further than their small town and their immediate position in the food chain had, of course, been rehearsed by Dean and Brando in American cinema. 'Exploitation' films, in England, had covered hard morality as soft pornography, but there was often the same message: self-realization was learned the hard way; for the tough to be truly tough there were bloody rites of initiation to be endured, to say nothing of public exile and humiliation in front of the whole tribe. *Violent Playground* (1958), *Room at the Top* (1959), *A Kind of Loving* (1962), and *The Boys* (1962) would all more than touch on this central idea. The theme would obsess American film-makers, up to and beyond Coppola's study of worry in the wasteland, *Rumblefish* (1983) – the film that launched a thousand adverts. As a theme, however, this was like Buddhism for teen nihilists, the discovery that, while boys might think you're the ace face, and girls form ragged queues to enjoy your indifference, you're not even a man until your recognize something deeper than the spiritual ergonomics of your own vain-glory.

This had been all very well in America, where Elvis and Jimmy Dean had mapped out the teenage dream and positioned themselves unknowingly for the last act of the tragedy, but in England, where boys wore socks the colour of cold porridge and girls thought thoughtful men were either queer or simple, it was a very different story. In their own sweaty way, the Angry Young Men of English theatre and film had done their best to show the relationship between territorial hostility, muscles and Meaning (*This Sporting Life* with its rage, romance and rugby had painted a particularly bleak portrait of love among the noble savages), but the struggle with masculinity as a fight with the self was still in its clumsy first round. What was a dispossessed man supposed to do beyond the terraces of his home town? How many collars could be turned up against the rain, and how many lives could be left because they simply weren't worth it? When neither *Summer Holiday* nor the kitchen sink could provide the answer, what was the question? Certainly, English cinema critics were becoming bored with the problem:

The British sociological film . . . is now firmly established: recipe plain-to-stodgy, final taste perfectly predictable; progressive but 'sensible' and all points of view given an airing. First and foremost it has a Problem (intolerance, colour, crime), and the people are there to illustrate it. Then you can expect good acting, with energy and conviction down to the smallest parts; plain, tough direction that isn't really going to offend Aunt Edna, a plain, tough script that ditto, and a lower middle class background. The family will live in a mean, small street, and the interiors will all look carefully right, half-heartedly comic relief being provided by the older members, who sit in corners, smoking enigmatically. It is advertised as searing, thought-provoking, blisteringly outspoken; but its impact is mild.

So said the *Spectator* in 1961, with reference to *Flame in the Streets* and it was not alone. Delinquency and social realism had become formulaic, as a box office trend, but there were still strong films raising strong questions.

The question, in fact, was a massive: 'Who am I?' The male sensibility in English pop, as it built its muscles through Mod, was both a reaction against adolescent (even teenage) conformity, and a belief that pop could be a spiritual quest through the boredom and hostility of modern English life in search of self-knowledge. This was fundamental to the no-nonsense polemic of the Who, whose earliest period delivered pop punches to the kidneys as well as combining a bisexual mixture of extreme violence and extreme sensitivity – the bad boy so worn out with the con-formism of the tribe that he turns on his peers as well as his teachers and parents. In this much, the Who smashing up their equipment could be seen as the English Mod equivalent, ten years on, of James Dean thumping the furniture in *Rebel Without a Cause* or Marlon Brando being beaten up by the praetorian guard of the dock bosses in *On the Waterfront*. When an outlaw turns his back on the other outlaws, you know that he's got something on his mind. So pop, despite itself, became arty. English society, high on the new convenience foods, allowed English culture to develop a kind of boil-in-the-bag popism as the successor to the beans on toast of social realism.

In England, throughout the 1960s, pop culture diversified to include

the other arts, marrying entertainment to protest while rearrang-
ing the social boundaries and cultural hierarchy. In the visual
arts, the intellectual audacity of the Independent Group had
given way to the echoes of American pop art proper, with its
election to art status of commercial brands, stars and urban
accessories. Then there was the suggestion (it was heavily limited
as a reality) of a new bohemian affair between working-class
creative types and the aristocracy, which brought the likes of
David Bailey or Mick Jagger into the country homes of England,
and laid the basis for new fables from *Darling* (1965) (in which
we find hip young bohemians, penniless, shop-lifting from Fortnum & Mason) to *Blow Up* (1966) – (in which the hip young
photographer drives a Rolls-Royce). On the new pop-aware television programming, also, we would find *The Avengers* combining
the institutional Englishness of Savile Row and vintage cars with
a deeply psychedelic notion of fragmented reality, in which the
underworld of crime, the underground of popular culture and
the hidden precincts of Cold War paranoia were compressed
into a Looking Glass world where nothing – to satirical ends or
not – was ever quite as it seemed.

Similarly, in 1967, Penguin Modern Poets 10: *The Mersey Sound*
would bring together the influential grouping of Adrian Henri,
Brian Patten and Roger McGough, whose pop art poetry brought
politics and contemporary satire to the hitherto refined world of
British poetry with varying degrees of success. (Larkin, however,
remained the High Priest of paradoxically subversive English
verse, blending the personal, the national and the universal with
a metaphysical genius that made his hymning dull Englishness
the mirror of his soul.) But in poems such as Brian Patten's
'Somewhere between Heaven and Woolworths, A Song' or the
more self-conscious popism of Adrian Henri's meditations on
love in Liverpool, London and along the East Lancs road, there
was an engagement with the vernacular idiom of High Streets
and supermarkets, new pop heroes and old pop precursors – to

say nothing of a horny (and, to contemporary eyes, corny) obsession with teenage sex. This was the young British artist as a pop troubador and modern free spirit, filled with righteous protest. In Adrian Henri's 'Hello Adrian (for Adrian Mitchell)', for instance, we find the standard index of fashionable reference points and political concerns in the 1960s:

> Very strange things have been happening to me lately. People keep falling off cliffs and into bed with me. Last night I met Paul McCartney in a suburban garden wearing a moustache drawn by Marcel Duchamp. I keep wanting to sign shelves of tins in Supermarkets. Everytime I go for coal the coalplace is full of dead Vietcong. Birds have eaten the berries off our plastic holly. I think it's going to be a hard winter.

The difficulty with all of this was that it was simply of its times as opposed to about its times – an early victim of seeking pop fashionability without thinking, and the 1960s produced much art which simply ticked the relevant boxes in the latest directory of received ideas: sex, peace, drugs, Maoism, and the Beatles. What was required, inevitably, were artists who could rise above the brightly coloured, dizzyingly seductive informants of their era and sum it up in a self-contained story, painting, film or song. And, as pop became the principal cultural currency of Englishness in the 1960s (a household phenomenon, like personal computers in the 1980s) as a means of buying the nation's attention, so the sophistry had to be separated from the hard crystals of genuine innovation and genuine subversion.

Improbably, one of the strongest voices in the 1960s came from the cartoonist, Ralph Steadman, whose early satirical cartoons (some of them published in *Private Eye*) were collected between hard covers under the title *Still Life with a Raspberry*. Steadman – a kind of protest-art court jester – was to England in the 1960s what S. J. Perelman was to New York in the 1940s and 1950s. Perelman's comic essays were less savage than Steadman's mixture of slapstick polemic and Hogarthian satire (he re-drew 'The Rake's Progress' as it might be pursued in England in the 1960s) but both did much to articulate, via the line of wit, the temper of their times. Steadman's targets were chosen from any manifestation of social, political or institutional humbug, ranging from the Catholic Church to the fashionable sophists of Swinging London and the burgeoning self-satisfaction of the lifestyle supplements in the Sunday press. But his work in the 1960s revealed not only an artist with a brilliant eye for the attitude and postures of modern British life, but also a definitive aesthetic. His idiosyncratic style – turning the ink-blot into an articulate creative statement – was coupled with his temperament as a politically motivated (if disillusioned) social realist, who used all of the traditions of British culture to question the England which had actually been delivered in the wake of Macmillan's boast of 1959 (by now a multi-purpose truism) that we had never had it so good.

It was ironic that an artist as English as Steadman should find himself best known in the canon of pop art as the illustrator of Hunter S. Thompson's famous essay 'The Kentucky Derby is Decadent and Depraved'. His illustrations for *Alice in Wonderland* and *Through the Looking Glass*, however, defined him as a pop artist with a mind wholly in tune with his times. English popular culture in the high summer of the 1960s had taken to the Alice mythology, finding in its mixture of Arcadian gentility and English surrealism a near perfect complement to the chemical counter-culture and that culture's fixed relationship with class, generational conflict and altered states of mind. Like Waugh before him, Steadman recognized in Wonderland the potential for satirizing England as he found it. His illustration for 'Father William' shows a sneering, lithe young hipster using Father William's legs as crutches to slouch between as he mocks; royalty and courtiers are clay-footed and ungainly in their pantomime-dame dignity, and Alice herself, wide-eyed and

Twiggy-legged, is not immune from caricature as a slightly dizzy and not wholly bright explorer. The whole effect is that of a film like *Darling* (with Julie Christie bouncing her way back to the bottom through Swinging London) as directed by Tenniel. As allegories of Englishness, Steadman's cartoons gave an insight into the social values of the 1960s that were sharpened by his ambivalence towards his subjects, bringing together (for example) the foppish languor of the Rolling Stones as pop aristocracy with his own portrait of Dorian Gray – 'the satirist consuming himself in an ever more beautiful world'. The Rolling Stones, as decadent dandies, had picked up the relevance to the modern age of Wilde's indictment by making a promotional film for their peerless anthem to snotty youth, 'We Love You', in which Marianne Faithfull played Bosie to Jagger's Oscar. After the Jagger drug trial, their choice of conceit in an English courtroom (complete with rattling keys and chains) took on an extra frisson of meaning.

Steadman's vision of England was similar to that described by Lindsay Anderson in his great diptych of films, *If* . . . (1968) and *O Lucky Man!* (1973). England's traditions and institutions are seen as deliquescent, corrupt or mad, and the landscape surrounding them is Alice-like in its sudden shifts of purpose. *O Lucky Man!*, especially, marked a high point in intelligent pop protest, and remains one of the most important documents of modern Englishness ever created. The idea of a journey, as an inner and outer quest, remains central. The film was best described by *The Times* at the time of its release:

> It is an epic comedy with music, in a traditional morality form. The hero of the film, Mick Travis (Malcolm McDowell), is a kind of modern Candide, or fairy-tale Younger Brother, whose innocently confident quest for success carries him through the length and breadth of a Britain of motorways, strip clubs, and atomic establishments, of rich industrialists, pop singers, down-and-outs and politicians.

By reviving the public school anarchist Mick Travis, Anderson had created a modern Everyman to figure in a contemporary Pilgrim's Progress. It was a grand gesture, to explore with Hogarthian vision and Dickensian scope the constitution and temperament of Britain. It flopped, of course. It was almost as though the period of British film-making which had begun with Albert Finney's defiant Arthur Seaton in *Saturday Night and Sunday Morning* came to an end with McDowell's brilliant performance as Mick in *O Lucky Man!*. It could also be argued that *O Lucky Man!* saw the end of popular socialism as a cultural force and the end of a particular sensibility of Englishness: there was less interest in realism (however translated into fable), and Hogarthian satire would be replaced by irony and the comedy of recognition. Cultural materialism was too in love with its own complexity to permit the forceful moral tales in which Anderson and his generation had believed. It was as though the 'Free Cinema' had been privatized or sold to Hollywood.

Like Pope's 'Dunciad', with its premonition of Albion gone mad, *O Lucky Man!* suggested that there was little chance for a young man like Mick. Using comedy as a Socratic lure with which to draw viewers to a reassessment of modern England, the film offered little hope of political redemption or the triumph of decency. Rather, chaos and corruption rise up to engulf the ordinary traveller who questions his position in the English scheme. Hence his Pilgrim's Progress into a nightmarish Wonderland where being a coffee salesman leads to Masonic corruption, atomic establishments have thugs in suits to beat up intruders, Arcady leads to the motorway and the motorway leads to a genetic research centre. Fancying a tycoon's daughter, inevitably, leads to being framed for selling chemical weapons; rehabilitation in prison leads to being beaten up by dossers. With chilling precision, a young mother (played by Rachel Roberts, who had starred in *This Sporting Life*) lists the cost of weekly groceries before committing suicide, unmoved by Travis's recitations from an anthology of moral philosophy – none of whose entries seem to have more worth than epigrams in sentimental birthday cards. The film was too dark for Britain in 1973, and too nineteenth century in its account of a young man's fortune at a time when intellectuals demanded cosmopolitan fine-mindedness. Steadman, sharing Anderson's view, could almost match the story point for point in his cartoon England and cartoon *Alice*. Not until Jarman's *The Last of England* would such territory be revisited.

Anderson's use of Malcolm McDowell as the star (and same character) in both *If* . . . and *O Lucky Man!* was a powerful and apposite piece of casting. McDowell's face could become the face of English youth in revolt – part anarchist and part innocent victim, both intelligent and naïve, meek yet set in opposition. His expression, blissful and enigmatic on the publicity poster for *O Lucky Man!*, was like a *tabula rasa* across which the imagined fate of a generation could be written. He could have been – as Marcello Mastroianni was for Fellini – Anderson's alter-ego, and there is an interesting excursion into Fellini-esque blurring of fiction and reality in the final scenes of *O Lucky Man!* Mick, now a derelict, wanders in to an open audition for people to act in a film. Anderson, playing the director, picks him out of the crowd, gets him to pose (as in *If* . . .) with a bren gun, and then begins to provoke him, trying to get a reactive smile. Hitting him with a clipboard (as the Zen master awakens the pupil), Anderson finally gets his reaction: 'What's there to smile about?' snaps Mick, as insistent as his questioner, and McDowell's face, already iconic from his controversial role as Alex in *A Clockwork Orange* (1971), fills the screen with an unwavering stare that might sum up the message of the film: learn the hard way. In this much, *O Lucky Man!*, and McDowell's relationship to Anderson, cinematically, can be likened once more to Fellini's filming of Mastroianni's enigmatic expression at the end of the equally bleak *La Dolce Vita*. Indeed, *La Dolce Vita*, as a journey into self-knowledge and a satire, was to Italy in the 1960s what *O Lucky Man!* was to England in the early 1970s, and the facial power of its star was of equal importance. The young man on his journey through society or national identity would have none of his illusions flattered, and his romanticism would return to mock him. The messages which were conveyed by Anderson and Steadman would be Soviet in their pessimism were they not so richly articulated by a vigour and humour which is common to all pop art statements. They did not reinvent so much as up-date the masculinity of the young English rebel, positioning his maleness as envied by his elders and challenged by his contemporaries.

The conundrum of modern masculinity had also been explored, albeit one-sidedly, in Michael Caine's embodiment of charm and viciousness in both the film of Bill Naughton's *Alfie* (1966) and in *Get Carter* (1971). The cockney Lothario of *Alfie* was a cartoon of chirpy chauvinism (a 'sex comedy' typical of the period that produced such horrors as *Here We Go Round the Mulberry Bush*, of interest only in its use of Stevenage New Town as a location) that turns, most definitely, into a sex tragedy of misogyny, abortion and social decrepitude, catalysed by an intermezzo on the terror of mortality. *Alfie* showed the sex-hungry male – Jack the Lad – as an ultimately weak figure, imprisoned within the suffocating locality of his conquests (his tiny topography of seductions) while believing it to be his kingdom. His man-of-the-world banter turns out to be woman-hating violence and his seducer's soft patter nothing more than self-obsessed sentimentality, as brilliantly described by the pitting of backstreet abortion against Alfie's eventual tenderness for his son. But buried within this deceptively moral fable there was a demand for male soul-searching; that cheery chauvinists, however empowered by a general permissiveness or a Cockney philosopher, could no longer get away with it. When one thinks of the abortion sequences in *Saturday Night and Sunday Morning* (all Hilda Baker, gin and knitting needles) or in Ken Loach and Nell Dunn's original Wednesday Play of *Up the Junction* (1965), one can see the rising protest against the hitherto unquestioned right of men to demand sex but deny the consequences. Thus, despite itself, *Alfie* challenged the male position on male authority. And it was all the more effective for making Alfie the typical geezer in the pub – as opposed to a liberal, artified modern male. Alfie's fear of domesticity, his fear of becoming 'poncified' and 'blown out', form the spur of his seducer's philosophy but leave him longing for 'peace of mind'.

> As I lean over the Embankment wall and watch old Father Thames steaming by, look at me now! I've got some money, haven't I, and I've got a few good suits, a fair car, and I've got my health back. But I haven't got my peace of mind. And if you haven't got that you've got nothing! There's one certainty: I'll go no more a-birding. I suppose I've just got to sweat this little lot out of me one way or another – what they call suffer it through. But what's the answer? That's what I keep asking myself. I suppose it's what everybody in this life is asking themselves.

Bill Naughton's character of Alfie fitted Caine like a glove, and he played the role with a dead-pan charm that Alfie himself would be far from possessing. *Get Carter*, on the other hand (with the playwright John Osborne playing a lazily sadistic gangster to Michael Caine's terrifying Carter, who arrives in Newcastle to avenge his brother's murder), showed the hit-man as a kind of Cockney Terminator, with a search and destroy programme set only to kill, interrogate or fuck. Once again, the story is based on a journey and a quest. *Get Carter* was a revenge tragedy for 1970s, describing a male underworld in which the levels of corruption and counter-intrigue were endless. Rehearsing the cold-light-of-day that *The Sweeney* would let in on the hitherto obscured or stylized world of gangland crime, the violence made all the more shocking by the banality or domesticity of its setting, the gangsters in *Get Carter* inhabit a strangely empty and pointless world, and they haunt their vice with the nervous boredom of ghosts, in which the killing and the fucking are as ultimately futile as they are compulsory.

Carter, like Alfie, is a reactionary beneath his sharp suits and his modern image, wanting an eye for an eye and a woman in bed, and this is a trait of masculinity which he shares with the character of Chas in Nicolas Roeg's mesmeric mêlée of dirty realism and psychedelia, *Performance* (1970). Chas, played with chilling conviction by James Fox, is another hit-man in the middle-management of London's gangland who is forced underground to avoid assassination. Chas, one could imagine, is a Mod made good (or bad) by his career as an executive in the protection business; he is a working-class Londoner who's made money out of crime, and his pride in his appearance is matched only by his viciousness. He holds the upper classes (with whom his gangster bosses, Kray-like, can fraternize) in contempt because he knows that they are every bit as corrupt as himself. Like Carter, he moves in a ruthless world of tarring and feathering before breakfast (symbolically, he drenches a rival boss's Rolls-Royce in hydrochloric acid before shaving the chauffeur's head and telling him to pass on the message to his 'owner'), where the men are violent, anal, but paradoxically steeped in tabloid moralizing about family values. The hit-men will ride to a contract killing like workers on the Central Line from Bow, about to carve somebody up but complaining of television programmes that might upset the kiddies.

When Chas takes a room, by chance, in the house of a reclusive former rock idol, Turner (played with effortless brattishness by Mick Jagger), the sexuality of this hitherto ultra-masculine film goes haywire. Turner is a foppish, Orientalist decadent, with a penchant for the occult and a bisexual household of girl-friends and child; his house is like a Kings Road boutique by way of Edgar Allan Poe – a *fin-de-siècle* hall of mirrors in which imperial sensuality is mixed with hardened seediness. Marianne

Faithfull's description of Brian Jones and Anita Pallenberg's Courtfield Road flat in 1966 (Pallenberg starred in *Performance*, and her friend Christopher Gibbs did the set design) as recorded in her autobiography 'Faithfull' (1994), is an obvious model for the neo-Wildean, psychedelic occultism of Turner's lair:

> A vertiable witches' coven of decadent illuminati, rock princelings and hip aristos. In my mind's eye I open the door. Peeling paint, clothes, newspapers and magazines strewn everywhere. A grotesque little stuffed goat standing on an amp, two huge tulle sunflowers, a Moroccan tambourine, lamps draped with scarves, a pictographic painting of demons ... A dissolute 'Night Watch' of mid-sixties swinging London.

Of course, by 1970, London had finished swinging and Turner inhabits the ruins of this environment like a dandified Miss Havisham on acid.

Chas, suddenly emasculated by this new context, with all of his threatening machismo either hopelessly square or open to instant reversal, becomes a pawn in a chess game of gender and psychological power. Mirroring a savage beating at the hands of a rival, in which sado-masochism is an obvious undercurrent, Chas's whole identity as a Mod reactionary is turned on its head by Turner's sexual mind-games and the near hallucinatory twists of the plot. This is a prime collision between two eras, in which Chas's physical and psychological safety-net is suddenly withdrawn. As a study of gender, *Performance* showed the boxing, East London male as ultimately vulnerable to sexual ambiguity but filled with instinctive contempt for the 'alternative society'. 'It's a right piss-'ole in 'ere,' confides Chas from a telephone in Turner's decadent mansion, underlining his traditional sense of values, 'foreigners, drugs, long 'air – the lot.'

Along with Malcolm McDowell's mould-breaking portrayal of the futuristic thug Alex, in Stanley Kubrick's film *A Clockwork Orange* (1971) (withdrawn in the UK by its director, after he and his family received death threats), which also dandified violence, Mick Travis, Alfie, Carter, Chas and Turner all embodied modern males on literal and inner journeys to a confrontation with their identity and their sexuality. As role models for modern young men, they had in common a fundamental loss of previously unquestioned (and unquestionable) male authority. We have come a long way from *The Leather Boys*, or Arthur Seaton's stone-throwing at the end of *Saturday Night and Sunday Morning*, but hints of this breakdown have been apparent all along. Catalysed by the pop interest in altered states of mind, the dissection of male heroes in English cinema between 1966 and 1971 described a psychological audit on modern masculinity and pronounced it to be in crisis. Even allowing for the artistic prejudice of fashionable, intellectual film-makers and critics, the reality of this crisis could be found elsewhere in the culture; and it did, at least, offer an alternative to the lingering machismo of James Bond or the imported buddiness of endless American police films. What was being hatched was a new kind of pop male, for whom life was a quest for identity and sincerity which doubled as an assault course between traditional masculine rites and the pop underground. This was the birth of the young soul rebel: a new breed of loner who pitted emotional idealism against emotional corruption. Importantly, he was a son of the suburbs or the provinces, and his philosopher's stone was most definitely the ordinary and the banal; herein lay his route to extreme states of mind and the retrieval of formative memories. To describe his journey, the cultural baton was passed from social realist cinema (and its mutations) to pop.

Still bloody from the womb, so to speak, the new pop male in England took a look around himself in the early 1970s – the decade in which space travel, boyishly celebrated in the 1950s, would be seen in popular culture as a metaphor for existential crisis – and found progressive rock and novelty singles wherever he looked. 'Grandad' by Clive Dunn, 'Mouldy Old Dough' by

Lieutenant Pigeon, 'Ernie (The Fastest Milkman In The West)' by Benny Hill and 'Amazing Grace' by the Royal Scots Dragoon Guards were all hugely successful Number One hits in 1971 and 1972; while the sprawling epics of musical virtuosity being created by Yes, Genesis and Emerson, Lake and Palmer held sway as grown-up music, as though validated by the sheer weight of their concepts and packaging. The obvious alternative for the thinking teenager was the futuristic pantomime of Glam rock being acted out by the luxuriously rampant teen anthems of T. Rex or the Sweet, but such besequinned extroversion and celebrated artifice was anathema to the ultra-masculinity that had been incubated in a youthful tradition of soul-searching dissatisfaction with the modern world.

Rather, the new pop male (with an identity crisis to get over) would spend his time on the fringes of the soul and Ska scene, close enough to skinheads and rude boys to see the tribalism of apprentice hard-men as one road to self-knowledge that might not turn out to be a cul-de-sac. What was required, according to the credo of method-acting masculinity, was truth in a false world and authenticity in a culture shot through with synthesizers and synthetics. Not even the birds, beer and Beelzebub brand of pop community on offer from the proudly self-contained (and culturally autistic) fraternity of heavy metal (still ruled in the UK by Led Zeppelin and Black Sabbath) had much to appease the new pop male who was searching for something to call his own in a modern world which seemed, to him, comprised of so many liars and fools. The failure of his own generation, despite the new values of pop, to resist yet further conformity and to sell one's convictions for herd-like complacency had been described in British films of the early 1960s − notably Colin's refusal to compete, ultimately, in *The Loneliness of the Long Distance Runner* − and would be revived in Franc Roddam's film version of the Who's *Quadrophenia* in 1979.

But there were two main factors which set the new pop male apart from his contemporaries. The first was his obsession with sincerity in a modern England which he saw as strangled by consumerism on the one hand and political failure on the other. (Hence his flirtation with extreme politics on either end of the political spectrum, and his eventual rejection of both.) And as pop was bound up in consumerism, and the life which pop might enhance or change was dictated, in part, by politics, the new pop male was faced with enemies on the outside and collaborators on the inside. The second factor was his fundamental distrust of fashionability, regardless of whether or not a fashion had evolved as anti-fashion. The new pop male, obsessed with the climate of his feelings, was searching for his soul in the closed order of his own mind. This was a monk-like, if melodramatic, occupation; it was uncompromising, scornful of indulgence and in favour of a discipline which would lead to the painful lucidity of 'true feelings'.

While punk rock would espouse some of the values that the new pop male saw as fundamental to his mission, it was the regional experience of punk – as opposed to its metropolitan base in media, art and fashion – which really galvanized the search for the young soul rebels. In London, the Jam and Public Image Ltd had held out in the late 1970s as groups who pursued intensity and conviction as opposed to cartoon anarchy or Goth–futurist style-mongering, while Sham 69, with their remarkable concept LP of 1978, *That's Life*, brought the social realism of *Up the Junction* to the three-chord skinhead protest song. *That's Life*, with its cover a collage of tabloid headlines, comprised ten songs linked by a miniature playlet about a day in the life of a working-class young man in London's outer suburbs. Beginning with his rude awakening in the family home, where he can't get into the bathroom because his sister has beaten him to it, and his parents are arguing over the breakfast table, the hero of *That's Life* proceeds to be late for work, get the sack, and wind up in a grotty disco where he picks up a girl whose boyfriend happens to be sitting at the next table. In the manner of social realism, everything and nothing happens, but both the songs and the dialogue between them conveyed the banality and violence which turn the commonplace into a suffocating tragedy of epic proportions. In this much, *That's Life* was firmly in the tradition of the kitchen sink, and almost too close to parody to be wholly successful. Indeed, with the exception of its rabble-rousing hit single 'Hurry Up Harry', with its endearingly minimal chorus of 'We're going down the pub', the record was a commercial failure. But there is a mesmeric squalor about its clumsy, simple tale, and in terms of defining the beer boy manqué on life's journey it delivered some lyrical gems, as in:

> Runnin' for the bus in my flash new suit,
> Someone shouts out 'Poof!' so I
> Put in the boot.

or:

> I've bin drinkin too many pints ov larrgah,
> I've bin gettin in too many bleedin fites;
> I come 'ome wiv sick all dahn me trarsurrs . . .

As a group who attracted a famously dangerous audience of Nazi skinheads, Sham 69, as the pulpit for Jimmy Pursey's well-intentioned sermonizing on social injustice and emotional frustration, were doomed to become victims of their own rhetoric. Pursey's ideal, for 'the kids to be united', was usually voiced in a hoarse scream at the end of a Sham 69 concert, as the seekers after truth became lost in a Bash Street Kids style punch-up of flying fists, chairs and beer bottles. But *That's Life* was a landmark record of method-acting masculinity, poised halfway between the innocence of *We are the Lambeth Boys* and the tragedy of *Quadrophenia* as a pop story about trying to be an ordinary bloke amid the litter, volatility and squalor of seemingly dead-end lives. Hence its lyric, 'Everybody's Right, Everybody's Wrong'; hence its revival of 'Angels With Dirty Faces' as a moral title first used in 1938 for Warner Brothers' teenage morality film about a gang of Brooklyn street kids and their idolizing of another local boy (Jimmy Cagney) made good as a gangster. Hence, also, a small cluster of like-minded post-punk groups, from the Cockney Rejects and Angelic Upstarts to the remarkably long-lived Chelsea, whose 'Right To Work' became a post-punk cliché. The overtly right-wing off-shoot of the Sham scene was a sub-section of 'Oi' groups, led by the notorious Skrewdriver, whose borrowed Nazi politics made them the house bands of the National Front. As a tribe within a tribe, the extremist Oi groups were disowned by as many 'true' skinheads as they were supported by 'fake' skinheads. Ultimately, they cast a much longer shadow than their significance deserved, being fomulaic speed punk groups with predictably repellent songs.

In terms of its politicized maleness, mutating the cliché of the working-class hero or the dead-end kid into a right-wing anarch-ist warrior, the Oi movement and its perceived *agent provocateur*, Garry Bushell (later to become the *Sun*'s television critic), were roundly denounced by the anarcho-hippie activists Crass, in their 1982 'Exitstencil Press' publication, 'A SERIES OF SHOCK SLOGANS AND MINDLESS TOKEN TANTRUMS':

Oi would have been harmless enough if its comic-book caricature of the 'workers' hadn't appealed so strongly to the elements that, inevitably, were drawn to its reactionary views – the so-called 'right wing'. Rather than rejecting its new and possibly unwanted following, Oi appeared to revel in its image of being 'nasty Nazi music for real men'. Defending the trail of blood and bruises that it seemed to leave behind itself wherever it went, the 'new breed' claimed that 'they weren't advocating violence, they were just reflecting the way things are'. Despite repeated evidence of Oi inspired violence, it became increas-ingly obvious that Oi the Bushell and Oi the bands were either perfectly happy with 'the way things were' or totally incapable of controlling the monster that they'd created.

Certainly, this was the problem that Sham 69's Jimmy Pursey – to say nothing of Madness, with their mixture of melancholy nostalgia for a London childhood and witty knees-up singalong numbers (Chas & Dave by way of Nell Dunn) – were forced to confront when their social realism met the right-wing fringes of real society. In the early 1980s, when politicized post-punk music seemed poised to pitch Red Wedge against Oi and the National Front, there was a sense that urban popular culture was echoing the confrontation defined by, for instance, the Spanish Civil War. Partly romantic fantasy and partly a social and political problem, more localized and complex than pop music, despite its best intentions, could hope to solve, the overt politicization of social realist pop groups began to flounder with the collapse of the Greater London Council (GLC) and the sub-cultural response to Thatcherism that either chose ironic glamour as the Trojan horse of protest, or went wholly underground with the burgeoning dance music scene that would be politicized as Rave culture.

But if *That's Life* told of male survival in Barking or Dagenham, on the outer limits of the capital, then provincial Britain was also developing post-punk pop that regarded the urban landscape as a metaphor for the state of youth and the condition of the soul. Away from the wealth and the perceived glamour of London (both the Fall and the Specials would identify London, with coruscating sarcasm, as the place where bedazzled provincials went to be fashionable) it was both harder to live out the fashionable values of punk rock and, consequently, more intense as an experience. In some ways, this was a repetition of the old chemistry of dandyism: distance from the capital bred fervour and originality; in London, as the social machine of aspirational culture, punk could be turned into cliché at the drop of a cat-walk fashion show or the conversion of a militant fanzine into a glossy magazine. The three punk rockers in a small town, on the other hand, would stand or fall by the talisman of a shared Sex Pistols

T-shirt, an old school tie with a safety-pin through it, or the sheer nerve to walk through the centre of town displaying some small badge of punk difference – a turned-up collar or a lapel badge. In provincial cities, where male orthodoxy was upheld by traditional masculine values, it was hardly surprising that the old gay clubs of the early 1970s (such as Shades in Nottingham or the Ranch in Manchester) were the only places where provincial punks could originally meet in safety, prior to the creation of their own clubs, such as Eric's in Liverpool or the Electric Circus in Manchester's Collyhurst – even if the bus ride home was to run the gauntlet of beery men and their jeering girlfriends who wished the non-conformists injury and humiliation for mocking their cherished domain of Saturday night on the town. Suddenly, every small town punk was a Quentin Crisp, trying not to make eye contact with anyone.

Having whizzed through the chicane of punk rock, and found it as false, within six months, as the pop and rock it set out to depose, the new pop male continued on the spiritual journey to the capital of his emotions. But where was that capital, and what did he hope to find there? The new pop male had an acute empathy with the city as he found it, and became the method-acting hero of his own *Bildungsroman*: the young man arrives in the city, bent on finding urban glamour and the girl of his dreams against all odds. Indeed, the city and the girl become one entwined emblem of success, and the capriciousness of both are used to chart the development of the young hero's spiritual journey to his own true personality. (When Billy gets off the train to London before it has even left the station, at the end of *Billy Liar*, and leaves Julie Christie to make the journey alone, he is neatly reversing the *Bildungsroman* tradition.) The *Bildungsroman*, as a literary genre, usually takes the form of a naturalistic account of naïve romanticism brought down by urban reality and the corruption within society. The heroes of such tales often enjoy a cruelly steep learning curve in which the metropolitan proximity of extreme poverty to flippant luxury is a decisive informant, particularly when seen through young eyes just learning the ways of the big city. Defined by Balzac's *La Comédie Humaine* (*Lost Illusions*, in particular) and Flaubert's *Sentimental Education*, to be reinvented by F. Scott Fitzgerald's *This Side of Paradise*, and, in filmed form by Lindsay Anderson's *O Lucky Man!*, the convention of the *Bildungsroman* casts the romantic, idealistic male as both at odds with and enamoured of his generation. Eventually, he becomes as successful and as corrupt as the city in which he has learned his hard lessons, and truth is located in the moral decisions he has taken to attain the city and the girl. This is the city as realism's Wonderland. For the Jam, from Woking, with their gritty fusion of pop, passion and politics, there was never any doubt that the heart of the self was described by London, and that to witness London was to study one's own soul.

In a more or less unbroken string of hit singles between 1977 and 1982, the Jam delivered four-minute epics of life and love in the capital, with Paul Weller's brutally focused writing (given wings by his harsh, suburban voice) creating polaroid snapshots of urban paranoia ('Down In The Tube Station At Midnight', 'Strange Town', 'A Town Called Malice'), social realism ('That's Entertainment') and political convictions ('The Eton Rifles'). Weller's Mod trajectory, from the home-town romanticism of Woking to his re-creation of the Angry Young Man as a hot-tempered fop, was driven by a suburbanite's vision of London and a literary talent for punk naturalism. He wrote from the *Bildungsroman* perspective of the ambitious and poetic young man who is both dazzled and appalled by the ceaseless contradictions and energy of the capital, which is at once seductive and indifferent (like the beauty queen of a small town or a society woman) to the determined youth who tries to understand it and, by understanding, possess it. Ford Madox Ford, in his book of 1905, 'The Soul of London', caught this relationship between the city and the bedazzled young hero of the *Bildungsroman* with uncanny accuracy: 'Above all, his London, his intimate London, will be the little bits of it that witnessed the great moments, the poignant moods of his life; it will be what happened to be the backgrounds of his more intense emotions.' Such, it could be argued, is the theology of those early singles by the Jam.

As such, Paul Weller could be regarded as an English romantic, combining the ecstatic melancholy of Wordsworth writing his 'Residence in London' section of *The Prelude* with the wonderment and eye for injustice which typifies a Dickensian boy hero. His pop vision was shaped by his ambivalence towards the constitution of English life; despising Thatcherism on the one hand but loving England and Englishness on the other. Hence, perhaps, his line in 'Start!': 'Knowing there's someone in this life, who loves with a passion called hate.' But, as his fame grew, he became a stylized Beat intellectual, setting up a small poetry press and bringing soul music to bear on protest singing. A decade later, in the mid 1990s, Weller would be reinvented as the Godfather of laddish nouveau in the flurry of pop-culture-as-metropolitan-PR that typified neo-swinging London.

But if Weller's suburban perspective gave an edge to his vision, then the provincial experience of Dexy's Midnight Runners, from Birmingham, and the Specials, from Coventry, put the fire in the belly of their particular pop projects. Dexy's were the definitive manifestation of English pop as method acting, but the Specials, if only on their first LP, gave a chilling account of early adulthood in a small city of dirty precincts and depressing discos, where the promises of pop were so foreshortened as to become a mockery. The Specials' 'Friday Night and Saturday Morning' chronicled a typical night out in the small town Locarno:

> Bouncers bouncing through the night,
> Trying to stop or start a fight;
> Sit and watch the flashing lights,
> Moving legs in footless tights.

Fuelled by the tuneless voice and depressive vision of their singer Terry Hall, the Specials had less to do with Ska revialism than they did with describing the world of mini-cabs and chip wrappers which lurked behind the electro-pop glamour of their peers, Sheffield's the Human League. As in (again from 'Friday Night and Saturday Morning'):

> Hope the chip shop isn't closed,
> cos their pies are really nice;
> I'll eat it in the taxi queue, stand in
> someone else's spew, wish I had
> lipstick on my shirt, instead of piss stains
> on my shoes . . .

This, clearly, is an Arthur Seaton for the 1980s, whose bravado and capacity for pleasure have been eroded by the inevitability of a boring night in a small but dangerous modern city. Not for him the conversion of a provincial disco on the Roxy/Bowie/New Wave axis into a glamorous techno-romance by way of synthesizers and face powder.

The Specials described narrow-minded, lumpen young men and their brassily shrewish girlfriends as the doomed youth of a doomed town – as nightmarish, in their own way, as the mutant partygoers in a painting by Georg Grosz or Otto Dix. And, while the group's politics were bred of a contempt for racism and Thatcherism (English Ska seemed always to be on a see-saw between the leftist bands and the rightish audience), the advice in their songs was traditional if not reactionary, in the punk style: 'Where did you get that blank expression on your face?'; or the kitchen-sink tirade of 'Too Much, Too Young' with its bitter mixture of sexual jealousy and despair:

> You've done too much, much too young
> Now you're married with a kid when you could
> be having fun with me.

Meanwhile, over in Birmingham, Dexy's Midnight Runners had reviewed their generation with equal disgust and were determined to make a Blast against what they saw as the complacency and self-satisfaction of post-punk English pop. Dexy's were an ultra-masculine conception from the word go, and their first LP, introduced with a radio collage of recent pop out-takes, including the Specials and the Sex Pistols, was a method actor's manifesto of anger, passion and introspection, brought into focus by the very title of one of its songs: 'Thankfully Not Living In Yorkshire It Doesn't Apply'. As with Paul Weller's literary persona, the Cappuccino Kid, Dexy's Midnight Runners put themselves forward as a bookish and intellectual group of soul boys, despite their self-invention as hard men, and herein lay the sensitivity which was to be worked out in the gymnasium of the mind, to complement the weight training and the heavy burden of emotional responsibility. Also, they revived the tradition of pamphleteering and essay writing as a protest against the orthodoxy of the music press; and, like statements of intent from a latter-day *Blast*, these collectively signed essays were virtually religious in their conviction. True to the method-acting masculinity of the new pop male, Dexy's Midnight Runners were concerned with emotional truth above all else, and they pursued their search for the soul with a fervour and a public manifesto which could produce only brilliance or disaster. And, in the way of these things, poised between passion and pretentiousness, the group delivered their share of both.

With a fan club that doubled as a kind of soul confessional, 'Intense Emotions Ltd.', based in Sutton Coldfield, Dexy's Midnight Runners were concerned with reaching the emotions of their audience with no external interference. On the reverse of the picture sleeve of their single 'Show Me' (1981) (a roaring

description of the rites of passage of a class of English schoolboys, comparing the alienation of the individual to the security
of the crowd), the Midnight Runners printed six statements to
help explain their approach to their music. This huddle of hard
men in hoods and boxing boots were as defensive as they were
evangelical:

> We're not talking specifically about 60s, 70s or 80s black American
> music, we're talking about soul as an emotional force. When
> you hear the record does it convince you that everybody involved
> in the making of the record truly believes what they're saying?
> For us soul goes much further than just records. We believe
> there are soul books (Seb lists John Steinbeck's 'Of Mice and
> Men'), soul films (Kevin swears by 'Mean Streets' and 'Midnight
> Cowboy') and soul life, we take strength from our soul.

The statements continued with the group's attitude to performance:
'We are obsessed with projection'; and self-discipline: 'We all
believe in self discipline, as a group we practise hard. We also
physically train hard together. Self improvement and self preser-
vation, that's what's important today.' The group would compound these sentiments with the lyric: 'I'm going to punish my
body until I believe in my soul.'
To back up these self-imposed commandments of excellence, Dexy's
Midnight Runners had to produce records and perform concerts
which were as passionate and as generous as their philosophies
were austere and confrontational. So long as the music – a
brass-and-keyboard-driven juggernaut, tugging the eccentric
trailer of Rowland's elongated vocal whine – held up, then the
group could refer all criticisms of their self-conscious stance to
the sheer power and atmosphere of their white soul sound.
But by reversing the traditional credo of pop, and being overly
bombastic about their dedication to their art, Dexy's were taking
a vast gamble on the security of their talent. The fall from grace
occurred with the release of their third LP, *Don't Stand Me*

Down, which remains to this day the *Finnegans Wake* of English pop: comic, unfathomable, touched by genius and weighed down with wanton obscurity.

Kevin Rowland, as the front man and architect of Dexy's Midnight Runners, had already earned a mixture of ridicule and admiration for his projection of the group as both a hard-hitting 'firm' of outlaw soul musicians and an austere fraternity of tough working men who were devoted to the pure communication of their feelings. Indeed, comparisons could be made between Dexy's Midnight Runners and either a team of travelling burglars or the characters in the television comedy drama *Auf Wiedersehen, Pet*, in which a group of dispossessed builders from depressed British cities find work in Germany and attempt to survive their dislocation through team spirit and self-policing. Above all, the group was an embodiment and articulation of the strengths and sensitivities of maleness, exploring precisely the same territory as American method acting and English Angry Young Men had before them. They were proto-New Men with muscles, challenging themselves to build a cult of the soul like Dominicans in donkey-jackets. Their material was their memories and their longings, a potent home-brew of autobiographical fragments, self-analysis and public confession. They evoked place as a portal to memory, and thus provided the clumsy yet brilliant pronouncement: 'I'm trying to get back the feeling I had in 1973.' If the group had a home, it was the Birmingham of the Bull Ring and failed, abandoned estates; the Birmingham known as a national joke because of its appalling town planning and the Spaghetti Junction intersection between the motorways. This mixture of banality, struggle and despair, encoded in the fabric of the city itself, gave Dexy's Midnight Runners an authenticity which anyone who heard their glorious soul fanfare would find hard to deny.

Don't Stand Me Down was released after the critical and commercial success of the group's spectacular involvement with fizzed up

Celtic folk, *Too Rye Ay*. Not only did *Too Rye Ay* give the group its biggest hit single, 'Come On Eileen' (the knees-up finale to many a student disco, not to be equalled until the Pogues breathed meths on the Students' Union), it also saw Rowland's soul vision – a breath-taking balancing act between musical discipline and a kind of stream-of-consciousness exercise in memory retrieval – mature and expand in the face of a misguided costume change into dungarees and felt moccasins. The sight of so many English white ankles (also displayed by Paul Weller in his Style Council period) was at odds with the intensity of the group. But *Don't Stand Me Down* would push reinvention to the outside of enough, as the group emerged in its third costume change, this time dressed in the garb of estate agents or building society managers, with neat haircuts, pure Young Conservative business suits and radiating the air of dependable young citizens. Was it all an ironic comment on Thatcherism? Eyebrows were raised.

Even the Snowdonesque portrait of the group on the album's cover looked somehow wrong. In the first place, this new look did not correspond with pop's recent appropriation of the business suit to either fashionable or ironic ends. When Heaven 17 had marketed themselves in the guise and language of proto-yuppie young businessmen, most notably in the annual-report-style illustration on the cover of their *Penthouse and Pavement* LP (1981), there had been a fashion for urban anonymity as either street style or ironic role-playing. But by the time of *Don't Stand Me Down*, with Thatcherism in full swing and English pop dominated by either Morrissey's Smiths, or huge corporate releases from huge corporate pop stars, the latest Dexy's disguise was opaque in the extreme. The group weren't known as fledgling critical theorists (such as Scritti Politti or Prefab Sprout – the post-modernism-with-a-fringe-on-top of English pop) making coded statements about narrative intentionality, and they certainly weren't linked to a technocentric stylishness which might have urged them to pose as bond dealers or computer operatives. But there were the young soul rebels, impassive as a row of besuited Mona Lisas on the cover of their record, and smiling purposely like a tray of passport photographs on the inner sleeve. Added to this there was the stretched expression of a veteran guitarist from Atomic Rooster, and a blurred photograph of a black session musician who looked, unfortunately, like a white man blacked up to impersonate a fleshed-out Prince. Even to an audience grown fluent in the language of pop mischief, none of this made any sense. Most worryingly, this new image was maybe Rowland's idea of normality.

The record was as perplexing as its cover, musical passages of grace and verve were mingled with spoken playlets in which, Beckett-like, nothing and everything might be implied. These conversational exchanges ('We were just discussing various topics, you know? This and that.') had all the uneasiness of poorly scripted 'found dialogue', in which small talk, confession and paranoid cross-questioning made a spoken paste with which the songs were glued together. Then, in the lyrics themselves, there was talk of national pride and personal pride, 'CND scum' and people whose soft political views made them contemptible. But when the songs took off, and Rowland's cracked voice strained to deliver his obscure, impassioned lyrics, there was a sense of such authority and craft that the record could not be dismissed as simply another bad LP.

The record (with dramatized scenes) was show-cased to pitifully small audiences, not least at the Dominion Theatre in London, and Dexy's Midnight Runners appeared to be finished even as the enigma of their strangled swan-song grew. But, echoing Blake's dictum that the fool should persist with his folly, there was a power in this spectacular failure which reflected a genuine maverick vision. Certainly, the most fitting conclusion to the story which the group seemed to leave unfinished was given by a fan who had taken up their invitation to share his emotions: he

sent a heart-felt letter of meditation and confession to Intense
Emotions in Sutton Coldfield; three weeks later the letter was
returned by the Post Office, the address scribbled out with the
words 'Gone Away'. 'I suppose it all got too intense,' he suggested,
later.

While Dexy's Midnight Runners had been co-ordinating their assault
on English pop complacency from Birmingham bedsits and
apathetic punk clubs, another equally intense project was being
hatched by the Pop Group, in Bristol. They, too, were determined to bare their souls through a fusion of post-punk, loose
funk and screamed despairing lyrics, and their flashily titled first
single, 'Beyond Good And Evil', was a four-minute hymn to the
connections between love and hate. With its swooping chords
(fancifully compared by the music press to the arc lights of
shell-fire in Coppola's *Apocalypse Now*) and vocals from the
underground (Dostoyevsky's as opposed to Paul Weller's London
Transport mindscape). 'Beyond Good And Evil' established the
Pop Group as young men deeply entrenched in a psycho-
melodrama, for whom torture and oppression were the pop the-
matic equivalent of runaround blondes and little red Corvettes.
This was uneasy listening, which would make Matt Johnson's
Soul Mining sound like *The Best of Clodagh Rodgers*.

Like Dexy's, the Pop Group saw sloganeering, propaganda and protest graphics as an extension of its mission to swap entertainment
for emotional aerobics. This was best realized on *Y*, the Pop
Group's first LP, which was originally sold with a fold-out lyric
sheet comprised of collaged photo-journalistic evidence of international atrocities. And, in this, the music press had been perceptive to liken *Apolcalypse Now* to the Pop Group's agenda;
their subject seemed to be amorality, guilt and man's capacity
for evil, and all the method-acting traits of expressing unbearable
emotional responsibilities were fully in place. This was Artaud-a-
go-go for the young depressive set. The Pop Group's liking for
protest pop which edified by way of shock was continued on

their second, over-indulgent LP, which had the jaunty title: *For How Much Longer Must We Tolerate Mass Murder?* This time, the record contained ten poster-sized sheets of protest slogans, montages and lyrics, which suggested John Heartfield by way of Amnesty International with a Situationist twist.

On the other hand, there was a sense in which the Pop Group's vaguely intellectual, emotionally exhibitionist and over-earnest pop was in fact defining the relationship between bookish insecurity and frustrated male anger. This was not necessarily their fault. But when the Pop Group screamed at the world there was the feeling that young men up and down the country, surrounded by Russian novels and love letters, were hijacking that anger to scream at girls who didn't like them or jobs that they didn't want to do. What was conveyed as virtually cosmic rage seemed to translate, within its complicit audience, into a metaphor for all manner of personal frustrations and domestic ennui. And perhaps the same could be said of all the high-blown, muscle-bound rhetoric of method-acting pop. In the end, perhaps, it was all for sensitive boys who wanted to be tough men.

The conversion of the glorious bloody-mindedness of English punk rock into the beery laddishness of 'New Wave', with its perky novelty singles by whacky young women (Hazel O'Connor, Toyah, Lene Lovich and Rachel Sweet), ruled over by the peevish maleness of Elvis Costello and Joe Jackson, had increased the opposition between the disparate inheritors of punk's legacy. Interestingly, the maleness of Dexy's Midnight Runners, the Jam or the Pop Group was often too introspective for the legions of proto-Lads who listened to Elvis Costello or Joe Jackson when in their cups and Ian Dury or the Pirates when they went out for a night with the other lads. There was little right or wrong in this polarization; rather, the supposed intellectualism of radical English post-punk was in danger of exchanging daring for pretentiousness, while the quirky accessibility of the New Wave was busily reinventing the dialogue between an audience and the 'stars' which punk had pretended to dismantle. All of which had cleared the way for the Smiths, and a complete reinvention of the English pop star.

As a male response to a long dark night of the soul, or as a cultural reaction to the eerie dawn of Thatcher's longest day, the sensibility defined by method-acting English pop was eloquent of fear, anxiety, introspection and morbid self-scrutiny. But once the dust had settled, the bedsit philosophizing had dried up, and the hospitals had finally been closed down, the method-acting, new pop male, for all of his testosterone and tears, muscles and moods, was left with his arms full of air. What was required – as ever – were bisexual icons.

crawley articulate:
the sound of the suburbs

> the suburb always has an abstracted quality, like a
> sentence learned by heart and repeated till the words
> are finally magical.
>
> JOHN BURNSIDE, *Suburbs* (1991)

Strange things happen on the edges of places, where two opposed
landscapes meet to create a mutant zone, lacking organic con-
sistency. English suburbia typifies this strangeness, endlessly
seeking new ways to feel at home with itself while engendering
contradiction and compromise. The suburbs, because of their
presumed orthodoxy, exaggerate the extremities of mood and
movement; the darkest alley in the seediest district of the biggest
city will lack the sheer oddness of suburban neatness, where all
that appears most settled conspires to make its own drama. And
reactive violence or melancholy appear to shape these suburban
dramas; from Betjeman's 'Croydon':

> The laurels are speckled in Marchmont Avenue
>   Just as they were before.
> But the steps are dusty that still lead up to
>   Your Uncle Dick's front door.

to Bromley-bred Siouxsie Sioux's 'Suburban Relapse', with its opening pronouncement:

'I'm sorry that I hit you, but my string–snapped.' English suburbia, in many ways, has become simultaneously synonymous with the sinister and the sad – the very opposites of its founding intentions.

The indifferent butt of metropolitan humour, the suburban realm of Perrin and Pooter has a history based on the convenience of commuting and the family man's fear of urban vice. The expansion of London's suburbs, in the early 1920s, saw advertising copy-writing stretch to new heights of lyricism to sell the virtues of 'Sunny Sutton' or 'Leafy Ealing'. The inference, of course, was that of moral cleanliness embodied in property, thus striking two targets simultaneously in the minds of middle- to lower-middle-income workers whose understandable desire to improve their quality of life was fanned by more than a light breeze of basic suburban snobbishness. The suburbs, as yet another new Eden, promised the whole package: status, moral standing, a selective sense of community, the chance to avoid other people's misery and the all-important English ability to define yourself through your property. Hence those standard villa names that mingle self-congratulation with statements of ownership – Dunroamin, Chez Nous and Mon Repos; hence, in the outer suburbs, of Surrey or Hertfordshire for instance, those surnames of suburban houses that imply a domesticated rurality, touched by the hand of Olde England: -mede, Cottage, -friar, -glebe, Lee, and Grange.

These grander names are reminiscent of the suburbia so beloved of Betjeman – of tennis clubs, Scots pines and erotically mysterious gravel drives. This was an older and more genteel version of the residential glue that was spread around English cities and towns immediately after World War One to join the town to the country in the name of peace and prosperity. Betjeman's suburbia was well-born but archaic, fussily proud of modern conveniences but

still thinking with the mind of a dowager or retired colonel.
The new suburbia, as exemplified by poor Slough, received
Betjeman's famous wish to see itself bombed.

But England's modernity can be usefully dated from the expansion
of the outer suburbs in the early 1920s (coinciding, interestingly,
with the publication of T. S. Eliot's *The Waste Land*) not least
because they were the precursors of the New Towns of the 1960s
and the regenerated or wholly invented towns and cities of the
mid-1980s: 'I've been looking all over Telford for you!', as the
slogan went. This new suburbia, of imitation, miniaturized
Lutyens and Voysey houses, of endless crescents, avenues and
cul-de-sacs, lined with brown semis, was the basis of residential
England as we know it today. The architectural historian Sir
Nikolaus Pevsner, in a particularly sniffy mood, put the case in
his guide to *The Historic Buildings of Surrey* (1962):

Outside the green belt, except for the Surrey hills, which have been
    protected, a particularly mean kind of village expansion has
    gone on all over the county, throwing out the old pattern,
    maybe pickling a few old cottages for appearances' sake, and
    not putting anything worth-while in its place. Meanwhile, the
    older suburbs have become geared to this juggernaut of mass-
    produced housing.

Such mass-produced housing comprised the affordable snippets of
respectability that were the logical and totemistic home of prefer-
ence for an expanding white-collar workforce who wanted to
conserve the rewards of respectable employment. Such colonization in the name of golf, God and gardening gave rise – as a
received idea, at least – to the basic conservatism of suburbia,
and of suburbia's enduring reputation for xenophobia, small-
mindedness and self-congratulatory moderation. In suburbia (all
'sub' and no 'urb') it is perceived that the local becomes the
universal, returning the language of Life to a reduced vocabulary
of domesticity and parish politics.

But surburbia, as John Betjeman described its formative history, and as the contemporary Scots poet John Burnside has described the quasi-mysticism of its psychology, has evolved an unique ambience that is derived from a convergence of ordinariness and the heightened responses of hope, ambition and nostalgia – the emotional by-products of the family home. The passage of seemingly eventless lives in a prettified, functional setting turns out to be a vivid and poignant procession of moods – inarticulate, maybe, and anonymous, but felt in what Larkin summed up as 'that vase', in his poem 'Home is So Sad'. The extremes of mood and emotion, contained (within 'that vase', so to speak) in the artificial formality of suburbia, give rise to a numinous Trinity of people, place and time.

This hidden numinosity is at the heart of John Burnside's anatomy of suburbia, in the 'Suburbs' sequence of his collection *Common Knowledge* (1991). Suburbia, tame and controlled without, is X-rayed – as though by psychic photography – to reveal itself as mystically supernatural within, its very ordinariness running parallel to invisible presences which make themselves felt through conjunctions of mood and seemingly everyday phenomena. In Burnside's suburbia, one arrives on the unexceptional scene just after the ghost or god has left, leaving the trace of its aura as a particular mood. Thus, an accretion of these invisible presences begins to inform suburbia as much as the evidence of domestic lives: routines grow close to rituals; ordinary objects lend themselves to shrines. And this is more than romantic poetics; here in the heart of security and bourgeois comfort one is fingertip to fingertip with a potency derived from an environment which is equidistant from the city and the country-side proper – a landscape that is informed by both but a part of neither. This collision of edges is central to the oddness of English suburban culture. Written in prose poetry, Burnside's responses to suburbia begin with simple defining statements, then deploy a literary impressionism to articulate the self in its surroundings; as such, his *Suburbs* becomes a directory of suburban numinosity and a carriage-lamp confessional:

> At night the suburb alters. The day-long, low-level action beneath the surface intensifies, like a bad wood warping under veneer: the garden is stolen by foxes rooting in turned dustbins, emptiness takes form and approaches from the centre of the lawn, a white devil, smiling out of the dark, and the realisation dawns that I live in an invented place whose only purpose is avoidance, and what I would avoid, I carry with me, always.

Burnside's investigation of suburbia becomes, finally, a theology: it presents the suburbs as a physical manifestation of a mystical state, where memories and moral audits are triggered and questioned, always seeking to define the presence of some invisible order.

> Sometimes its simplicity is deception: the distance arrives in a thread of cool perfume between two curtains, and I think I am already present somewhere else, having made a journey of some kind, as if any journey could end somewhere other than here, in the suburbs, where everything is implied: city, warehouse district, night stop, woods emerging from mists.

English suburbia, ultimately, has been described by an awareness of those inner journeys between present time and memory across a landscape where 'everything is implied'. Fecund with felt absence ('the suburb is no more substantial than a mirage in a blizzard', writes Burnside) but laced with erotic traces of hope, nostalgia and elsewhere, suburbia articulates potential and loss in the same breath, proposing romance in the midst of an unreal reality.

Culturally – to say nothing of spiritually – suburbia has been a place to come home to that doubles as a place to escape from; it embraces a condensed history of English architecture, in which a single suburban street can represent strata of social history, from Edwardian mansions to post-modern artisan cottages. But suburbia has seldom been a subject for artistic expression, despite its role as the primary incubator of English outsiders and artists. Rather, suburbia's role is reactive; a state of state-lessness in which environment presents itself as a proposition of conformism, the weight of which inspires rebellion as much as obedience. And suburban moderation has always waved a red flag to certain young bulls. As Celia Johnson remarks to Robert Newton in Coward's *This Happy Breed* (1944), when communism comes to the kitchen table in the shape of one of the teenage children's mouthy chums: 'It's wrong, isn't it, this Down With Everything business.' But the suburbs have produced a great many subscribers to the Down With Everything movement, not least in Sutton-born Quentin Crisp, whose refusal to conform was a steel rule tempered in the forge of suburban etiquette.

Unlike England's provincial cities, suburbia has no centre – no civic steps for local outlaws to congregate upon, displaying their difference to studied indifference – but simply an endless repetition of shops and houses, generationally reinvented to the same order, the familiarity of which breeds insularity and introspection in the face of its founding ethos of neighbourly sociability and security. In suburbia, the teenage outsiders must make do with taking over the bus-shelter from dusk till midnight as a meeting-place and a venue for illicit activities – reversing the creed of suburbia's shrine to respectable commuting by having nowhere to go, and leaving their own bored art of graffiti as defiant evidence of their act of desecration.

Over the eighty years of its existence as a major tract of residential England, suburbia and suburban principles have both expanded and adapted to accelerated consumerism. Now, rural suburbia – sprawling in red shallows between pylons and grey fields – has made its own conurbations of hypermarkets and housing estates, where mothership retailers offer total consumer environ-ments on reclaimed farmland or the hinterlands of motorways and industrial parks. The essential melancholy of these places

– the quietude of the ordinary – has become entangled with a scientific strangeness, which enhances suburbia's role as the battleground of boredom and the existential theatre of adolescence. And it could be argued, in fact, that the pop sound of suburbia has been defined by the melodramatic, monolithic, music of the Cure, in which an eerie monotony gives service to morbidity.

The Cure are from Crawley, redeveloped in the mid-1940s as an early suburban New Town in the colourless countryside between the North Downs on the edge of Surrey and the South Downs overlooking the Sussex coast. Quiet and respectable, yet lacking the bourgeois superiority of neighbouring Haywards Heath (home town of Suede), Crawley is a near perfect example of England at its least surprising. It makes no claims to being distinguished in any way, and there is little to distinguish it if it tried. Until a few years ago, however, one could find the words 'Robert I Love You/Cure Forever' written in white paint beneath a bridge not far from a roundabout, whose turfed island was greying and sparse beneath a slender, solitary streetlight. The Cure, in their twenty-year career, have sold many millions of records; their particular brand of depressive, percussive, down-in-the-mouth suburban romanticism has carried a breath of Crawley from Texas to Tokyo, somehow articulating the suburban condition as an international esperanto of mildly disaffected youth. The Cure's front-man, Robert Smith, is both a suburban anti-hero – famous for his smudged lipstick and back-combed shock of hair – and a beer-drinking football enthusiast, who moans his lyrics about blood, death and loneliness with all the plaintive weariness of a person whose library books are eternally overdue. There is neither insight nor polemic; there are no messages and no rallying anthems. Rather, the Cure are the musical expression of suburbia itself: a dense and repetitious sound, carrying a mesmeric dirge of infinitely transferable songs, all of which sound as though they could go on for ever – like endless avenues, crescents and drives.

In terms of pop credibility, at least, it was never really acceptable to like the Cure. Despite their portentous, drum-driven sound and their hymning of rage and despair, they lacked the sinewy venom of the Only Ones, the minimalist intensity of Joy Division or the violent absurdism of Wire – of all whom were their musical peers. The Cure, lacking the crackle of urbanity, were always regarded as the commercial end of post-punk psychodrama, and something of a cartoon at that. In this much, they have shared the fate of the novelist Lawrence Durrell, whose febrile and richly romantic novels of twilit psychological intrigue among profound and beautiful people were considered absurd and senti-mental – the Mills & Boons of NW3 – by the literati, despite being written within a high-minded genre and selling in vast quantities. Durrell, like the Cure, offered a seductive aesthetic that was seen as too in love with its own richly-coloured despair, and his 'Avignon Quintet', for example, shot through with mists, moods and melodrama, could be regarded as sharing the same bombastic territory as the Cure's equally stylish and equally formulaic third LP *Faith*.

But if the Cure (or Lawrence Durrell) did lack the verve, sparsity and vision of the real innovators in their respective fields, they offered instead the chance to indulge a middle-brow taste for high romantic mawkishness. And with tremendous success. The Cure's 'The Drowning Man' was 'The Lady in Red' of the sub-urban outsiders, describing a passion play of adolescent melan-choly which could be experienced, vicariously, through a pantomime of depression and emotional collapse. Like Durrell's neurasthenic diplomats and aristocratic occultists, the ubiqui-tous 'I's and 'you's of the Cure's lyrics implied being on the edge, but being in little danger of actually falling. It was all – to repeat one of Burnside's statements about suburbia – 'implied'. And the Cure's morbidity, like Durrell's gnostic safari across the landscape of the highly-strung mind, was always more implied than really felt as an exercise in emotional tourism. This was armchair catharsis and safe self-hatred – a popular package holiday to the darker reaches of the human condition, where death and despair comprised little more than the ghost train at a Club 18–30 for the younger depressive set.

By the end of the 1970s it had seemed as though many of the groups that were wandering around rather aimlessly in the ruins of punk were involved in styling a collective *de profundis*, with varying degrees of authenticity. Joy Division's genuinely disturbing expression of nervous exhaustion and frenetic rage on *Unknown Pleasures* (1979) was echoed in a softened form by the Cure's *17 Seconds*; but where Joy Division's Ian Curtis seemed to be flashing a torch in the dank warehouse of his soul, searching for something, the Cure's Robert Smith was essentially a purveyor of filmic ambience – a role the Cure underlined by touring in 1980 with an instrumental set to a short, abstract film called 'Carnage Visors'. The sound was repetitious, portentous and eerie, in keeping with the stylized seriousness of its era, hinting at drama but leading nowhere – a suburban soundtrack if ever there was one.

When Smith did sing, it wasn't so much his doom-laced lyrics as the actual sound of his voice which lent the Cure their mesmeric monotony; it was the voice of nervous boredom in a small town bedroom, muffled beneath suffocating layers of ennui. Alternately peevish and petulant, breathless with anguish or spluttering with incoherent rage, Smith's voice was unique in making monotony malleable – a quality which granted his somewhat boneless performances a sympathy and energy which his singing, by rights, denied. Also, however abstract a Cure song might strain to be, the result was never that far from swishy pop with a dash of moody film soundtrack; the songs were about isolation, boredom, sadness, anger and claustrophobia, but these themes were usually boiled in the bag of style to make them more palatable.

And yet Robert Smith – the Chatterton of Crawley – had created if not a wall of sound then a very high hedge of sound, over which he seemed to peer at the world like a boy who couldn't be bothered to ask for his ball back. Time and again there is a wistfulness and nostalgia in the Cure's songs which seem to hint at the continued, or even obsessive, denial of a formative trauma. Much of the Cure's morbidity and rage is in line with the emotions of the jilted teenage lover who can't quite realize that the autumn romance is over and winter will bring no Christmas. There is the proximity of love and hate, the yearning to rest, and the admission of defeat in the face of finally acknowledged truths. But there is no rallying command, however hoarse, self-deluded or sentimental, to fight back. The soul is not so much bared as reduced to wandering around in its dressing gown.

Despite their massive international success (and it was shocking, somehow, to see a full-page colour advertisement for the Cure's *Kiss Me Kiss Me Kiss Me* LP in Andy Warhol's *Interview* magazine), the Cure would appear to be locked, as an idea, in the late autumn of 1980 – the year that their first hit single, 'A Forest', hit the UK chart at Number 31 – with the chill mist of Crawley still damp upon their pullovers. Shambling and shock-headed, they lacked the glamour of their fellow, darkling suburban punks, Siouxsie and the Banshees (indeed, suburban Siouxsie, in the proto-Goth equation, was Morticia to Robert Smith's Uncle Fester) primarily because their pallid, boyish sensibility did not share Siouxsie and the Banshees' glittering teenage obsession with Roxy Music. The Cure were very much a boy's group, and, while Robert became something of a post-punk pin-up, younger women were often drawn to the more croonerish depression of Depeche Mode or Echo and the Bunnymen.

Despite themselves, almost, the Cure became linked to the Goth movement of the early 1980s that defined Robert Smith (along with Pete Murphy of Bauhaus) as the embodiment of the alternative pop star: a pseudo-occultist, pallid romantic, trapped in the haunted semi of his unbearable memories.

The English relationship with Gothic revivalism had always been an aesthetic response to the formalism derived from Reason and Science. The exuberant medievalism of Pugin's Victorian architecture, for instance – all vivid encaustic tiles and leaded casements – could be seen as a fantastical denial of modernity and an attempt to recapture the romantically historical or supernatural mysteries that science had in fact already solved. From such reappropriations of the Gothic came a vogue for ruins and ghosts, where high passions were matched by sepulchral surroundings, as could be seen in the romanticism of Mrs Radcliffe and Mary Shelley, to say nothing of the Gothic parodies by Thomas Love Peacock, such as *Nightmare Abbey* (1818) – the *Spinal Tap* of the Romantic movement. English Gothicism, however, has often done the bulk of its cultural work on a metaphorical level. And, translated into a metaphor to serve the late 1970s and early 1980s, Gothicism became cartoon-like in style and fed vampirically on a host of spooky informants from US psychobilly rock-'n'-roll to corset fetishism; pop Goth, born in punk with Dave Vanian's the Damned, could be seen as a tribal attempt to become the Living Dead – either Thatcher's teenage victims or post-punk refuseniks of the brighter, camper, electro-pop and disco boom that was just around the corner. With the constancy of Teddy Boys, the Goths declared their style to be indurate to the capriciousness of either fashion or pop, preferring to worship at local shrines before such minor gods as Alien Sex Fiend or the Sex Gang Children. Goth took hold as both a suburban and provincial cult, in which young men and women with heavily powdered faces, mourning clothes and Robert Smith's hairstyle could be seen at domestic ease in towns like Littlehampton and Ipswich. Their chosen pop style was quickly and fittingly pronounced a tomb on the agenda of fashionability, and the movement as a whole could be likened to the vast garden cemetery at Brookwood, in Surrey, where the London Necropolis Corporation laid out a suburbia for the dead in the middle of the nineteenth century, with room, ultimately, for a quarter of a million graves. It is there still, expanding weekly.

By the early 1980s, as provincial suburban Goth and metropolitan suburban New Romanticism were merging to create a whole new era of club-based pop culture, anticipating the jazz revival and dance scene that would grow towards the middle of the decade, the Cure became a monolithic Pink Floyd of the post-punk confusion, ploughing their deep dark furrow alone in a very grey field on the edge of credibility. Faced with the usual problems of internationally successful pop stars (internal politics, addiction, solo projects and stadium concerts in Belgium), the group clung – as if by habit – to its credo and aesthetic of violence and despair. But English pop, reinventing itself on faster and faster cycles of trend, was out of love with the ethos of despair that the Cure – drab and apolitical – appeared to have set in amber. Introversion had given way to clubbing, and plangent romanticism had been succeeded by a pop cultural playfulness (and cleverness) in which irony would be the key note. The political camp of Frankie Goes to Hollywood, held in place by Paul Morley's applied semiotics, would soon seem far more relevant than the Cure's latest articulations of nervous break-downs and failed identities.

If the Cure can be heard, fancifully, as the sound of the suburbs, then what prepared suburbia to produce such dispossessed spirits? In England, where culture seems concerned with depth (in America it seems more in love with breadth), one begins with a local sense of place – which absorbs repeated patterns of experience like a psychic tape recorder, listening out for errant bleeps and squeaks which denote disturbance. Suburbia, born of convenience and the demands of market forces, has a potent sense of place which is derived from its uneasy colonization of chalky downs, inhospitable marshes or flinty hinterlands. Then, becoming a DIY Eden, surveyed by so many round-eyed Adam and Eves, suburbia did not reckon for such a fall from grace; aiming at perfection, suburbia arrived at Purley, describing the suburban soul in an intricate social architecture. E. M. Forster, ever the apostate high priest of suburbia, defines the situation with timeless accuracy at the beginning of *Maurice*:

> Maurice's mother lived near London, in a comfortable villa among some pines. There he and his sisters had been born, and thence his father had gone up to business every day, thither returning. They nearly left when the church was built, but they became accustomed to it, as to everything, and even found it a convenience. Church was the only place Mrs Hall had to go – the shops delivered. The station was not far either, nor was a tolerable day school for the girls. It was a land of facilities, where nothing had to be striven for, and success was indistinguishable from failure.

Fair or not, Forster's anatomy of the suburban condition suggests a breeding ground for disaffection. But this is not the suffering and struggle for reform provoked by the industrial or inner cities, bringing with it its own cultural response; rather, it is a reflective state – a brooding non-conformity in which preparation for rebellion may well be foreshortened by the very comfort and complacency of the suburban surroundings. If cities can explode like cultural bombs, then suburbia, more often than not, is the blue touch paper. Domesticating a not-so-rugged wilderness, English suburbia was concerned with security above all else, thus making it – as a popular notion – the place where nothing can ever happen. And it is this security which primed suburbia as the venue for a particular brand of reactive English culture. Suburban writers such as Stevie Smith and Edinburgh-born Shena Mackay caught the spirit of suburbia by locating an existential crisis, or a crisis of faith, in the cushioned basin of suburban life; they lacked the hatred of the young Graham Greene or Evelyn Waugh for the 'Tudorbethan' and the leaded windows of the solid fuels office, and they avoided the sophisticated ambivalence of Betjeman, for whom suburbia was a complex ambiguous joke, as laced with self-reflective irony as it was held in place by love – the Surrey sports girl sensually entwined with the scent of Surrey pines. But Stevie Smith and Shena Mackay brought a new understanding of the suburban condition – the compromised soul, almost – which exposed the psychology of a uniquely suburban malaise. Their thesis, while not official, was implied by applying the sensibility of suburbia's poignant placelessness to tragi-comic treatments of the theme of mortality. And this was a suburban response which J. G. Ballard – the William S. Burroughs of Shepperton – would take to even darker, metaphysical extremes: 'There's a certain sort of logic leading towards these immaculate suburbs. And they're terrifying, because they are the death of the soul. And I thought, My God, this is the prison this planet is being turned into.'

Mackay's heroines can be seen as the suburban equivalent of the working-class women in Nell Dunn's south London stories *Poor Cow* and *Up the Junction*; pitted against a given society, they do their best to cope within the limits of that society. But where Nell Dunn's Clapham or Battersea were vivid and volatile, Mackay's suburbia is a place where deliquescent gentility, urban over-spill, hypocrisy and ennui are encoded on to the landscape; the demarcations of class and convenience are as fixed as they were in Forster's fictitious suburb of Sawston, eighty years earlier, but the shops no longer deliver and the ritual of commuting has become a deadening routine. Suburbia has been synonymous with boredom and stillness – a suspension of morbid speculations such as the Cure translated into foggy post-punk. Hence this description in Mackay's 'Redhill Rococo' (1986):

> A Brighton train arrived at platform three, and departed. She walked
> to the end of the platform and stared at a house standing in a
> waste garden of dross, the last one of a demolished terrace which
> the occupants had refused to leave. Pearl had read about them
> in the Surrey Mirror. Smoke was coming from the chimney and
> Pearl wondered what they were doing in their brick shell,
> marooned in rubble under their damp spiral of smoke. At last a
> train did arrive and Pearl got on, hoping it stopped at Purley. It
> did not and she had to go on to East Croydon and change.

Here we find a near documentary account of the suburban rail
system becoming a mesmeric chant of monotonous facts, the
lulling effect of which (touched by helpless irritation) lures the
mind into the sombre conjecture; what is occurring in this
suburban hypnosis (Burnside's 'abstracted quality' from the
'sentence learned by heart') is akin to a psychiatric process of
transference, in which the marooned suburbanite transposes
herself into the unknown lives around her. For Mackay,
Betjeman's attractively arcane Metroland has become a pop age
no-man's-land, stifled by the rigidity, however rotten, of its original advantages of convenient shopping, respectable housing and
position within the Greater London commuter belt. Reading in
her morning *Guardian* of a mass execution by hanging in a
distant country, Pearl's acquaintance Helen links the atrocity to
an item on knitting, and the stories entwine in her mind. Once
again the mesmeric qualities of the banal and the boring, in this
case knitting, trigger a transference into morbidity:

> There was an interesting article on the revival in popularity of hand
> knitting but, as she read, the skeins of wool kept twisting into
> ropes.

> Imagine such an occurrence in Reigate, or Redhill: it would merit
> more than half a column inch in the Surrey Mirror. Outside
> the Old Town Hall would be the best place, she mused, or
> the Priory Park, or on the roundabout near Redhill Station;
> scaffolding and ropes erected in an obscene gymnasium on the
> grass. Pastoral scene of the gallant South East.

The ultimate destination of Helen's mesmerized suburban daydream is to find the suburb synonymous with death – a theme which is echoed by Pearl's suspicion at her daughter's burgeoning involvement with a group of local charismatic Christians. The equation that relates English suburbia to meditations on mortality and religion was also central to much of Stevie Smith's poetry, so much so that she becomes the Emily Dickinson of Palmers Green, in terms of her pessimism and personal theology, at least. Stevie Smith was both dependent on suburbia and at a loss within it, commuting to and from her job in London as a secretary at the magazine publishing company Newnes Pearson, while nursing her 'Lion Aunt' in the unchanging house at Palmers Green. But Smith was anything but a recluse, socializing widely and – as was dramatized in Hugh Whitemore's play of her life, *Stevie* (1977) – always finding someone to run her home to her inconvenient suburb. Smith defines the notion of the insular suburban misfit artist, yet points up a creative chemistry that is derived from the relationship between the city and suburbia. The suburbs, working on the metaphorical level once more, became womb-like in their offering of a constant security, and commuting – an oscillatory existence between the two opposed states of the urban and the suburban – permitted the suburban artist a peculiar kind of freedom. Peter Pan-like, the suburban artist can avoid commitment to the reality of urban life, travelling between the city as NeverNever land and the infantilist comforts of the suburban home as the safe harbour of Kensington Gardens. The commuting becomes internalized: a psychological traversing between innocence and experience.

But this response, in the suburban artist, offers no real safety from the doubts and fears (Stevie Smith attempted suicide) that their art must confront: the price of such statelessness, however useful as a safety valve in the creation of art, is a personal limbo and a search for faith. (Remarkably, the post-punk art group This Heat would record an interpretation of Stevie Smith's famous poem on suburban suicide, 'Not Waving But Drowning', on their self-titled LP released in 1979.) In her poem 'The House of Over-Dew', Smith uses the polarity of urban and suburban to describe the religious fanaticism of a former accountant who has moved his family beyond the suburbs to a kind of living death of spiritual servitude. Despotic in his misguided saintliness, attempting to run the House of Over-Dew as a retreat for resting missionaries:

> Mr Minnim, released suddenly
> From the routine of his accountancy
> Suffered in his head a strange numbness,
> He moved about in a dream, would take no hand with
> the dishes.

Settling at Over-Dew in the dead of winter, Mr Minnim's family are broken apart by his scheme as the thaw brings 'mud and slush'; their former neighbours laugh at them, and Mrs Minnim's last security – their vacated but unsold house in the suburbs – is denied her because its value could have been contributed to the running of the retreat. Deeply morbid, 'The House of Over-Dew' is on the one hand a metaphysical poem, in keeping with Smith's religious themes, on the difficulties of faith. But then there is a choice of imagery within the poem (not least Mr Minnim's 'strange numbness' in the head) that places its story within a psychological, outer suburban wilderness, where even faith is translated into a symptom of desperate malaise. Tellingly, the Minnim son's fiancée, withdrawn to the sanity offered by London, gets the last word in the poem:

> In London
> The girl who should have been Georgie's wife
> Hears all; understands; loves Georgie, is helpless:
> reads to her class
> The Latin prayer: I devote to Hades and Destruction.

From the Cure's *Faith*, to Pearl's engagement with the suburban charismatic Christians, to the strange numbness in the House of Over-Dew, there is at least a punning of shared concerns which support John Burnside's suburban theology, that 'what makes it beautiful is what makes it dangerous, like the spirit of the fish pool which flares out and taints our children'.

That the suburbs, as opposed to the city, have been the prime incubator and kindergarten for principal players in English popular culture is as certain as the equally strong role of the provinces. Around the extreme south-east of London, along the Bromley, Croydon and Sutton belt (a suburban curve, linking the urbanity of Lewisham and New Cross to the quasi-ruralism of Epsom and Leatherhead), the suburbs would become famous as a launch-pad for punk rock. Jamie Reid's proto-punk situationist newspaper *Suburban Press* was launched in Croydon in 1970 as an anarchist critique of suburbia: the cover of issue 1 was simply a photocopied image of a new semi, while issue 5 displayed a similar image of the Croydon flyover, entitled 'Lo, a monster is born!' Running until 1975, *Suburban Press* rehearsed the graphical style that Jamie Reid would later use for promoting the Sex Pistols, and the newspaper's 'sticker campaign' ('Keep Warm This Winter, Make Trouble', for example) anticipated the sloganeering used to advertise 'Pretty Vacant' and 'Holidays In The Sun'. Meanwhile, in neighbouring Bromley, the 'Bromley Contingent' would provide punk rock with its first famous diva in the shape of Siouxsie Sioux.

Away from the glowing embers of legend, suburbia produced punks who were devotees of a finely honed amateurism, turning themselves into their own comic victims, like walking satires of their own condition. Suburban punks wound up running pig farms or working for the Post Office; it was hippies, interestingly, who made good businessmen. The fact that suburban life, particularly for teenagers, can be a vicious cocktail of boredom, compromise and frustration was deeply sympathetic to pop culture and to

punk culture especially. Art schools, historically, had linked creative thinking to pop since the early 1960s, reinforcing the road
from Nowhere to Somewhere in terms of pop's suburban formula; but if Malcolm McLaren and Jamie Reid (both students
at Croydon Art College) would go on to become the aristocracy
of punk, who applied 'detourne' situationist technique to suburban pop culture, capitalizing on their art school educations,
then there was also a serfdom of separatists (and imitators) for
whom fame remained elusive, and for whom the semi rather
than the salon would remain the principal inspiration. While a
yob among the snobs will always go far in England, the ones
who never got out of their bedrooms can sometimes burn with
an equal intensity.

One group which seemed to personify emotional frustration on the
suburban edge was the Television Personalities. Formed by
Daniel Treacy, a native Londoner, in 1978, with his friends
Edward Ball and Mark Sheppard, the Television Personalities
mined English popular culture from Lindsay Anderson's *If* to
the rock legend of Syd Barrett to produce a remarkable catalogue
of alternately comic and despairing pop songs. Dismissed by
some critics as little more than purveyors of punk novelty singles,
the Television Personalities were in some ways a victim of
their cult hit, 'Part Time Punks' – which sold 24,000 copies
on the strength of its catchy tune and uncomfortably recognizable punch-line: 'And I think it's a shame that they all look
the same.'

Commenting on the suburban search for punk credibility, the Television Personalities began with a faintly spurious comedy of
recognition but then developed their songs to describe an interior
darkness in which the part-time punks of their first hit could be
seen as a generation of Billy Liars – frustrated by banality and
boredom but alienated by their imagination, timidity and intelligence. These were the people for whom the anarchy of Crass
seemed like the same hippie dog but with different fleas, and

for whom the glamour of Kings Road fashionability would simply be another exercise in commuting from suburbia. In 1980, the group released its first LP, *And Don't The Kids Just Love It*, to a hurricane of indifference and sales of just 12,000 copies; but the record contained an elaborate code of reference points in its song titles alone: 'This Angry Silence', 'Look Back In Anger', 'Geoffrey Ingram', 'A Picture of Dorian Gray' and 'I Know Where Syd Barrett Lives'. Saturated in imagery from popular culture of the 1960s (quotations from David Sherwin's screenplay of *If . . .* were featured on the album sleeve, and the cover stars were Twiggy and Steed), the record lacked the sheer speed and attitude of other punk debuts (*Crossing The Red Sea With The Adverts*, for instance, or Wire's magnificent *Pink Flag*) but stood alone on the edge of the dance floor (or the playground, come to that), wiping its nose on the back of its sleeve and being hopelessly incapable of joining in with even its pop peers. The vocals were a thin whine and mumble, starting into sudden viciousness, while the guitar solos and drum rolls lurched uncertainly between amateurish interpretations of the polished sound of the Jam or the Buzzcocks.

But it was the very clumsiness of the Television Personalities which made their records so telling of a particular suburban sensibility. Somehow doomed to comparative obscurity, the group was unfairly consigned to minor cult status; its mixture of punk social realism (in the style of Sham 69 or the Jam) and pop cultural aestheticism had the effect of making it sound like a pub band with obscure lyrics. Their definitive statement, however, could be found on the cover of their LP *Privilege*, which was a Victorian portrait of three Aubrey Beardsley-style aesthetes, dressed in Wildean velvet knee-breeches and jackets, their heads leaning weakly to one side in attitudes of effeminate languour. The picture was an example of the late Victorian ridicule of Oscar Wilde as conveyed by hearty satires in *Punch* magazine, which ran a popular campaign of aesthete taunting and mockery of the

Aesthetic movement in general. The Television Personalities, it seemed, were finally pillorying themselves as latter-day aesthetes – marginalized by their own culture as limp-wristed, ineffectual and ridiculous.

Despite creating a fascinating cul-de-sac within the maze of English popular culture, the Television Personalities lacked the musical force and glamour to become as significant as they deserved to be. Certainly, as pop psychologists of the suburban condition, they were lucid and witty, but it would require a Samson – in the shape of Morrissey – to bring down the pillars of English pop complacency and turn sensitivity into a violent celebration which would unite the dispossessed on an international scale. But the Television Personalities must be acknowledged for rehearsing pop's obsession with its own history (which would be very much a feature of 'BritPop' in the 1990s) and for bringing not only the tragedy but the comedy of English kitchen-sink cinema to the pop song. Their cry in the cold light of morning (rather than the long dark night of the soul) was articulate and poignant, achieving such unexpected and forceful images as 'My brother's anorexic, but no one seems to care about the state he's in' – which lesser groups would miss by never conceiving of anorexia as a male illness. The detail is more literary than lyrical, as were, perhaps, members of the group themselves.

-▦-

England's ambivalence towards itself has selected suburbia as the principal setting for satire and comedy over the last forty years; the kitchen sink could be up-graded to the three-piece suite when it came to comically anatomizing the 'little man' as the descendant of the shrewd first-time buyer of the 1920s – popularly perceived as the bowler-hatted pioneer whose stockade was his villa and who tamed the wilderness in the name of car-boot sales. Suburbia bred a mock heroic comedy, in which lost dogs, eccentric vicars, embarrassing neighbours and unexpected dinner guests could be seen as the alpha and omega of the human condition. The reduction of life to the comfortably – and terminally – local was taken up as suburbia's comic function (a neat reversal of the city's role as a catalyst of grand gestures and dangerous passions) and it was this obsession with the local that fuelled the farce which launched a thousand situation comedies.

In the earliest 'Carry On' films, such as *Carry on Cabby* and the hospital 'Carry Ons', we are presented with suburban townscapes and local institutions which are still ruled by the regimented spirit of National Service or even World War Two. Sid James employs Charles Hawtrey in *Carry on Cabby* (1963) because of his service record, while in *Carry on Nurse* (1959) the patients on a male ward rouse themselves to oppose the tyrannical Hattie Jacques to the accompaniment of military band music and a distinct revival of the attitude which won the war. These early 'Carry Ons' continued the ethos of Ealing comedy in terms of the rights of the Little Man to defend his freedom (a scenario established in *Passport to Pimlico*, 1949, and *The Titfield Thunder-bolt*, 1952) but modernized the situations to satirize the post-war common enemies of galloping bureaucracy, inefficient local services and, ultimately, teenagers and young people.

As the worried features of Richard Wattis were often used to sum up the new threat of the 'man from the ministry', so the glorious trail that was blazed by the 'Carry On' team, through dating agencies, toilet factories and hospitals, described the new suburban society as a vision of England in which everything looked boring and nothing worked properly. Always looking as though they were filmed in Morden on a wet Tuesday afternoon, the 'Carry Ons' were the basis of a popular English cynicism which the cartoonist Giles also made famous: permanent bad weather, grouchy British Rail staff, and the common people (as Jarvis Cocker, of Pulp, would later define them) endlessly satirizing the discrepancy between their own ordinariness and the messages beamed back down to them from the stratosphere of freshly mediated High Society and government.

The 'common people', in 'Carry Ons' and early situation comedy, at least, were scripted to be complicit with their humdrum lives; indeed, self-improvement as much as rebellion was grounds for a good laugh and a lesson in humility. The cheeky chaps and saucy women in the 'Carry On's' eternal suburbia would prove themselves reactionary and intolerant of the counter-culture in the deft way that they get rid of an open-air pop festival at the end of *Carry on Camping* (1969). Disguised as hippie ravers, Sid James and Bernard Bresslaw tie all the concert-goers' love-beads together and have them towed off the camp site, *en masse*, by a tractor. And here are shades of Chas in *Performance*, with his contemptuous pronouncement of 'drugs, foreigners, long 'air, the lot . . .' But Sid and Bernard have also learned a moral lesson: they lose their illicit young girlfriends as the ravers are dragged off through the mud, but can now return to the legitimate (and, by implication, socially orthodox) affections of their nice suburban partners. Humility is all, once again. Even in the 1970s we would find Sid James, in the amiable suburban sit-com, *Bless This House*, hopelessly at odds with his love-bead-wearing, art student son and his hot-pants wearing, dolly-bird daughter.

The brilliance of the 'Carry On' films lay in the innuendo-laden dialogue, the brash brass soundtracks and the long-suffering characters: Hattie Jacques and her budgie that can pick race winners, Lance Percival's 'cake of many countries' (in *Carry on Cruising*), and the classic pantomime of outrage enacted by Joan Sims when taken to a documentary about nudist camps at the start of *Carry on Camping*: 'You'd know all about it if your lolly fell in your lap!' she upbraids an indignant Sid. As monuments to popular suburban attitudes, reflected as comic enlargements, these films were without equal; but the series was as good as finished by the early 1970s, when the descent into mere crudity was hastened by the increasing defection of the original cast into other jobs or no jobs at all. By the time of *Carry on Girls* (1973), with its lampooning of the women's movement in June Whitfield's unforgettable pronouncement (as a militant 'women's libber'), 'We will squat on this erection!', there was more than a sense that the 'Carry Ons' could not survive the modern age – most notably because the modern age was becoming increasingly complex and multi-cultural, and could not respond to the postwar sensibility of tea urns and tandems that early 'Carry Ons' had defined so well.

Throughout the 1960s and the 1970s, English comedy would struggle to find a language which put its finger on the pulse, culminating in the phenomenal success of *Monty Python's Flying Circus*. Worn thin by familiarity, Monty Python can be seen as a classic example of class-bound English comedy going through yet another phase of reinvention; but more interesting, in many ways, was the children's television programme *Do Not Adjust Your Set*, where several of the 'Pythons' started their TV careers and the neo-dadaist Bonzo Dog Doo-Dah Band had a weekly slot. Vivian Stanshall's Bonzo Dog Band was both pop and pop art, combining nostalgia for novelty numbers by jazz bands of the 1920s with distinctly psychedelic musical collage. More than mere satirists, the group looked at the present by way of the past, anatomizing Englishness with a creative range which stretched from 'Hello Mabel's' tea-room jauntiness, through the melancholia of England's seaside towns ('Postcard'), to the positive freak out of 'We Are Normal And We Want Our Freedom'. Unlike most pop humorists, who are doomed by definition it seems, the Bonzo Dog Band mixed wit and pathos in a way that would not be repeated until Madness wed the comedy of recognition to the tragedy of growing old.

Like an English version of Frank Zappa's Mothers of Invention, only funny and to the point, the Bonzo Dog Band applied pop absurdism to national notions of normality. This could be twee and irritating, but it could also – when the project took wings on mimicry and lyrical cleverness – deliver neat, anecdotal or epigrammatic assessments of the English condition. The group's definitive work was its LP of 1968, *The Doughnut In Granny's Greenhouse*, with its magnificent sermon of suburbia, 'My Pink Half Of The Drainpipe', which began with the stentorian protest:

> You! Who speaks me to me across the fence
> Of common sense

to be answered:

> I've a sister in Toronto who's a nurse.
> And I've had a bit of bother laying turf.

Nineteen sixty-eight was also the year that the Beatles delivered their ultimate pop art statement, *The White Album*, with its debts to Fluxus and Dada as well as nostalgia for tea-room dance music. It is tempting to see artistic similarities between these two pop art LPs of 1968, but the monolithic significance of the Beatles – particularly the deliquescing Beatles of '68, whose fame rendered even their photographed portraits as opaque transmissions from a distant planet of celebrity, beyond common reality – makes any comparisons difficult. What was shared, however, was a sense of Englishness which had one foot in the future and the other in the past; one half of the brain engaged with the banality of daily life in rainy old England, the other pioneering within extreme states of mind to bring back reports from the edges of consciousness.

The heavily documented history of the Beatles shows us a guinea-pig phenomenon; as with Elvis, there had never been that sort of celebrity before, and the celebrities themselves, like animals sent into orbit to see what might happen, were beyond our reach almost before the rocket was launched. A group like the Bonzo Dog Band, however, never really made it out of the laboratory – a fate which it shared, in terms of comedy, with the great 'lost' sit-com of the early 1980s, *Big Jim and the Figaro Club*, and its depiction of post-war corporation builders in an England 'before the world turned rotten and sour'. The Bonzo Dog Band's last project was the unwanted *Excerpts From The Brain Opera*, and they played their last concert at Loughborough University in the dead of winter, 1970; the creators of the Urban Spaceman (their only hit) would find no place in Ziggy Stardust's silver decade.

As English comedy had shown suburbia as a battlefield that doubles as a plastic Eden, the effective comic anti-hero was seldom better than Leonard Rossiter's sublime performance as Reginald Perrin – a character in which Hamlet, Billy Liar and a cartoon Cromwell were recklessly mingled to turn a prime-time situation comedy into a near Chekhovian study of nervous collapse. With his morning walk through quiet residential roads named after Romantic poets (echoing the 'semi-detached torture chambers' in Ellesmere Road, west London, described by George Orwell's precursor of Perrin, George 'Fatty' Bowling), the inevitable seven-minute delay of his commuter train, his pointless job at Sunshine Desserts and his existential frustration, Reggie Perrin was a brave, if pessimistic portrait of suburban life within the consumer democracy. His eventual faked suicide was closer to classic tragedy than situation comedy, while his re-emergence as the founder, managing director and guru of Grot (a retail chain that sells expensive rubbish of no actual worth to fad-crazed customers) was both anarchistic in its apocalyptic cynicism, and utterly prophetic of the venture capitalism boom in the 1980s which would see over-priced bric-à-brac and quack herbalism being sold in every post-modern precinct and heritage-driven shopping mall from Covent Garden to York. By fixing Perrin's despair and mental imbalance on to the absurdity and gullibility of advanced consumerism, the character managed (despite the weakness of the later scripts, in which Grot became a quasi-mystical commune; from Ruskin to the Moonies in one queasy go) to describe the conversion of old suburbia into the new suburbia of hypermarkets, total consumer environments and fad-dictated consumption.

As Evelyn Waugh had perceived the death of honour in his description of the Allied retreat from Crete in 1940, and Noël Coward saw the Festival of Britain as a cross between a confidence trick and the selling of advertising copy to a nation in denial and despair, so Reggie Perrin, trapped in a society which gave no quarter in its sophistry, revealed the rat race as beginning in the home: suburbia was the rats' dormitory, just as Croydon could be seen as London's filing cabinet, with its brutalist towers marked out by *Suburban Press* as totems of imprisonment. Indeed, Perrin's half-hearted war cry seemed to rehearse Soft Cell's lyric on 'Frustration', that: 'I work for a firm but I want to burn it down.'

The new suburbia, taking hold from the end of the 1970s, would be monolithic in the scale of its retail parks and the sphere of its influence. Sweetened by the heritage industry (what Alan Bennett defined in his short TV film about a restored arcade in Leeds as 'shops that sell out-of-the-way mustards') and attempting to tame an eerie psychological hinterland that closes in when the shops shut, the new suburbia would be the setting for a new kind of precinct pop, from the Human League to jungle. It would be either Utopia or Dystopia, depending, paradoxically, on your credit rating within the computerized consumer democracy. But Leicester-born artist David Shrigley, in his text *Burn Out* (1995) described the suburban future with a violence and despair to which suburbia, by now, must be accustomed:

Experimental rock music came and went. Girlfriends picked up their clothes and left. There was no milk and no bread . . . I noticed people coughing and vomiting outside by the bins. The pox had come to town and it was having a good time. We all took a bus to the centre of town, bought some petrol and burned down the hotel, the church, the hospital and the orphanage. More jackboots. Nothing is or ever was sacred.

6

iʃ shakeſpeare had a sister

I was working as a waitress in a cocktail bar,
That much is true,
But even then I knew I'd find a much better place.
Either with or without you.

'DON'T YOU WANT ME' (1981), *Human League*

If we can speculate on the post-war career of Waugh's Captain
Hooper, positioning him as the amiable and comparatively
classless modern patriarch in the New Elizabethan age, then
what might we think of Mrs Hooper – whom Waugh never
got around to, but whose place at Hooper's side seems almost
inevitable? Waugh's conception of female characters seemed
tinged with a grim misogyny which, one suspects, derived more
from his disastrous first marriage to the socialite Evelyn Gardner
('She Evelyn' to Waugh's 'He Evelyn' in the androgyny-friendly
parlance of Mayfair's Bright Young Things) than from a disillusionment with women *per se*. But as a creator of fictional
female 'types', he provides a recognizably pre-war cast of women.
Waugh's female characters are either signifiers of sophisticated
selfishness (Brenda Last in *A Handful of Dust* and Virginia Troy
in the 'Sword of Honour' trilogy), hopelessly domestic stiflers of
male brilliance (Celia Ryder in *Brideshead Revisited*) or tragic

beauties – such as Julia Mottram (in *Brideshead Revisited*) – who weave a hair shirt of boredom and melodrama in which to protest their disaffection with high society and mourn their lost youth. The exception to these roles would be Cordelia Flyte, in *Brideshead Revisited*, who is virtually excused gender on the grounds of her Catholic piety. All products of Mayfair and the county estates, Waugh's women, whether active or reactive, are convincingly drawn but exist primarily to serve the wholly masculine institutions of English society prior to World War Two.

The only clue to Waugh's definition of modern wives can be found in the character of Daisy Leonard in the 'Sword of Honour' trilogy, whose shrewish determination to have her husband excused overseas service and take a barracks posting in England leads, tellingly, to him being blown up by a stray bomb. As the particular attitude of an individual novelist, mirroring a social orthodoxy in which the visibility of women had been held in check by a largely patriarchal society, Waugh's engagement with femininity and feminism can be seen as typical of his period and class. But World War Two, as a catalyst of social change, would broaden the directive of English culture to include more fully the specific experience and contributions of women. In this much, the imagined Mrs Hooper might well have identified, romantically, with Celia Johnson in Noël Coward's *Brief Encounter* (1945), but would find herself presented with a very different version of the same story – working-class social realism over mannered, psychological romance – in 1957, in Ted Willis's *Woman in a Dressing Gown*. Indeed, by the time of *Woman in a Dressing Gown*, in which a cheerful, working-class wife and mother is in danger of losing her husband to a better educated and more sophisticated young woman, the 'problem' film and Free Cinema would have turned attention away from the upper-class stereotypes, both male and female, that had evolved within English culture as an historical consequence of bourgeois writers and artists, to focus more widely on a new society in which gender, no less than class, was undergoing reinvention. In order to appreciate the impact of this reinvention, particularly with regard to the role of women within English culture, Virginia Woolf's essay 'A Room of One's Own' provides a famously pivotal text which refers back to the pre-war feminine condition while anticipating much that followed.

When it came to giving advice to young women on how to make a career as a writer, Woolf diluted her usual brackish tisane of snobbish high-mindedness with a drop of cooling realism: 'a woman must have money and a room of her own if she is to write fiction.' This famous phrase occurs within the deceptively conversational opening of Woolf's incisive essay on the status of women in English literature, and provides the essay with its title. Delivered first as two lectures to the women of Newnham and Girton colleges at Cambridge University in 1928, 'A Room of One's Own' was published in an expanded form by the Hogarth Press in 1929. As the central figure of the Bloomsbury Group clique, who by means of excessive mutual admiration and high birth had elected themselves to be a metropolitan repository of fine intellectualism (the Fortnum & Mason of belles lettres), Woolf was not given, often, to dismounting from her extremely high horse. But on this one point, of the historical impossibility of England producing a female Shakespeare, she reveals herself as a hands-on feminist and a democrat. To translate this achievement, fancifully, into the language of pop, 'A Room of One's Own' is Woolf's blistering Top Five single in an otherwise somewhat patchy discography: her 'Running Up That Hill' as opposed to her 'Wow', to borrow from the chequered career of Kate Bush.

Powerfully argued and poetically written, 'A Room of One's Own' pursues the imaginary life of Shakespeare's sister as its central conceit: assuming this sister to be as talented as her famous brother, Woolf suggests that Elizabethan society would have been so structured as to forbid her genius to flourish. Her fate

– 'killed herself one winter's night and lies buried at some cross-roads where the omnibuses now stop outside the Elephant & Castle' – becomes politicized in Woolf's anecdotal pronouncement (untypically levelled at the traditions of Cambridge, where the Apostles were an outpost of Bloomsbury): 'Literature is open to everybody. I refuse to allow you, Beadle though you are, to turn me off the grass. Lock up your libraries if you like; but there is no lock, no bolt that you can set upon the freedom of my mind.' The romance of Shakespeare's sister, for Woolf, becomes a parable about the reality of life for women artists in England.

One does not have to look far to test the truth of Woolf's axiomatic essay. Mrs Gaskell records, in her *Life of Charlotte Brontë* (1857), the advice passed on to her subject by the then Poet Laureate, Southey, in March 1837, when she had written for guidance in the business of writing poetry. As an exercise in networking, Charlotte's approach to Southey was doomed from the start. With withering condescension, the great man replied to his humble correspondent:

> The day dreams in which you habitually indulge are likely to induce a distempered state of mind; and in proportion as all the ordinary uses of the world seem to you flat and unprofitable, you will be unfitted for them without becoming fitted for anything else. Literature cannot be the business of a woman's life, and it ought not to be. The more she is engaged in her proper duties, the less leisure she will have for it, even as an accomplishment and a recreation. To those duties you have not yet been called, and when you are you will be less eager for celebrity.

The humility of Charlotte's reply (again, recorded by Mrs Gaskell) describes the complicity with patriarchal despotism expected of Victorian women, and illustrates the social and cultural impasse that has been created entirely by gender:

> In the evenings, I confess, I do think, but I never trouble any one
> else with my thoughts. I carefully avoid any appearance of
> preoccupation or eccentricity, which might lead those I live
> amongst to suspect the nature of my pursuits. Following my
> father's advice – who from my childhood had counselled me
> just in the wise and friendly tone of your letter – I have endeav-
> oured not only attentively to observe all the duties a woman
> ought to fulfill, but to feel deeply interested in them. I don't
> always succeed, for sometimes when I'm teaching or sewing I
> would rather be reading or writing; but I try to deny myself, and
> my father's approbation amply rewarded me for the privation.

The tone of Charlotte's self-rebuking 'confession' is almost proto-
Maoist in its admission of guilt as a necessary component of
punishment. But most eloquent of all, in this nervous exchange
of letters between a parson's daughter and the Poet Laureate, is
the bat-squeak of defiant conviction, barely audible, that echoes
about the final sentences of Charlotte's reply to Southey; beneath
the humility there is a hint of independence, all deriving from
the power of authorship and signature:

> Again, I thank you. This incident, I suppose, will be renewed no
> more; if I live to be an old woman, I shall remember it thirty
> years hence as a bright dream. The signature which you sus-
> pected of being fictitious is my real name. Again, therefore, I
> must sign myself,
>
> C. Brontë

Southey's unwarranted suspicion, in the fundamental matter of
names, has been gently but firmly turned against him; the
rebuke, with a deft touch, has been returned.

Between Charlotte Brontë's letter of 1837 and Virginia Woolf's essay
of 1929, it would seem as though little had changed in most
women's roles in English society and culture. Women had gained
some political recognition, and those who could afford it were
allowed a university education, but the audible voices of England
were primarily bass and tenor. Woman was the helper of man:

part muse, part mother and part servant. The rigidity of these roles can be seen in the moralistic schoolgirl fiction of Angela Brazil, whose social values would be inherited by Enid Blyton, and thus passed on through the mainstream of popular fiction to generations far removed from the Victorian orthodoxy in which they had evolved. In Brazil's *The Madcap of the School* (1916), the progressive Miss Gibbs is clearly seen to be something of a crank:

> She had attended an educational congress during the Easter holi-days, and came back primed with the very latest theories. She was determined to work on the most modern methods, and to turn her pupils out into the world, a little band of ardent thinkers, keen-witted, self-sacrificing, logical, anxious for the development of their sex, yearning for careers, in fact the van-guard of a new womanhood. Unfortunately her material was not altogether promising.
>
> A few earnest spirits, such as Maudie Heywood, responded to her appeals, but the generality were slow to move. They listened to her addresses on women's suffrage without a spark of anima-tion, and sat stolidly while she descanted upon the bad con-ditions of labour amongst the munitions girls, and the need for lady welfare workers. The fact was that her pupils did not care an atom about the position of their sex, a half holiday was far more to them than the vote, and their own grievances loomed larger than those of factory hands.

Written at a time when the anti-Suffragette movement was distribut-ing leaflets and posters that described the fledgeling women's movement as a social evil, not only impeding men from carrying out their war work (one contemporary poster, 'Not at Home!', depicted an exhausted factory worker returning to his parlour, only to find the children playing with matches beside a note on the kitchen table which reads, 'Gone to the Suffragette meeting') but also inciting immorality in its darker existence as a crime against nature itself. The official acknowledgement of such

prejudice can be seen, for example, in the indefinite hospitaliz-
ation, by the authorities, of working-class girls who become pregnant under age – a reality of life that even Enid Blyton's 'Five
Find-Outers', in the late 1940s, would get wind of when they
attempt to cross-question a dismissed housemaid about her
former life prior to moving to the Arcadian village of Peterswood:

'I did something very foolish and bad, you see, and I had to be sent
away.'
'I think I understand,' said Fatty.

Similarly, in Jack Lee-Thompson's film *The Weak and the Wicked*
released as late as 1953, in which Glynis Johns plays a middle-
class prisoner learning the error of her ways by edifying her
fellow (primarily working-class) inmates (including the young
Diana Dors, who becomes a better person by realizing that her
boyfriend has led her astray), we are shown imprisoned mothers
having their babies taken away from them, at nine months old,
for adoption. This was a scene which even British film melodrama could not rob of its tragedy and brutality.

Throughout the 1950s, women became the principal targets of the
latest trends in advertising, with their place in the new consumer
democracy being shaped by products that claimed fashionability
and convenience while implying a family morality, for which
the lady of the house was beamingly responsible. The world of
launderettes and supermarkets, synthetics and frozen foods,
would serve as the backdrop for 'Mother's Little Helper', by the
Rolling Stones, in which 'the little yellow pill' is taken in ever
larger quantities by the housewife whose nameless depression
('she's not really ill') has been brought on by the boredom and
claustrophobia of her domestic routine. That women were
increasingly resistant to their continued subordination was even
acknowledged, but held in place by comedy, in *Carry on Cabby*
(1963), in which Hattie Jacques and Sid James, as work-obsessed
husband and neglected wife, set up rival cabbying companies.

Hattie's all-women cab company is staffed entirely by mini-skirted dolly birds who more or less solicit their male fares with a flash of thigh and false eyelashes; sexual independence is partially gained by the use of sexuality.

Within the reactionary world of the 'Carry On' films, in which women's libbing would merely provide another vehicle for their tried and tested formula of comedy, one can see a continuation of the English need to use satire and ridicule as a weapon against either radicalism or rogue elements. And the early lampooning of the women's movement can be compared to the cheerily chauvinistic way in which modern art had been denied any seriousness by sketches in *Punch*. This link, between the reception of modernist art in England and the advancing claims of women for broader acknowledgement, had been encoded at the start of the century – as a near fable – in the public hostility towards Epstein's relief statuary on the upper frieze of the British Medical Association in the Strand. Executed between 1907 and 1908, these figures aroused the indignation of an independent watchdog Committee for Public Morals, who worked in league with the London *Evening Standard* to have them removed. Particular distaste was levelled at the figure of 'Maternity' – an austere, serene carving of a pregnant woman, in Epstein's early Primitive style – because of the visibility of the pregnant belly. After nearly three decades of argument and counter-argument, the figures – already pronounced 'indecent' – were finally condemned as 'unstable', and were drilled off the façade to cheers from a small crowd in 1935. In this manner, Epstein's open-handed depiction of 'Maternity' was destroyed in the name of public safety and civic morality.

London, by the turn of the century, was heavy with Victorian and Edwardian allegorical statuary which depicted women as idealized figures: square-jawed, muscular and Britannic, or thinly-clad nymphs. George Frampton's statue of Peter Pan in Kensington Gardens (1911) was typical of the latter genre, possessing within its folkloric charm a sexually suggestive tickle of sensual girl-ishness. The perceived superiority, in sculptural terms, of the male figure over the female figure was an aspect of hand-me-down Anglo-Hellenism which kept the female form upon its customary pedestal. With Epstein's primitivism, it was almost as though the charges of instability and indecency being brought against the pregnant belly of 'Maternity' were officializing the belief that ideologically advanced femininity in itself was a moral lapse – the evidence for this being seen through the attitudes of Brazil and Blyton, to say nothing of the mute protest in *The Weak and the Wicked*. The weapons against this moral failing were comedy (one of Epstein's sculptures would be exhibited in Blackpool, on June Bank Holiday 1925, as a side-show under the title 'Freaks of Modern Art') and a distrust of Modernism that derived, in part, from an identification of progressive expression with German, and therefore decadent, notions of psychiatry. That Epstein had been commissioned to carve Oscar Wilde's Parisian tomb could not have counted in his favour.

During the 1920s, and the scandal attending Radclyffe Hall's lesbian romance, *The Well of Loneliness* (1928), which was banned on moral grounds, the androgyny of the Bright Young Things served more to caricature the advance of English women within the pantomime of aristocratic fashionability than to produce any coherent change in their actual status. Largely a question of chic, at a time when fashion was only distantly related to politics (as opposed to sharing its bathroom), the loosening of sexual behaviour and sexual stereotypes described in the early novels of Evelyn Waugh or Nancy Mitford's novellas reveal an infanti-lism that was common enough to the flapper mentality. The Savoy Orpheans defined this fashionable androgyny in their popular song 'Masculine Women, Feminine Men' (1925), with its punchline 'Which is the rooster? Which is the hen?', and it was only with the outbreak of World War Two that the greater society of English women (as opposed to aristocrats and the upper-middle classes) would find themselves taking a step towards parity that was hard to reverse come the peace.

By 1946, ordinary women who had served in the forces or worked in factories found it difficult to be broken back down the ranks to housewife and helpmate, and their place in the new society – with or without a Beautility kitchen – occupied an ambiguous mezzanine between the strived-for comforts of traditional family life and an acknowledgement of some greater progress. By the time of *Woman in a Dressing Gown*, in which the betrayed wife's ability to face life alone is matched by the desire to keep her husband and family, there was more than a sense that the wives and mothers of the immediate post-war period (the Mrs Hoopers, in fact) would comprise a transitional generation between the Victorian notions of duty that had shaped their mothers, and the burgeoning permissiveness and liberality which would fall into the laps of their children. In terms of the female condition, the young working women in *Up the Junction* (1967) or *The Family Way* (1966) – products of the youthquake – are still hemmed in by male orthodoxy but have exchanged domesticity for sexuality as the language of their protest. Sexuality, needless to say, was the province of pop.

As the 1950s began to produce some home-grown rock-'n'-roll to challenge the supremacy of crooners and the student-driven obsession with 'trad' jazz (the teenage son in *Woman in a Dressing Gown* is a keen Chris Barber fan), young women were allotted their latest roles as socially commodified Girlfriends. Within the narratives of early pop and rock-'n'-roll, women were indispensable as the capricious pedestal-dwellers of a new breed of courtly love. As Girlfriends, young women became modern muses to inspire the best, and worst, of early English pop; but this was a clearly sanitized condition, pitching the pinky blue of girlish sentimentality against the black leather edifice of young male pin-ups. The few young women pop stars – Alma Cogan, Petula Clark or Helen Shapiro – were sold as jolly elder sister types, with New Look dresses, sweet smiles and a lingering impression of lavender bath salts. Unlike, for instance, Billy Fury, or even the young Cliff Richard, the women in pop – as representatives of the Girlfriend class – were not expected to sneer, snarl or in any way ruffle the surface of their femininity. This was Finishing School pop, with a duty to be eternally, breathlessly and hopelessly in love. And, gathered in the National Milk Bars, Roxys and Locarnos of England, a mass of lumpy hair and National Health glasses, the Girlfriends of Britain could dance away the heartaches while pursuing their secondary official role, as Fans.

Presented, as the first teenagers, with a lifestyle (the term was a modern invention in itself) that was two parts swooning to one part blooming, the young women of pop's infancy were bombarded with products which made being plain or overweight a virtual hanging offence, despite the homely and sensible advice being offered to girls in new magazines such as *Date*. In 1960, *Date* magazine was a teenage handbook for girls and young women, with the word 'teenager' being used in advertising and editorial copy alike to represent a strictly codified and labyrinthine world. 'Teenage Skin Cream' prompted the slogan, 'I've had a lovely time, Mummy!', while Clarks Teenage Shoes presented the buyer with the problem: 'How can you choose when you love them all?' With miniature interviews, in the fan-club style, with Billy Fury, Adam Faith, or even Jimmy Logan, the regular 'Coffee Club' spot – with fashion tips (including, in issue 2, an interview with Adam Faith's boot-maker), pop and film gossip – and romantic fiction ('Object – Marriage!'), *Date* magazine established shopping and romance as the template for young women's magazines in the pop age.

'Object – Marriage!', as an example of the typical romantic fiction in *Date* magazine, is worthy of closer attention in the way that it rehearses the world of dating that would obsess, by the late 1960s and 1970s, such situation comedies as *The Liver Birds*, *Man About the House* or Jack Rosenthal's *The Lovers* with Paula

Wilcox. The problems of sex, cohabitation and marriage, as a comedy of errors and a battle of the sexes, fondly acted out between the young men and women of the first nervously permissive generation, were seen as a pitting of ideals against reality – with the landscape of shop and office-work providing the social and domestic points of recognition.

Thus, in 'Object – Marriage!' (written by Samuel Grafton) we find Estelle Hardy pursuing the determinedly bachelor Stephen Wallace with the following proposition: 'Let me come to your flat every day for a month and cook for you and do your washing and mending and handle your money – and then you decide if you can get on without me. Fair?' Scandalized, Stephen endures this arrangement until he realizes that Estelle is indispensable to him: 'We had steak and mushrooms for dinner. The room glowed.' Eventually, Stephen realizes his true feelings and the story concludes: 'I'm a normal young man of twenty-six, and I can get married just like anyone else.'

Within the perky world of *Date*, aimed at young women with either pocket money or a junior salary, blooming and swooning are the alpha and omega of the female experience of popular culture. But prior to the onset of a more casual attitude towards sex, in the later 1960s, the result of so much romance and so little sexual freedom made a cult of dating, as a mythology, that seemed to lead straight up the aisle to a Tip Top kitchen – and, presumably, a bottle or two of mother's little helpers. In a magazine advert from 1960, issued by the Gas Council, we find Peter wooing freshly bathed Jill (courtesy of 'Mr Therm's' gas water heater) with the following admonition: 'Darling, you look simply wonderful tonight. And you were ready when I called. Promise you'll stay punctual after we're married?' To which Jill replies, blushing at her forwardness, 'I promise – if you promise I can have a gas water heater in our home!' This fetishizing of romance, coupled with the febrile advertising pitched at young people, must have made for frustration with a less glamorous reality, as we can see

in *A Kind of Loving* (1962), with its constant pitting of the dream
of sex against the fragility of love ('You've got wonderful breasts,
Ingrid,' gasps Vic, 'I've always thought so') and the struggle for
emotional independence and adult freedom.

Throughout the first half of the 1960s, sex and sexuality became a
favourite topic within the English psyche, replacing mere teen-
agerdom as the venue for sensationalist or social realist speculation. The inevitable element of titillation in this new problem
would pave the way for 'sex comedies' such as *Here We Go
Round the Mulberry Bush* but also – by way of *The Family
Way* (1966) – see the ultimate end of the kitchen sink and its
replacement with metropolitan-based, psychedelic and psychological films in which sexual freedom and sexual experimentation
were taken for granted along with the LSD. But before the
screen turned day-glo, the last of the 'problem' films (creaking, by
now, beneath their formulaic characters and predictable issues)
would attempt to come to terms with the dangers facing pro-
miscuous teenagers. In *That Kind of Girl* (1963), we find a sexual
problem film that was best described, at the time of its release,
by the *Monthly Film Bulletin*:

> There is much padding and surplus material before the film arrives
> at its main theme – the dangers, through ignorance, of VD.
> Directed to adolescents, the propaganda element is reasonable
> enough, even if the medical profession is depicted in rather
> too glowing and sympathetic terms; but the story is sheer melo-
> drama, running the weird gamut of anti-nuclear demonstration,
> striptease, pre-marital intercourse, rape and the improper use
> of the telephone – scarcely a digestible mixture.

What was clear, as pop ideology struggled to keep on a footing
with the social orthodoxy, was that young women were being
confronted with sense and sensibility in the same breath; sooner
or later, something had to give, and it wasn't going to be the
industrial webbing of a Snug-Fit liberty bodice.

In films such as *Cosh Boy* (1953), the problems of juvenile delinquency had been seen as male in origin and male in solution:
''Ee's the boss now!' says Cosh Boy's Gran, as his recently
acquired but defiantly opposed Canadian step-father prepares
to thrash him before handing him over to the police. Up until
the arrival of the step-father, vicious little Cosh Boy has ruled
his female household of weak mother and exasperated grand-
mother with a mixture of emotional blackmail and tantrum-laced
bullying. Also, having got the young Joan Collins pregnant and
left her to jump in the Thames ('Oh, she'll be all right,' says the
arresting officer, 'we want him for something far more serious
than that!'), Cosh Boy's reign of terror is clearly facilitated by
the war-denuded number of male authority figures. Borstals and
Boys' Clubs are the new homes of bad and good boys respectively, with the suggestion that dates and debates will occupy the
latter, while hitting old ladies over the head and taking advantage
of nice girls will hasten the incarceration of the former. And to
what extent *Cosh Boy* was a good example of titillation pretending
to be dramatized sociology seems less important than its depiction of a male world in which women are weak or stupid or
both.

It is only with *Beat Girl* (Cosh Boy's dream date, it could be argued),
in 1960, that we see a slightly different parable of teenage femininity beginning to emerge. In several ways, *Beat Girl* is the
mirror image of *Cosh Boy*, with the spoiled daughter of a successful and idealistic architect reacting violently against the sisterly
solicitude of her new French step-mother. As *Cosh Boy* was set
firmly in working-class London, so *Beat Girl* takes place between
genteel Chelsea and bohemian Soho, where a young group of
Beats jive-talk from boredom to boredom in search of real hip
kicks. Beat Girl herself (Jennifer, to her father and step-mother)
is a bratty English Bardot whose lust to shock is matched only
by her girlish naïvety. She remains convinced, however, that her
wild friends and wilder behaviour will drive a wedge between

the workaholic father who has neglected her (his dream is to build an ideal city, the model for which anticipates Milton Keynes while echoing Brasilia) and her glamorous Parisian step-mother. But what is most telling in this brew of child psychology and teenage delinquency is its explicit use of the sex industry (scenes set in a Soho strip club met the censor's scissors, but remain graphic for their time) and sexuality in general as the language and plot through which Beat Girl and her step-mother must confront one another.

Jennifer uses her precocious sexuality to similar effect as Cosh Boy's cosh when it comes to getting her own way in the heady hinter-land of teenage disaffection. The fact that, before her marriage and distressing inheritance of a stroppy teenage step-daughter, the architect's Parisian bride used to work as a striptease artiste ('I 'ad to; I deed nuffing rong!') ties in with Jennifer's increasing infatuation with a strip club in Soho, which is run by dinner-suited spivs who use expressions like, 'Scarper, sonny, yew 'erd the man' and, 'You'se ment to be strippin', Dolly – not just pullin yer blahse orf!', and who represent, to her, the twin fascination and repulsion of the low-life proper. With Adam Faith playing a beatnik strummer ('I ain't fightin' no Teds! Fightin's for squares!'), and a proto-Happening in Chiselhurst Caves, Beat Girl, while addressing the 'problem' of children growing up with-out sufficient parenting, at least acknowledged the existence of sex as a weapon in the socio-emotional arsenal. Jennifer attempts to use her own sex appeal as a means of blackmailing her new step-mother into admitting her draughty past. Thus, the Soho striptease club becomes the actual and allegorical venue for the denouement of this power struggle, and the melodramatic climax of the film maintains the world of vice as a perilous chamber in which nice girls (unless they are rescued by rich architects) can lose themselves for ever in a gin-sodden penumbra of degener-ation and easy morals.

Beat Girl, despite the censor and the melodrama, put female sexu-

ality into the pop medium in a way which was largely unaltered
by the time Marianne Faithfull failed to convince as a sexually
liberated hell-raiser in *Girl on a Motorcycle* eight years later.
To contemporary eyes, *Beat Girl* is a somewhat risible (to use
Halliwell's economical adjective) delinquency film, but seen in
the context of the 1960s issues of *Date* magazine, or even the
sixth-formers-in-suspenders titillation of another film from 1960,
The Pure Hell of St Trinians, the depiction of a sexy girl with a
short temper, as opposed to a short skirt, was reasonably radical.
Born to be neither Bardots nor bobby-soxers, the first generation of
English teenage girls were expected to be alternately homely and
hysterical; like their male counterparts, they looked under-
nourished and awkward featured, caught in a spiral of aspirational culture which had yet to deliver the constancy of
cosmetics and teen fashion with which they could armour themselves. As we can see from the footage of early Beatles concerts,
in which the shots of the audience are somehow more interesting
than the close-ups of the group, the release of hysteria from
hordes of Helens and Hilary's describes a generation of young
women who had suddenly found a sexual pressure valve through
which to emit the pent-up frustration of centuries. Teen girl
hysteria, channelled through boy pop groups, could be diagnosed
as two parts growing pains to one part collective hysteria: a
potent brew of chemical and physiological reactions, heavily
laced with peer pressure, social conditioning, gender construction and primal rage. The boy groups are appropriated to be the
vessels for this powerful emotional cocktail. And, for the first
wave of commodified teenage girls, the distance between childhood and adolescence was still barely acknowledged. But the
Beatlemania girls would also grow up to include the 1960s foun-
ders of the women's movement as a practical, theoretical and
political body – a prospect which must have seemed remote at
the start of the decade, when young women were being reinvented but not yet released, and the choice between conformity

or rebellion boiled down to the social labels of housewife or whore.

The bleakness of this conundrum was described by Lynne Reid Banks in her novel of 1960, *The L-Shaped Room* (filmed by Bryan Forbes in 1962), which managed despite its straining for colourful characters to convey some idea of the isolation facing the single and pregnant Jane Graham, as she nurses her shameful secret in a Fulham bedsit. In *The L-Shaped Room* we find the first inklings of an alternative urban society – pre-Swinging London bohemia – that offers support to social and family outcasts because being an outcast is the common denominator: black, lesbian, struggling author and so forth. Prior to agitprop, *The Female Eunuch*, the underground press, the hippie communities and the directory of urban survival techniques listed in Nick Saunders's *Alternative London* handbook, which would become alternative institutions between 1960 and 1970, the cast and setting of *The L-Shaped Room* represented the first direct account, by a woman author, of abortion and alienation in England since Rosamund Lehmann's *The Weather in the Streets* published back in 1936. Lacking the northern darkness of Shelagh Delaney's *A Taste of Honey* (filmed, famously, by Tony Richardson in 1961), *The L-Shaped Room* has dated less well, but both Delaney and Lynne Reid Banks were responsible, in the early 1960s, for positioning the reality of pregnancy, as opposed to the virginal romance of sexuality, at the centre of English society's somewhat blinkered view of modern young women.

It would seem, particularly with the far more brutal *Up the Junction* and *Alfie*, that the only way to confront orthodox attitudes towards sex appeal, sex and marriage was to create female characters who were young, rejected and pregnant. Interestingly, films such as *A Kind of Loving* and *The Family Way*, both set in Lancashire, saw the actual sex act, as the consummation of marriage (and the fetishized destination of dating), as the principal problem that drove the problem film. Pressure from peers and family alike creates a claustrophobia and self-consciousness that creates a tragi-comic false start to the dreams of legitimate sex that the boyfriends and girlfriends have striven to realize. There is always a crisis to be overcome before the couple can proceed: Vic has to be sick on Thora Hird's carpet in *A Kind of Loving* before his young bride will leave the wholly feminine world of her mother's home; Hywel Bennett has to have a fist-fight with his domineering boss before he and Hayley Mills can finally have their honeymoon in Blackpool. Ultimately, the translation of romantic dating into marriage is seen as a compromise between the promises of pop and the conditions of social reality. The divide between North and South, London and Manchester, was vividly pronounced in the handling of these stories, with London's rush towards Swinging capital of the world providing a sympathy that the dark North rejected with folkloric philosophies born of hardship. It was grim up north, after all.

In John Schlesinger's proto-punk classic of 1963, *Billy Liar* (adapted from the novel by Keith Waterhouse, published in 1959), in which a disaffected and romantic young man spins endless fantasies in order to cope with the dull reality of his northern town, Stradhoughton, Billy's three North Country muses – Barbara, Liz and Rita – each define a specific embodiment of English pop's first daughters. Barbara is cloying, practical, sentimental and repressed; oblivious to Billy's 'passion pills' but addicted to oranges, she is a bloomer and a swooner of the *Date* generation who has shot off the conveyor belt of northern orthodoxy to become engaged to a man whom she thinks she loves, but does not think to question. A devout handmaiden of cultural materialism, for whom curtains are 'my department, pet', and who dreams of a cottage in Devon, Barbara is the girl-next-door who longs to be married and living next door to her mother. Gullible to Billy's lies – or deaf to them in the one-dimensional world of her romantic fantasies, where men's sexual 'feelings' are incomprehensible as a reality – Barbara is unaware of his simultaneous engagement to the sexually available but equally despotic Rita. Rita (peroxide blonde to Barbara's natural brunette, foul-mouthed to Barbara's aspirational politesse) sees men as unreliable, weak but necessary, and confronts the hopelessly compromised Billy with the glorious pronouncement (on his parents' doorstep), 'Yeah, you! Yer rotten lying cross-eyed get, yer nothing but!' But Rita, for all of her vivacity and fierce temper, is still a social conformist, locked in her place and her class but turning the violence of her frustration inwards, as opposed to at her small-town peers. Told by Billy that he cannot take her dancing because he 'has to stay in and play Monopoly with me Uncle Ernest', she cuts him short: 'Oh? Yer Uncle Ernest? Well I'll tell you what you're doing, you're taking me dancing, at the Roxy, and don't be late!' Billy's hatred of his small-town life finds no sympathy from either of these matriarchs in the making, who seem to represent the pop northern equivalents of Waugh's Celia Ryder and Daisy Leonard, respectively.

It is only the bohemian Liz (memorably played by the handbag-swinging Julie Christie) whose soft-core beatnik *joie-de-vivre* offers Billy his third chance of romance and a true empathy with his boredom and misery. Liz ('She's crazy, man!' exclaims Billy to Arthur, admiringly), appearing like a stem of heliotrope in Stradhoughton, is set apart from the conventions of her contemporaries and promises – with her suede jacket and hitch-hiking ways – the delights of London and the greater world. Her defining line is her comment from the balcony of the Roxy, after Billy's 'Twisterella' has been performed by the visiting band and the drunken locals are united in the last conga: 'It's this *town*, Billy – it's the people we know . . .' Her meaning is that they are watching young people of their own age, messily growing up to become just as prejudiced and complacent as their parents. Billy, with an indecision that marks an epoch, is too addicted to his imagination to dare confront the reality of escape with Liz. True to its native culture, but a violent reaction against the traditions of northern England and the inherent conservatism of youth, *Billy Liar* provides the three female characters who seem to represent the three faces of early pop's eternal feminine: the nice girl, the tart and the beatnik.

▦

Within the visual arts, between 1956 and 1963, London experienced and inspired an explosion of creative activity which saw painting, sculpture, action painting, 'auto-destructive' art, situationist activity and the arrival of Pop Art proper, all taking their lead from the European and American avant-garde but quickly harnessing the energy and social upheavals of English popular culture, and, more specifically, the new network of clubs, small galleries and pop personalities which was becoming established within the capital. True to the ethos of Swinging London, this colourful renaissance saw a dialogue between the old-established, somewhat aristocratic institutions of English culture – the Royal College of Art, the Tate Gallery – and the classless, up-to-the-minute bohemia that would soon comprise an underground society. As ever, swinging London would be best defined as an obsessive but ambivalent relationship between youth and old age, the traditional and the newly Pop. Along with pop music, American notions of consumer culture and radical means of reinventing both the artist and the art object, sexuality would be central to this vivid and compartmentalized development in British art.

While the leading artists of the period were male – Peter Blake, David Hockney, Robyn Denny, Derek Boshier et al. – the new blurring of media within art, which encouraged new processes of documentation and comment to contextualize subjects and attitudes, created a place for a female contribution which was never fully occupied. There remained a lingering machismo, even within pop art society, that preferred women to remain in their place as models, in keeping with their traditional role as the subjects and muses of fine art. With the exception of Bridget Riley, whose Op Art techniques would place her in a school of her own, unconnected to self-conscious polemicizing about sexuality and gender, there was little new art from English women.

The painter Pauline Boty (who would die of cancer, aged twenty-eight, in 1966), however, became an iconic figure within the visual arts and media action scene at the beginning of the 1960s. Boty had graduated from the Royal College of Art having gained more of a reputation for her Bardot-like beauty and her secre-taryship of Anti-Ugly Action (a pressure group opposed to the socially and aesthetically hostile aspects of urban development) than for her paintings, which described the pop commodified sexuality of women – as pin-up models or starlets – in a style reminiscent of her contemporary, Peter Blake. In her paintings '5–4–3–2–1' (1963), 'It's a Man's World II' (1963–5) and 'The Only Blonde in the World' (1964), Boty showed herself to be the only artist in Britain who was dealing directly with pop sexuality from a woman's point of view. As a perfect pop muse (dancing with Derek Boshier on *Ready, Steady, Go!*, for example, and eventually marrying the founder of *Black Dwarf* magazine, Clive Godwin), Boty was considered more of a personality than an artist – more sexy than serious. David Mellor, however, in his peerless book *The Sixties Art Scene in London* (1993), points out that Boty's project was 'to look forward – in a feminist manner – to the issues which concerned women's art in the following two decades: identity, pleasure, critiques of patriarchy, and the establishment of a distinctively female iconographic programme that concerned her.' In this much, Boty can be seen as a pop precursor of female conceptualists such as Helen Chadwick, and the social critiques through self-portraiture that have distin-guished women artists in the 1990s in the work of Jane and Louise Wilson, Georgina Starr, Sarah Lucas and Gillian Wearing.

By 1966, as London poised to swing like a pendulum to the limit of its arc, the class-bound rituals of seduction were being replaced by a fashionable permissiveness that acknowledged youth – free, now, of the morally policed youthquake – as its principal concern. While Free Love would be put forward as an intellectual or political paradigm, drawn from hippie notions of tribalism or a convenient reworking of existential freedom, and the Pill would offer women the choice to have sex when they chose, the movement of sexual liberation had produced hippie men who were every bit as chauvinistic as their post-war fathers, expecting their 'Ladies' to endorse some system of fashionable polygamy. These Lotharios in love-beads were less advanced than their ideologies of freedom might suggest, and it is telling that throughout the conversion of Mod to progressive rock there were no alternative female rock stars in Britain. England had not produced a Joni Mitchell, a Patti Smith or a Janis Joplin, and with the exception of Dusty Springfield's magnificent succession of soul-bearing singles ('You Don't Have To Say You Love Me' or 'I Close My Eyes And Count To Ten') it seemed that women would remain as either fans or girlfriends in the world of pop.

Women as political artists had seldom succeeded in England, and the demonization of Yoko Ono by the British media, back in 1969, had set a new low in the suspicion with which any fringe activity by women was treated. Ono, popularly believed to have broken the very heart of English pop by breaking up the Beatles (who were barely speaking to one another by this time, anyway) found herself placed beside Epstein's 'Maternity' as an avant-garde representative of woman as the unsettler of gender roles and aesthetics. Her art, derived from the spiritually centred but confrontationally absurdist directive of the international Fluxus group, was unlikely to win mainstream approval; more revealing, however, was the hostility directed towards her for bringing England its first taste of celebrity feminism. Marrying into an English institution such as the Beatles could only work against her.

And the inference remained, beyond the glorious pop moments provided by Alma Cogan, Twinkle or Petula Clark, that women in English pop were entertainers as opposed to artists. Had David Bowie been a real woman, the course of English culture would probably have been radically altered.

But Bowie would have been a catalyst for changing this situation by 1976, when Siouxsie Sioux performed 'The Lord's Prayer' at the 100 Club. Sprung from the precincts and High Streets of suburban England, the first wave of punk women turned their sexuality into power by appropriating fetishism and cut-price cosmetics to make a parody of themselves. For Siouxsie Sioux, mixing the eroticism of a pub stripper with a succession of cultural reference points from Ziggy Stardust and Louise Brooks, to Malcolm McDowell's portrayal of Alex in *A Clockwork Orange* (McDowell's false eyelashes, for that iconic role, had been bought by the yard from Biba), the plastic glamour of her image was both a subtle extension of feminist protest and an ironic challenge to notions of sexual fantasy and sex symbols. And this made Siouxsie a self-contained and self-reflecting private world, embodying the chemistry of stardom in a new language. If the body could be read as a text, then Siouxsie combined von Masoch's *Venus in Furs* with an Ann Summers catalogue, turning herself, as much as her fledgeling punk rock group, into a situationist slogan offset by glittering expressionism, as revealed on their debut LP *The Scream*. Siouxsie was punk rock's Helen of Troy – the face that launched a thousand clubs, an updated version of Oscar Wilde's image of Lillie Langtry as the embodiment of modern beauty. As Wilde has called Langtry 'formerly of Troy now of London' so Siouxsie was formerly of Bromley, now of the 100 Club – with a similar translation of status.

But the tone and temper of Timothy Whites was never far away from the reinvention of pop women which punk rock, pioneered by Siouxsie Sioux, Jordan, Cat Woman and Poly Styrene brought about. This was not a self-consciously intellectual, political or artistic protest; rather, this was the revenge of the Saturday girls – the disaffected fifth-formers who were bored and misrepresented by pop fashion's existing idea of sex and glamour. Unlike the hippie rejection of artifice and consumerism, punk women relished the cheap, the gaudy and the disposable, utilizing all manner of traditional household products to create a female anti-fashion: neat bleach to dye hair, transparent rain macs to wear over leotards and fish-net tights, gaffer-taped bin-liners worn as skirts. The stroppy tart had replaced the doe-eyed earth mother.

With an example (however unaffordable) set to them by Westwood and McLaren's tit T-shirts, bondage trousers and rubber-wear, consumers of punk androgyny could turn gender into a hall of mirrors and create fashion classics as though by accident. Poly Styrene, performing 'O Bondage Up Yours' dressed in a plastic tablecloth with the cutlery and condiments glued on to it, was drawing attention to the domestic routine in a way which was either deft, daft or Dada, depending on your point of view.

By the end of the 1970s, despite the fact that punk had elected Gaye Advert, from the Adverts, and Pauline Murray of Penetration to be its unofficial pin-ups, the rock-against-virtually-everything ethos permitted feminism to take its rightful place on the altar screen of pop's newly raised consciousness. The Raincoats, the Slits, the Au Pairs and Ludus were outspoken in their concerns about women's issues, but were vastly different in their musical styles and attitudes towards performance. While the Slits, ironically, espoused the rampant sexism of Rastafarianism to lend their bitter songs a bouncing bass and industrial-strength dub, the Raincoats produced a fractured, viola-driven intensity which achieved sublimity on their first, self-titled LP. The Slits, having arrived with standard punk numbers such as '(I'm going to be) Your Number One Enemy', developed a disdainful brattishness which lent their best songs – 'Typical Girls', 'Love Und Romance' and 'New Town' – a tuneless opacity that reversed the notion of the harmonizing girl group into a minimalist ensemble of breathless chants and barked statements. Photographed by Pennie Smith as semi-nude mud wrestlers for the cover of their first album release *Cut* (they had previously shared a Rough Trade LP with the Pop Group), the Slits continued their sardonic ritual of shaming men into an acknowledgement of their voyeurism; but increasingly self-indulgent lyrics and production values, to say nothing of the cultural absurdity of playing at white Rastas, swiftly sunk the group into the post-punk mire of the early 1980s.

The Raincoats, too, could hold their own only for one glorious record. As pared down as the Slits were over-produced, their Rad Fem disaffection reached its apotheosis in a cover of the Kinks' 'Lola', in which any fixed sense of predatory sexuality was exchanged for a narrative free-for-all with redirected gender. And this turning on its head of sexual expectation was fundamental to the Rad Fem punk groups: when Linder, from Ludus, performed at Manchester's Hacienda Club wearing a dress made out of raw meat and a black dildo, she was giving the crowd what they wanted in a way that they weren't prepared for, thus subverting the sexuality of female pop entertainers. Above all, the women of punk and post-punk were united by a musical radicalism (Laura Logic's frenetic jazz or Linder's Yoko-esque vocalizing) which stuck in the craw of even independent pop's pundits. There was to be no female equivalent of pop method acting in England, and the radical was imported from abroad, with cult recognition for Nico, Patti Smith and Nina Hagen.

Sliding between the opposed factions of commercial pop and the avant-garde, however, was Kate Bush, whose faintly Victorian sensuality, mixed with a training in mime from Lindsay Kemp, gave her a Number One in 1978 with 'Wuthering Heights'. As pop's equivalent of the mad girl in the attic, exuding a mysticism and morbidity that were at once sexual and infantilist, Bush was covering the territory of Angela Carter's *Company of Wolves* in the guise of a pre-Raphaelite raised on *Jackie*: folkloric fable and disturbed dreams, focusing on the rites of passage between girlishness and womanhood. Bush was neither Rad Fem nor pure pop, her themes were the retrieval of memories and the solitary passion, gift-wrapped in a mixture of mawkish sentimentality and ultimately seductive melodrama. Her particular brand of romantic Englishness ('Oh, England, my Lion Heart,' she sang, with feeling, on her second LP) made her an early example of heritage chic, but the undercurrent of Carteresque allegory and journeys through the sub-conscious landscape of memory and desire snatched her best songs from the perky eccentricity that distinguished her worst. Bush could be seen as a cross between Christina Rossetti and Lynsey De Paul, representing the independent brilliance of the girl outsider on the one hand, and the gauche exhibitionism of a wrongly encouraged drama student on the other. Her moment of greatness would arrive in 1985, when 'Running Up That Hill' delivered an eerie marriage between her plea for passion and the hopelessness of hoping. Ultimately, Bush conveyed an impression of romantic isolation that was far from comfortable, suggesting that her attempts to escape from the attic of memories or the dank forest of sexuality would be a long time in succeeding. And as pop's representative of the Brontë's romance or Carter's magical realism, Kate Bush remains an enigmatic figure.

By 1982, when Bananarama (as yet unpeeled) first minced down a subway with the Fun Boy Three in matching grey tracksuits, tunelessly chanting 'It Ain't What You Do It's The Way That You Do It' in a forlorn attempt at gamine pertness (the beginnings of indie-pop girls as sulky boys), punk feminism had fizzled and black sports bras were only a video away. Siouxsie was waving with one white arm as she drowned in Gothic melodrama, the Rad Fem groups had packed up their trumpets, and the burgeoning jazz revival that centred round the reinvention of Soho as a 1980s version of its 1950s heritage (a kind of death by cappuccino for *The Face* generation), saw performers such as

Carmel and Working Week taking the club spotlight in a way that reasserted pop as fashion-conscious entertainment and little else. The future would bring success for commercial artistes such as Annie Lennox or Sinead O'Connor, with their arch 'n' angry divadom, but they were somehow contained and commodified, producing officially alternative music for conservative young people with officially alternative lifestyles – Sade with attitude, to be reincarnated in the professional pixiedom of Bjork. Their brand of female performance was on an axis with misery-mongers like Elvis Costello, who had turned his soap-box soliloquies into thinking man's soap opera.

-⊞-

As Shakespeare's sister, according to Woolf, would wind up buried at some cross-roads near the Elephant & Castle, and as literature, according to Southey, was not the business of women, so in English pop it seems as though the bulk of the glittering prizes have been awarded to the men. Women, it appears, have achieved brilliance in supporting roles, be that fair or not, and while literature, theatre and film have produced female stars and innovators, from Margaret Rutherford to Angela Carter, pop's girls have remained in the blooming and swooning business. In this much, if a cheer can be raised for Rita's denouncement of Billy Liar as a lying cross-eyed get, then it should be repeated for Joanne Catherall and Susanne Sulley of the Human League, who ascended from their technical position as mere backing vocalists to embody a kind of feminist consciousness that could either dance around a handbag or hit you with it. Recruited from a Sheffield nightclub, Joanne and Susanne brought a genuine street credibility to the otherwise ponderous sound of the Human League, and this was a High Street credibility which spoke of the shopping precinct and the tungsten-hard rituals of working for low pay and dressing to kill.

Poised on the provincial clubbing axis of Roxy Music, David Bowie and Manhattan Transfer, Joanne and Susanne possessed an independence and home-grown glamour which made their seeming banality somehow iconic; their dancing had the Warholian mesmerism of always seeming to be the same dance, swinging arms and hips from left to right for as long as each song lasted without any variation. Their blank expressions were strangely disconcerting, and their passivity seemed to mask an unspoken pronouncement that summed up modern England: 'It's this town Billy; it's the people we know . . .' The spirits of Rita and Liz walked abroad in Joanne and Susanne, surveying their roles with an ancient wisdom.

7

Luꞓifer over Lancashire:
Billy Liar, Branwell Brontë,
john cooper clarke,
mark ε. smith & the north

For the young Malcolm McDowell, looking down from the top deck of the 28 bus from Ellesmere to Liverpool Lime Street, it was the glimpse of unaffordable, bright red electric guitars, hanging in the window of a music shop, 'that gave you hope, somehow . . .' McDowell was the son of a Liverpool publican, and inspired to act by the screen presence of Salford-bred Albert Finney, whose Memorial company would later produce Lindsay Anderson's *If . . .* and *O Lucky Man!* Anderson, a devotee of Humphrey Jennings and the documentary film movement, travelling in the mid-1950s by night train to visit friends in Wakefield, had been moved by the sight of a guard on the foggy northern station who was holding up his lamp and chanting the name of the stop in a rich, flat dialect. As a new breed of English intellectuals were turning towards socialism and Marxism in the 1950s, so the north of England, assuming a near Soviet function of providing the social reality for social realism, became the principal setting for the first modern fables of the dawning pop age. Newcastle-born Neil Tennant, of the Pet Shop Boys, would remark in 1995 that 'the story of pop is essentially a northern story'. Today, beyond 'The Beatles Experience' at the regenerated Albert Dock, perhaps the strongest monument to Liverpool's projection of early British pop is the austere Billy Fury memorial lectern, standing in the cavernous choir of the Anglican cathedral.

The industrial heritage of the north, shaping the monolithic Victorian mill towns and ports, had produced an architecture which was simultaneously mean, and dramatic with civic grandeur. The wealth of the nineteenth-century industrialists had been immense, deriving from a near feudalism that mixed the somewhat self-celebrating philanthropy of providing town halls, libraries and dwellings for the workforce, with also paying their wages and collecting their rents. In this manner, the northern cities provided marvels of pattern-book architecture: factories, offices and warehouses were commissioned from fashionable young architects who, on virtually unlimited budgets, could, for instance, mix the Gothic with the Venetian to suit the grand schemes of their clients, or design on a monumental scale not known outside the City of London. The discrepancy, in architectural and political terms, between the immensity of the workplace and the terraced cottages of the workers created the image of the northern townscape, surrounded by a wilderness of moorland, that would become as predominant a cultural force in England as Edwardian Arcadia or Swinging London. The old ruling families shaped their industrial kingdoms with a firm hand, building with a faith in dynastic longevity. 'There's always been a Holroyd at Holroyd's Mill,' twits Arthur to Billy as they lurch through Stradhoughton on their coffee break from the Shadrack & Duxbury funeral parlour, 'and by 'ell there always will be!' The first generation of northern teenagers were adept at mimicking the self-satisfaction of their elders.

The moors which give way to the shallow acoustic basin that spreads around north Manchester, and join the west and east of the north of England, provide a brooding influence that has been seen as a *tabula rasa* upon which is encoded the indifference of nature to the good or evil of historical events. Open to the weather and the immensity of the sky, the moors are like a desert landscape of the north, their rugged inhospitality barely leavened by their natural beauty. In northern culture they become the theatre of rumination, transcendence and alienation, as Mrs Gaskell identified in her description of the road to Haworth Parsonage.

All round the horizon there is this same line of sinuous wave-like hills; the scoops into which they fall only revealing other hills beyond, of similar colour and shape, crowned with the wild, bleak moors – grand, from the ideas of solitude and loneliness which they suggest, or oppressive from the feeling which they give of being pent-up by some monotonous and illimitable barrier, according to the mood of mind in which the spectator may be.

This 'monotonous and illimitable barrier' was echoed by W. H. Auden in his poem 'Roman Wall Blues', in which he imagined the experience of a Roman foot soldier, bored to tears in the shadow of Hadrian's Wall, even further north:

> The rain comes pattering out of the sky,
> I'm a Wall soldier, I don't know why.
> The mist creeps over the hard grey stone,
> My girl's in Tungria; I sleep alone.

The moorland, for Auden's sentry, bends agoraphobia to morbidity and eventual fatalism – a case, perhaps, of home-sickness over-shadowed by a deeper sickness of spirit which the mesmeric monotony of the landscape has induced:

> When I'm a veteran with only one eye,
> I shall do nothing but look at the sky.

As a vital informant of the northern sensibility, the ambiguous potency of the moors can be seen as a doubling of landscape as conscience and consciousness, and not only in the novels and poems of the Brontës. For Billy Liar, the moors are a place of burial for the good-will calendars which he has failed to post for his employers at the funeral parlour:

> There was a circumference of sparse yellow grass where the old men walked in summer, and I took the path they had worn towards a pocket of stone cottages, mostly condemned, that huddled miserably together in a corner of the Moor. Behind the cottages Stradhoughton Moor rose steeply again, out of an ashpit, to meet the scraggy allotments, and, beyond them, the real moors of Houghtondale, such as were illustrated in the Council yearbook. I intended to drop my parcel of calendars down a pothole.

This fringe of moorland is the setting for Billy's virtually Sophoclean encounter with Councillor Duxbury, whose undelivered calendars he still has under one arm. With the symmetry of destinies common to classical tragedy, the young man, weighed down by guilt, frustration and existential angst, finds himself face to face with the elderly monarch of Stradhoughton, who is lost in his memories and his witnessing of change. If we think of Billy as attempting to bury the past (each leaf of each calendar is printed with a prim aphorism, imposing the thin voice of conscience), while Councillor Duxbury is actually living in the past, then we can see the moor as the neutral wilderness in which they try, but fail, to communicate:

> 'Aye, ther' were nowt like that,' he said. His memory has been jogged by so many 'Echo' interviews that he now regarded every statement as a cue for his reminiscences, and no longer bothered to add 'when I were a lad' or 'fot'ty year ago', 'Ther' were nowt like that. We had to make our own music if we wanted it, else go without.' He rattled on as though he were

himself an old gramophone that had just been kicked back into
action. I was not sure that he knew who I was.

That Billy, suddenly trusting the older man's solicitude, attempts to
unburden himself ('My grandma's poorly . . .') does not enable
an exchange that might save him; the rift is too wide, but 'I
walked happily along the rough stone path through the allot-
ments to the quiet moorland beyond, and even while I was
burying the calendars the feeling was still with me.' Billy's 'feeling' is a sudden tenderness for the older man, rendered mute,
perhaps, by Mrs Gaskell's 'monotonous and illimitable barrier'
of the moorland landscape.

⊞

Beyond the famous settings of Emily Brontë's *Wuthering Heights*,
and the fictional worlds written from the isolated confines of
Haworth Parsonage, poised between its churchyard and the
moors, it is Branwell Brontë whose life and temperament seem
most eloquent of the relationship between the moors and the
soul. Branwell, as the brother whose early promise was never
fulfilled, and whose deterioration of mind and body was more
tragic than anything conceived in his sisters' novels, has claims
to having embodied the northern anti-hero. In her biography of
Charlotte Brontë, Mrs Gaskell writes intriguing sub-headings
for her chapters that mention Branwell, indicating a hapless
and ultimately self-destructive rebel: 'Deplorable conduct of
Branwell Brontë and its consequences'; 'Branwell Brontë still at
home'. Branwell's degeneration is described, with little sympathy
and some moralizing, as the consequences of a fatal collision
between his romantic temperament, artistic leanings, and some
claustrophobia within Haworth and the northern landscape to
which he was particularly sensitive – a sickness of spirit derived
from the dreariness of his surroundings: 'The black gloom hung

over what had once been the brightest hope of the family – over Branwell, and the mystery in which his wayward conduct was enveloped. Somehow and sometime, he would have to turn to his home as a hiding place for shame.' Branwell, as a northern anti-hero, is as much an ancestor of Billy Liar (whose grammar school education, in his father's opinion, brought nothing but conceit, 'suede shoes and fountain pens') as aspects of Billy's rage are rehearsals for Mark E. Smith's exclamation, on the Fall's 'Cerebral Caustic' (1995) of *Shadrack!* – the name of the employer that Billy screams into a sample urn.

In Daphne du Maurier's biography of Branwell, *The Infernal World of Branwell Brontë* (1960), she describes a young man of acute sensitivity and artistic ambitions who becomes somehow lost in a middle mist of lowly employment on the railways, from which he was dismissed for 'careless book-keeping' (Shadrack finds similar faults with Billy's accounts of the postage money), and, crucially, a hopeless infatuation with his subsequent employer's wife – the aptly named Mrs Robinson. Du Maurier chronicles Branwell's descent from child prodigy – as a poet and story-teller – to emotional collapse and drug addiction. The mythology of the suffering artist is turned, in du Maurier's biography, into the nightmare of the mediocre artist, whose imagination is too fatally strong for the limits of his skill. For Branwell, his suffering was not validated by either the production of great works or a posthumous fame – save that of being the shadowy dypso brother of his celebrated sisters.

A gauge of Branwell's frustration can be taken from the fact that while Charlotte's letter to Southey brought forth a significant dialogue between an unknown woman writer and the Poet Laureate, Branwell's letter to Wordsworth (again, seeking advice or sponsorship for his own writing) brought no response at all. According to du Maurier: 'His letter disgusted the ageing poet, who told Southey that it contained "gross flattery and plenty of abuse of other poets".' Added to this was Branwell's failure to be admitted to the Royal Academy of Art, and his equal failure to establish himself as a portrait painter in Bradford. Thus, in du Maurier's account: 'In February 1842 Charlotte and Emily left for Brussels. Anne was away as governess near York. Brother and sisters had never been more divided and apart. It was at the end of March that Branwell was dismissed from his post as station-master at Luddenden Foot because of negligence.' (He had already been moved from the same post at Sowerby Bridge, in the hope that a smaller station might be easier for him to manage.)

Branwell, like Billy Liar, lived through imagined alter-egos, some heroic and some satanico-romantic; the more that the real world closed in – his 'shameful' relationship with his employer's wife, the failure of his writing, art and career, endless debts, the final attempts to keep him off drugs and alcohol – the more he was tortured by his imagination. As a child, it had been Branwell who had invented the exotic 'genii' of the Brontë children's games, an imaginary city called Glass Town and a character called Alexander Rogue. Overexcited by the swing boats at Keighley Fair, the little Branwell had screamed out, 'Oh! My nerves . . . my nerves . . . my nerves . . .', with some indication of the terrifying collapse that would come in later life. Writing in 1847, a year before his death, Branwell stated:

after a fit of horror inexpressible, and violent palpitation of the heart, I have taken care of myself bodily, but to what good? The best health will not kill acute and not ideal, mental agony. Cheerful company does me good till some bitter truth blazes through my brain, and then the present of a bullet would be received with thanks. I wish I could flee to writing as a refuge, but I cannot, and as to slumber, my mind, whether awake or asleep, has been in incessant action for several weeks.

He died in 1848, aged twenty-nine, his failure summed up in his own words: 'In all my past life I have done nothing either great or good.' His sister Charlotte wrote: 'All his vices were and are nothing now. We remember only his woes.'

Branwell Brontë and Billy Liar can be seen as culturally related: both were weighed down by their native environments and longed, romantically, for the glamour of metropolitan bohemia; neither of them made it – Branwell was refused admission and Billy got off the train before it had left the station; both of them were hapless seducers for whom the rewards of seduction were the small-town shamefulness of being 'found out'. Both of them created imaginary kingdoms (Branwell's embattled African colony of Glass Town, and Billy's war-torn but constantly regenerating Ambrosia); and both of them found their real lives to be eclipsed and oppressed by the dreams of their imaginations. That Billy could have wound up a drug addict seems just as plausible, within this twinning, as Branwell finally meeting the right girl but failing to leave with her on the train from Sowerby Bridge. Indeed, what the booking offices at Sowerby and Luddenden Foot were to Branwell, so the funeral parlour of Shadrack & Duxbury must have been to Billy.

The morbid tragedy of Branwell Brontë, however, is at least updated into tragi-comedy by *Billy Liar*. Lancastrian humour, as much as northern fatalism, shapes Billy's perception of the north: 'I don't mind dark satanic mills,' he remarks, 'but by gum when it comes to dark satanic chip shops, dark satanic housing estates and dark satanic police stations . . .' Along with being received in the pop age as the cradle of social realism, built as a consequence of industrial hardship, the north has been distinguished by its comedy of dialect from George Formby to *Coronation Street*. And, like the results of a cross between Branwell Brontë and Billy Liar, northern culture, as one of the richest seams of cultural expression within Englishness, can be seen as a fine balance of comedy and tragedy across the unique fulcrum of its regional sensibility.

In the case of George Formby, the comedy of despair was inherited from his father, who was also a highly paid music hall entertainer, and who based his act on the bronchitic condition of a typical mill worker. With his gruesome catch-phrase 'Coughin' summat champion tonight!' (he would die, with tragic irony, from a respiratory illness), George Formby Senior bequeathed a comedy based on the assumption of common hardship, which his son would transmute into a studied impersonation of the homely clown whose gullibility and innuendo could wink towards the unsayable and chuckle in the face of fate. In Formby's romantic or absurd musical comedies, it is his awkwardness and colloquial lack of sophistication that make him both the stooge of exotic villains and alluring *femmes fatales*, and their eventual undoer. George Formby, like his spiritual home town of Blackpool, was unconcerned with irony but could hone bluntness into rhinestone brilliance. While Formby came to signify a version of northernness which was as locked in its own language as Betjeman's descriptions of metropolitan suburbia or provincial gentility, there is a sense in which that language revealed dialect as a social weapon. Nuance and intonation, as much as vocabulary and syntax, could convey the complex constitution of northern pessimism and vernacular protest.

Such a cult of fatalism can be seen as the consolidation of the north's older reputation for depression, ill-fortune and occult or demonic presence. If the north, historically, has been regarded as a psychic lightning conductor for suffering and random evil, informed by legends of witchcraft (as at Pendle Hill, with the torture of witches at Lancaster gaol), the exploits of Brady and Hindley on the Moors, the horror of working conditions in the eighteenth and nineteenth centuries, the botched redevelopment schemes of the 1960s and 1970s and the collapse of the local industries throughout the 1980s, then you have a region of mythological darkness. Even the high rainfall (that was good for the old textile industries) became as much a depressive feature of 'kitchen-sink' cinema as the moaning factory whistle or the brooding terraces. And, if the suppression of language by suffering had created a society in which violence and anger – as well as good humour and fortitude – were always close to the surface, then the north had developed a vernacular culture that was quick-witted, yet steeped in despair and the history of protest.

-╫╫-

In John Cooper Clarke's finest writing – the poems and texts written between 1977 and 1980 – we find one of the strongest voices and most accomplished narrators in post-war British poetry. In keeping with the mythology of romantic poets, Cooper Clarke has become a marginalized figure, remembered more for the witty doggerel with which he entertained on the campus cabaret circuit than for his vivid contribution to vernacular realism. In Cooper Clarke, a former laboratory technician at Salford Technical College, we can find the bitter visions of the early Eliot, redefined in the potent language of a working men's club, subverted by the sensual melancholy of the late Keats. A reflex to self-destruction threads portentous menace and tension through Cooper Clarke's lucid selection of images and subjects, enabling his best poems to describe the fag-end of northern consumer society with a perception which is as opposed to the instant gratification on offer from cheap hedonism as it is to the moralistic cobweb of northern Catholicism.

When Cooper Clarke released his first EP, 'Psycle Sluts', in October 1977, he was taken up as a 'punk poet' and could have become bogged down in the wave of novelty acts (such as 'Jilted John' or 'Alberto Y Los Trios Paranoias') that were a colourful by-product of punk rock. As it was, his dramatic use of dialect, which fired the expressionistic black comedy of his writing with the force of a linguistic revolver, raised him above mere regional caricature and defined his voice in its own right. Accompanied by the Narks, Cooper Clarke delivered 'Psycle Sluts' as a frenetic

Mancunian parody of Beat writing, stripping that idiom of its
near-legendary pretentiousness by describing a state of drug-
fuelled urban paranoia in the flippant argot of a northern spiv.
Cooper Clarke advanced masked beneath his skill as a humorist,
out-one-lining his hecklers with the foul-mouthed invective of
any cheap comedian in a northern pub; but this invective, its
language and its *raison d'être*, were also the subject of Cooper
Clarke's poetry: the walk from the bus stop late at night, the
fifth-rate discotheque, the small-town gangsters and the gap
between lust and love. Within this landscape, realistically poised
between comedy and despair, Cooper Clarke wrote himself as
both a critic and a victim, presenting cartoon narratives on the
one hand and poignant observations on the other. At the comic
end, describing himself as the infatuated lover of an alien monster, he levels a thrust at the prejudice against mixed marriages
while catching the temper of local orthodoxy by way of its diction:

> They'd go nudge, nudge
> when we got on the bus, saying,
> 'It's extraterrestrial, not like us,
> and it's bad enough with another race,
> but, fuck me – a monster from outer space.'

As Betjeman had discovered that he would be tolerated by the upper
classes because he could mimic them and make them laugh, so
Cooper Clarke could present poetry by armouring it with comedy. By the end of the 1970s, taken up by the variety billings
that would link him to Linton Kwesi Johnson, Cooper Clarke
would suffer the mixed blessings of a cultural ghettoization
which gave a hearing to 'minority' poets on the one hand but
presented them as self-consciously political on the other. The
pop-driven agit-prop of Red Wedge and Rock Against Racism
achieved a temporary fashionability which, ironically, also
brought about its sophistry, self-satisfaction and apathy. Cooper
Clarke, as unique to British poetry (save for a distant and tenuous

ancestry in the Mersey Beat poets of the 1960s), would develop his poetry and performance to move away from vernacular and directly political satire and towards a greater empathy with his subjects. This found expression in a greater economy of language, a slowing of pace and a more impressionistic collaging of detail. Recording with Martin Hannett's Invisible Girls (who would also back Pauline Murray, formerly of Penetration, on her romantic, self-titled pop LP of 1980), Cooper Clarke found a muscular and polished musical vehicle for his recitations.

After the deft misanthropy of 'Gimmix!':

> beauty aids, commodity art,
> And things that are the thing,
> Teasmaids, cushions that fart,
> The Lord of the Rings . . .

and the modern melancholy of 'Valley of the Long Lost Women':

> A truck turns into a cul-de-sac,
> Spring time turns to ice,
> ruck sacs turn into hunch-backs,
> muscle men turn into mice,

Cooper Clarke finally wrote his *Waste Land* in a poem called 'Beasley Street', which he recorded with the Invisible Girls on his 1980 LP *Snap Crackle And Bop*.

With 'Beasley Street', Cooper Clarke's poetic vision found perfect harmony with his language, producing a work as realized as Larkin's 'Whitsun Weddings' or Auden's 'Atlantis'. Most tellingly, there are no jokes in this evocative description of a Mancunian street; Cooper Clarke anatomizes the urban landscape with an acuity and sympathy which makes 'Beasley Street' a universal comment on consumer society's equivalent of slum housing. While the pathos within the poem is on a par with the scenes of East End poverty described by Dickens, the language is neither sentimental nor judgemental; the landscape is both figurative and psychological, thus placing it within the tradition of Eliot's 'unreal city'.

As dialect, Cooper Clarke's Salford accent lent an expressive intonation to the strict rhyme and metre of his verse. In 'Beasley Street', as in the other less comic poems collected on *Snap Crackle and Bop* (most notably 'Belladonna', 'Limbo Baby Limbo' and 'A Family Affair'), this dialect served to heighten both the plausibility and sentiment of Cooper Clarke's delivery by opposing the traditionally elevated speech patterns of the professional poet. His use of 'found language' – the ready-made poetry of Mancunian conversation at its most expressive – allowed the seemingly slight to make a greater comment upon itself.

'Beasley Street' begins with a vivid description of the street as both a real location and as a metaphor for stagnating consciousness; like the Thames for Eliot or Conrad, Beasley Street is a river to the heart of darkness:

> Far from crazy pavements,
> the taste of silver spoons,
> a clinical arrangement
> on a dirty afternoon;
> where the fecal germs of Mr Freud
> are rendered obsolete –
> the legal term is Null and Void
> in the case of Beasley Street.

Cooper Clarke's Waste Land is a place where love and procreation have not only worn out but become their reverse; Beasley Street is a state of living death, as removed from drama as it is from hope. It is a place for the discarded, the lost and the forgotten, where nothing ever happens save further decay. Such a depressing theme, in less accomplished hands, would become hysterical or an exercise in social realist cliché, but as Cooper Clarke builds image upon image and scene upon scene, dipping between vignettes of modern hopelessness and details that tell of the empty passage of time, the poem acquires a momentum of sympathy and truthfulness that avoids either journalistic truisms or political finger-wagging. The only reference to the political disregard of England's least fortunate is powerful enough to stand on its own:

> In an X-certificate exercise,
> ex-servicemen excrete;
> Keith Joseph smiles
> and a baby dies
> in a box on Beasley Street.

The horror of the poem lies in its subject's mute acceptance of boredom as the lobby of death:

> OAP, mother-to-be,
> watch the three-piece suite;

and:

> Beauty problems are redefined,
> the doorbells do not ring.

This is a place where the living have become ghosts, haunting the ruins of home and hope; their situation is described through images of domestic decay, playing on humour in a way that twists the comic punchline into tragedy:

> Vince the ageing savage,
> betrays no sign of life,
> but the smell of yesterday's cabbage
> and the ghost of last year's wife.

As Beasley Street reverses life and confounds hope, so there is no chance of redemption; the dream – if it can be called a dream – is simply to be a different person in a different life:

> The boys are on the wagon,
> the girls are on the shelf;
> their common problem is
> that they're not someone else.

and

> Eyes dead as vicious fish,
> look around for laughs;
> If I could have just one wish,
> I would be a photograph.

There is a final, glancing blow in this description of an urban oubliette for society's lost souls, and that is a sarcastic reference to the sociological solution:

> It's a sociologist's paradise –
> each day repeats . . .

Thus, Beasley Street's only value to modern society would be as a model for some social theory; life itself, as a gift turned into a burden, must simply be endured. For Cooper Clarke, combining the realism of Larkin with the secular despair of early Eliot, 'Beasley Street' brought together all the themes of his earlier poetry and defined them with a new simplicity. Beasley Street itself, though recognizably northern, could be anywhere English and urban; the poem is a violent protest, achieving its conviction through an absence of judgement and a tightness of focus. Cooper Clarke bears witness to all of the banal suffering that is rendered invisible by its very familiarity; there is neither metaphysical cleverness nor romantic glamour in his meditation on modern squalor – he does not make himself the hero of his own fable, but leaves us (as did Chekhov) to draw our own conclusions.

In keeping with English romanticism, Cooper Clarke's eventual destination is an uncompromising realism; at his most lyrical, he relates a tenderness that is shot through with symbolist morbidity, as in 'Belladonna' (1980) with its couplet refrain:

> Arm in arm down Hemlock Row,
> Walking together in the purple snow.

This mixture of beauty and suffering, never too distant from a pharmacological background of cocaine, heroin and amphetamines, casts Cooper Clarke as the Rimbaud of Salford – a poet for whom the argot of Manchester is just as rich as the street slang of Paris. In terms of defining the northern sensibility, Cooper Clarke's subject is the fate of vulnerable humanity at the hands of advanced consumerism in a depressed or archaic region; his particular balance of comedy and protest is drawn from the increased vulgarity of cut-price glamour in a local culture weighed down by economic collapse and a redundant industrial heritage.

▦

Within the first generation of Mancunian punks, Howard Devoto – the man who invited the Sex Pistols to Manchester, co-founder of the Buzzcocks and subsequently frontman of Magazine – revealed himself to be a lyricist and performer of barbed literary accomplishment, paraphrasing emotional experience with an accuracy that was intensified by the simultaneous commentary, within the songs, of accusation and confession. Having written two of punk rock's classic songs, 'Boredom' (which shared with Richard Hell's 'Blank Generation' the assertion that dumb was smart) and 'Orgasm Addict', Devoto had laid the blueprint for his developing themes of the fragility of identity and the violence of love.

With Magazine's first two LPs, *Real Life* and *Secondhand Daylight*, Devoto's performance and lyrics put forward an attitude of displacement which would survive the conversion of punk rock into social cliché. Simultaneously awkward and menacing, witty and reserved, he seemed to represent the lucidity of the lost philosopher as pitted against the classic nervous boredom of the English punk, and provided a rallying anthem for this condition in 'Shot By Both Sides' and 'A Song From Under The

Floorboards'. Devoto delivered aphorisms ('I know the meaning of life and it doesn't help me a bit', for example) which suggested the ambiguous arrogance of supreme intelligence and the pain of self-awareness. Unlike most of his Mancunian peers, he had no interest in regionalism as either style or content; Magazine were less a Manchester group than an idea that originated in Manchester.

The perception of the north as a willing dumping ground for the sophistry of southern fashionability was central to Mark E. Smith's conception of his group the Fall. The Fall have used the rock form as a vehicle for Smith's unique recounting of lucid dreams that double as a form of mass observation; they are both the unencumbered sound of a regional sensibility, and, in Smith's seemingly refracted but wholly focused use of language and narrative, as important to the history of English pop as Cubism was to the development of European painting. And, as genuine innovators in a medium too used to graceless mavericks, they have remained within a largely marginalized sphere of influence.

On the sleeve of the Falls first live LP, *Totale's Turns* (1980), there is an acerbic note entitled 'CALL YOURSELVES BLOODY PRO-FESSIONALS?', penned by one of Smith's many alter-egos, Roman Totale. The note describes the hostility with which the Fall were met by their local audience on the working-men's club circuit. Rather than the 'northern white crap that talks back' (as Smith introduces the Fall), 'cast out, cast out as if from Heaven', the local youth, according to Totale, believe that 'Everyone knows best groups come from't London'. In short, the vorticist violence of Mark E. Smith's Fall was initially rejected by the very culture that it was articulating with such force, oblique lucidity and mordant humour. Smith remains a regional visionary and ex-ponent of political surrealism; his writing combines the malevol-ence of Wyndham Lewis's satires on the Bloomsbury Group with the polemicizing of a revisionist historian. Indeed, the Fall could be seen as a vorticist Blast against the design-conscious professionalism and Mancunian elitism of Anthony H. Wilson's Factory Records. Smith wrote in 'Cash and Carry':

> Even in Manchester. There's two types of factory there. One makes old corpses. They stumble around like rust dogs. One lives off old dying men. One lives off the back of a dead man. You know which one. You know which Factory I mean. You know . . . You know . . . Psychedelic brain mushes offers the alternative. They're all good boys, regular wages. The boss does the covers. They are OK by me. They just don't talk to me.

Smith keeps the Fall at arm's length, because, he claims, 'that's our mentality'. A former communist and ex-dock-worker, Smith named his group after the novel by Camus. This was his first and last engagement with self-consciously 'intellectualized' pop culture. In what could be seen as an act of Class War, Smith, as the 'prole art threat', would reject or ridicule all attempts by cultural pundits either to appropriate or to deconstruct the Fall. To this end, Smith added a pointed note on the reverse sleeve of the Fall's *Slates* 10-inch mini-LP (1981): 'Academic thingys ream off names of books and bands.' This hostility towards bourgeois critiques is as pronounced as Roman Totale's disgust at a would-be fashionable northern audience who hide their conformity beneath 'straight leg Lee Coopers'. Smith, like Lewis, has adopted the artistic persona of the Enemy of one and all. He has described his artistic project – which is laden with wit, as well as bile – as a product of the 'dock mentality': an insular bloody-mindedness which doubles as an epic vision of England (and Europe) beset by corruption, decay, absurdity and hypocrisy. Backed by the disciplined repetition of his group ('Don't start improvising, for God's sake', Smith barks on 'Slates, Slags etc', 1981), Smith could narrate or sermonize in a semi-codefied language that made philosophical comedy out of intellectual short-hand. He assumes various characters within these narratives: Riddler, the Man Whose Head Expanded, Carrier-Bag

Man, the Hip Priest, Wireless Enthusiast, Roman Totale – to name a selection; these characters are both his fictional puppets and his alter-egos. Smith, like Fellini, sub-contracts different aspects of his vision to a cast of personal representatives who can explore states of being in a succession of lucid dreams. And, as with Fellini's dreams transcribed to film, it is often difficult (and unnecessary) to distinguish these dreams from reality. There is always a plausibility which makes the seemingly illogical or absurd make poetic sense.

From their first LP, *Live At the Witch Trials* (1978), the Fall were committed to an unvarying course through dreams, protest and paranoia. In literary terms, Smith has been compared with James Joyce as an innovator within the English language, but he remains protective of his gifts, as he hints in 'Room To Live':

> Foreigners and experts go in
> And through my place
> Turn my home into a museum
> And like the murder squad
> They scan the room for the well of inspiration.
> They don't tolerate ordinary folk
> And folk look at me strange;
> But I'll give them this at least
> They pay for what they eat.

As this lyric suggests, surveillance is a major theme in Smith's writing, positing him as both sleuth and criminal, but always in possession of suppressed information. 'There used to be a statue of Cromwell outside Victoria Station in Manchester,' he said during an interview with *Frieze* magazine, 'but they moved it and put it behind some fucking bush in Wythenshawe.' Smith, as a reactionary republican, describes evidence of hostility from the opposition as ubiquitous. English and Scottish history (to say nothing of Dutch, German and Italian history) becomes a sinister source for Smith's open file on treachery and corruption. In his experiments with theatre and ballet, *Hey! Luciani* and 'I

Am Kurious Oranj' (1988), Smith has tackled murderous plots in the Vatican and over the Dutch succession respectively. In some ways, these historic dramas were extensions of Smith's primary metaphor of England in decay. In *Kurious Oranj*, sharing a song-writing credit with William Blake for 'Dog Is Life/ Jerusalem', he narrates:

> I was walking down the street when I tripped up on a discarded banana skin, and on my way down I caught the side of my head on a protruding brick chip. It was the government's fault. I was, ah, very let down by the Budget. I was expecting a one million quid hand out. I was very disappointed. It was the government's fault.

'The Fall', in Blakeian terms, could be regarded as Smith's perception of England's fall from grace and descent into self-pity or fashionable liberalism – two sins of equal gravity in Smith's writing.

His theatrical projects saw Smith working with Michael Clark's ballet company and the late Leigh Bowery, an Australian eccentric who elevated going to nightclubs as a reconstructed art-work (through elaborate costumes and make-up techniques) to a form of performance art which hailed the absurd and the transgressive as its primary aesthetic. But the metropolitan fashionability of these projects could not have been further removed from Smith's defiantly northern stance, and of the two works it was the less grand *Hey! Luciani* that was the most effective, and the most faithful to Smith's clever appropriation of amateurism and *arte povera*.

The Fall had always made use of a Luddite tendency to reverse the slick professionalism of pop as product – hence their artistic opposition to the luxurious minimalism of Wilson's Factory artefacts. Each Fall release was sleeved with cover art (designed or directed by Smith) that extended the marriage between Blake and *Blast* in the graphics of an underground samizdat (best realized, perhaps, in the art-work for *This Nation's Saving Grace*, with its implication of chariots of fire riding over the Mancunian cityscape), replete with dry wit. Throughout the early 1980s, as the Fall grew in reputation while confounding the heavily produced and brightly packaged pop culture of that period, their artistic vision was unyielding to fashionability. From *Hex Induction Hour* (1982) to *This Nation's Saving Grace* (1985) and *Bend Sinister* (1986), Smith appeared to be working on an epic diagnosis of his times, relating the dispossessed to a delight in contrariness which said as much about the failure of socialism as it did about the effects of fad-led consumerism. Hence, perhaps, his eerie revival of 'The British Grenadiers' on *Bend Sinister*.

As removed from the ground-breaking house and techno scene that would develop from the Factory's club, the Hacienda (and Factory's imprint on an era with New Order's best-selling 'Blue Monday') as they were from the later consolidation of rave and independent pop that became the proto-laddism of 'Madchester' (despite Mark Smith's occasional sorties into the world of dance music), the Fall maintained a fierce independence with a smouldering hatred of the high-riding aristocrats of pop fashionability. Smith's twisted comedies and perverse visions saw a landscape of deliquescing precincts, portakabins, blank British countryside and lurid psychological interiors. These were the dreams of Branwell Brontë as self-inflicted time-travel, touched by the arcana of local journalism. Smith's writing was peopled with social misfits, mutants and autistic enthusiasts; their first-person narration, more often than not, played with lunatic conviction as cock-eyed shamanism – delivering accounts of fantastical or disturbing occurrences between the pub and the Post Office, the High Street and the hotel. Writing from the point of view of an anxious victim of hostile forces, recounting his strategies for psychic self-defence while pronouncing judgement on the enemies, Smith became the hero of his own allegorical comedies. We are not that far, in fact, from an apocalyptic view of Billy Liar's Ambrosia.

If we take Smith's writing and his plosive, side-of-mouth delivery to be the underground press (or local paper) of his own psychological vision, we can see that he is Editor, Chief Correspondent and full cast of most of his stories. In 'Village Bug', for instance: 'I cannot account for this village bug/ Smoke hangs like clouds of slugs/ Gossip spreads.' And in 'Wings' we find Smith as time-travelling historian and as psycho-journalist:

I ended up in the eighteen sixties.
I've bin there for one hundred and twennyfive
years. A small alteration of the past can turn time into space.
Ended up under Ardwick Bridge. With some veterans of the
US Civil War. They were under Irish patronage. We shot a
stupid sargeant, but I got hit in the cross-fire . . .
. . . So now I sleep in ditches. And hide away from nosy kids.
The wings rot and feather under me. The wings rot and curl
right under me. A small alteration of the past, can turn time
into space.

Smith's subject is seldom love, but his writing leaves traces of tenderness among the surreal comedy and grape-shot philosophizing. 'This is the finest time of my life,' he admits in a tuneless croon on 'Bill Is Dead', while 'Mark'll Sink Us' comes closer to confession:

A message mesmerised
on all English breath
The crux pretty grasped
but mostly misunderstood.
Mark'll sink us!
I am desolate. I live the
black and blue of the night.
Friend depression comes
now and again. Once in a blue moon.
It points backwards, thus: Mark'll sink us!

Ultimately, perhaps, Smith's target is what he perceives as the failure of English pop to change anything:

> All the English groups
> act like peasants with free milk;
> On a route, on a route to the loot,
> Five whacky English proletariat idiots.
> Californians always think of sex
> or think of death.
> Five hundred girl deaths . . .

Smith's hatred of pop nostalgia ('Vimto and Spangles were always crap-uh,' he pronounces on 'It's A Curse', 'Regardless of the look back bores') lends an air of caustic topicality to each record. Lampooning the re-emergence of open-air pop festivals in 'Bonkers In Phoenix', or baiting the music press in 'CAC Mithering', he resembles the later, solitary Lewis who was producing *The Enemy* journal more or less single-handedly. And yet Smith's northern pop *Blast*, fed on the mutant landscape of north Manchester, is still underwritten by a sense of regional identity as cultural metaphor, 'Lie Dream Of A Casino Soul', 'Hit The North' and 'Lucifer Over Lancashire', with its acknowledgement of northern demonism, take the local and pronounce them universal, suggesting a prophet in Prestwich: 'I can see. I have dreams. And the secret of my life: Is . . . Secretive' ('Cash & Carry').

lipstick & RObots

'Give a man a mask and he will tell the truth.'

OSCAR WILDE

'Down in the Park with a friend called '5'.'

GARY NUMAN

By 1973, in terms of fashionable household interior design, the damp autumn of domestic psychedelia had finally given way to the warming sirocco of home-building Habitat. The Mediterranean touch of off-white, wickerwork and terracotta would replace the arcana and Victoriana of bedsit mystic chic; the fetishized and mutated art nouveau of imported West Coast poster art would be usurped by the straighter lines and more worldly styling of rediscovered Art Deco, Martini chic and urbane dandyism. And similarly, in popular culture and pop music itself, the 1970s would see as drastic a change between the sensibilities of its first and second halves as had the 1960s. In terms of style, chemicals were out and cocktails were in – and this shift would be as important as a metaphor, with regard to the submerged agenda of English pop, as it was in the burgeoning industries – fashion, advertising and media – which spread pop's message and had claims to being pop in themselves.

Most importantly, English pop culture would open itself up on a far broader scale to European influences and stylized time travel, courting the implied sophistication of abroad, the past and the future, despite providing a host culture that was slow to lose its self-consciousness in the face of a technologically shrinking planet. Even within the painted world of Glam rock there seemed to be a deeply English championing of reality: however flamboyant or effete in appearance, the teen heroes of Glam – Mud, the Sweet and Slade – were laddish good-timers, returning to the harder values of basic rock-'n'-roll and stomping out the hippy sensitivity and pedantic virtuosity of Yes or ELP with their impudently caricatured platform boots. In a Trinity of breathless sophistication above the pilgrim soldiers of Glam were T. Rex, Roxy Music and the reinvented David Bowie, all of whom were accomplished time-travellers, and would bring a preview of the future to the present. And, as ever, there would be a Tiresian court jester dipping in and out of the spot-light, this time provided by Steve Harley of Cockney Rebel.

Indurate to all of this, however, were the orgiastic rituals of heavy metal. Heavy metal music, developing during the late 1960s from rhythm and blues to the elevation of monolithic cults around Led Zeppelin (whose Celtic cowboy occultism had a weight of genuine darkness which was summed up in the density, as an image, of their name) and Black Sabbath, had declared itself a proudly independent republic within the states of popular culture. Part of its appeal lay in simple extremism – of scale, volume and imagery – which supported its principal conceit of rock supremacy. And, as such, heavy metal became the self-proclaimed sound of English machismo, while appealing to the boyish sensibility of role-playing within a culturally autistic realm of fantasy kingdoms, in which the heavy metal hero was a triumphant, death's head warrior. The cover art of LPs by Iron Maiden, for example, would revel in this notion, promoting a bad boy image of ultimate strength and terror. Wholly dismissive of fashionability, heavy metal could be seen as a form of musical miscegenation, in which runic saga, pseudo-satanic imagery and hymns to destruction became the soundtrack of fantasy epic, underwritten by legends of equally heroic hedonism among its principal practitioners.

But heavy metal appeared to take its strongest hold in out-of-the-way places, where boredom or isolation redoubled the need for rock fantasy; it was, if anything, the true sound of rural England, updating the folk tradition as much as race-tuned trucks had usurped the horse and cart as the principal means of transport for bored country boys. Terminally adolescent but touched by the hand of the Hell's Angels, heavy metal, for all of its outward bravado and volume, was more of a passage to personal and tribal insularity, in which the codes of heavy metal were sufficient unto themselves, and little dialogue was assumed with the outside world. Hence the partial truism that heavy metal co-existed with model-making and fantasy war-gaming as a cult of make-believe and a safe haven from social responsibility. Few of its converts would defect to punk rock or Goth; the juggernaut of heavy metal would trundle on, in love with excess – as though it alone knew where it was going.

Of all the groups assembled under the generic label of heavy metal, only Led Zeppelin would endure as a touchstone of some Viking sensibility which reached out to the extreme edges of conscious-ness to wrestle or couple with whatever demons or angels might be found there. Led Zeppelin, steeped in the blues, purveyed a disciplined intensity which became easy to caricature but hard to write off as pomp rock bombast. Their first three LPs, as with Jethro Tull's *Aqualung*, *Thick as a Brick* and *A Passion Play*, Hawkwind's *In Search of Space* and even *From the Witchwood* by the Strawbs, marked out a territory between the dusk of the Sixties and the dawning of the Seventies which called upon the folkloric or the fantastical to describe a nihilism attendant on the end of an epoch and an establishment – that establishment

being the University of Rock which seemed to have been established in the latter half of the 1960s. Tull's child prodigy poet,
disqualified on grounds of taste, in the concept of 'Thick as a
Brick', or their baroque tramp Aqualung, were as close to a world
going out of control as the frozen landscapes of Led Zeppelin
were to a world that was dead already. This was epic fury,
underwritten by cod-mysticism, which was floundering or defiant
between the distinct musical sensibilities of two eras. It would
be the last time before the arrival of ambient techno and acid
house, over a decade later, that pop music would foreground
the interior journeys through self-sealed psychosis and fantasy.
The Led Zeppelin, with eerie persistence, would drift through
two decades towards the corn circles of the New Age.

But there were two iconic record sleeves in the early 1970s – one
American, the other British – which could be seen to oppose
one another as banners beneath which to march towards the
life to come. The first of these was Carole King's *Tapestry* – a
classic portrait of domestic melancholy straight from the heart
of the Earth Mother. King, barefoot and placid, was seated on
the sill of a rustic interior which suggested hearth and home;
behind her inscrutable mask of serenity there seemed to be the
shell-shocked quiet of a person in recovery from the rites of
passage. Without a visible trace of make-up, the great composer
of rock-'n'-roll love songs looked as though she had finally settled
down, exchanged bohemia for baking and worry for weaving. It
was all very natural; a kind of 'getting back to' something (the
soil? the soul?) which rejected the youthful clamour for modernity with a firm but gentle smile of refusal. Her life had been
a tapestry of rich and royal hue (the portrait suggested) and now
she was going to sit back, take stock, and speculate on the
patterns of life and love. With the melancholy maturity of songs
like 'You've Got a Friend' and 'It's Too Late', Carole King's tapestry was ready to be hung in the homes of young married
couples everywhere. It spoke of old loves and possible futures.

This was the *A la recherche* of the spice-rack generation.

Facing the figurative portrait of Carole King on the cover of *Tapestry*, across a slender gap in time but a chasm of sensibility, was the figurative portrait of David Bowie on the cover of *Aladdin Sane*. America's reflective priestess was up against the mute mask of Beckenham's space boy. The cover of *Aladdin Sane*, as an iconic image, was the precise reverse of *Tapestry*. As a white humanoid on a white background, his face a lightning-flashed, absurdly prettified skull, hair a carrot-red late Elvis and pink-shaded, mascarared eyes closed, Bowie exchanged human for inhuman, heterosexual for any-old-sexual, domesticity for statelessness, nature for artifice, nostalgia for futurism, and the pastoral for the urban. Carole's sleepy gaze was not returned by the slumbering, shy or weeping Aladdin; Bowie's pop product made no eye contact with the consumer. It didn't have to: a new generation, having watched Ziggy Stardust mutate into Aladdin, were already looking at the world through Ziggy's famously screwed-up eyes (one of Bowie's pupils having been bashed into its trademark luminescence during a fist-fight with George Underwood); it was their vision. And the future, it seemed, as a vivid premonition of apocalyptic artifice above all, *contra mundum*, began with Aladdin. Carole's naked sincerity – the worldly self-knowledge of early middle-age – seemed like an infantilist nostalgia for a personal Arcady, when set against Bowie's pronouncement of an androgynous adolescence with one white foot in the future.

David Bowie, up until what seemed to be his artistic suicide note of 1980, *Ashes To Ashes*, was the single most important figure in English pop. He was the link, effectively, between proto-Mod and post-punk – a definitive icon of England in transition and the popular embodiment (after an early obscurity in London's underground art scene) of the avant-garde. Hence the advertisement in the music press, during punk, which stated: 'There is Old Wave. There is New Wave. And There is David Bowie.' And, by 1973, Bowie had already rehearsed much of the aesthetic that would eventually lead him to a lonely walk as Pierrot, choreographing his own requiem to a secular Sanctus.

-⊞-

Above all – above his influence on fashion and music – David Bowie was a unifier of pop youth: he brought together a massive faction of lost romantics and disbelievers in the rock orthodoxy; he built a bridge between the sexes that inspired mutual identification and adoration from boys and girls, in a way that neither the Beatles nor the Rolling Stones had ever achieved. Hence, perhaps, his line in 'All the Young Dudes' referring to the brother still at home, lost in archaic ideas of rock-'n'-roll revolution; the young dudes themselves were more than happy to surf on the rising wave of simply being young. To identify with Bowie, in 1973, was to make a decision that turned bedroom dreams into personal politics. To be a Bowie fan made further labelling unnecessary. An army of outsiders, from Basingstoke to Burton-on-Trent, had discovered a leader who could stamp their passports to a parallel reality.

A sociological model had been created, for Ziggy's children, which saw High Street futurism and plastic decadence – Rimmel and Robotics – as the pop cultural esperanto of the disaffected young romantics of Britain. Bowie, the Sun King of advanced consumerism, blurred the boundaries between the present and the future, male and female, and offered a DIY disguise for the pursuit of glamour in a synthetic age. Here, too, was an exercise in audacity that fledgeling punks would cut their teeth upon, laden with hinted-at profundity, flashy references to Braque, Burroughs and Warhol, highly-charged sexuality and a confrontationally stylish cult of alienation. In an era of football terrace violence, the exchange, in drug culture, of cannabis for amphetamines, and Kubrick's *A Clockwork Orange*, when the tower block

Utopia of post-war town-planning had deliquesced into a city-scape of bruised brutalism and broken lifts, Bowie, as a pop idol, was like the ghost of a dead future coming back to haunt a present *in extremis*. No wonder people got excited, and *The Times* described him as 'T. S. Eliot with a rock-'n'-roll beat.'

Bowie, like Marc Bolan, was a suburban boy who had progressed from the sharp individualism of Mod, through psychedelic mysticism, to wrap trashy rock-'n'-roll pantomime in tinfoil. English dandyism reached an apotheosis with Bowie, and dandyism, in England, had always suggested the suburban outsider's subtle revenge on home and high society alike – a mask behind which to advance. But the pop dandyism of Kubrick's droogs or Ziggy Stardust was as English as a pub sandwich; it saw the future as a dressing-up box and put science fiction into bed with the suburban aesthete or the Dickensian thug. It suggested precinct mutants from Hulme or Stevenage rather than teenage rebels with an eye to America, and it was steeped in a makeshift glamour that spoke more of Croydon than California. Bowie's Aladdin might hymn the decadence of Beverly Hills, but his heart, one felt, was in Beckenham.

Pop had been playing around with sex and sexuality from the moment when Elvis wore eye-shadow, but the costume drama of gender-bending for the masses had its opening night with Bowie's whole-hearted rejection of gender. The Star Man, England decreed (as Bowie slipped an arm around Mick Ronson's waist on *Top of the Pops*) was obviously a real homosexual. Or was he? No fool, Bowie fuelled the flames of this debate with ambiguous statements about his bisexuality, and the nation held its breath. Bowie's ascendancy, colourful even by pop's standards, implied a society out of control. Beach-fighting Mods and flag-burning hippies had probably done more actually to worry the government, but there was something mainstream – something High Street – about Bowie's new androgyny and all that it stood for. It splashed over the brim of known pop faddishness and suggested an amorphous, mass-media and wholly new brand of *fin-de-siècle* decadence. Sexuality itself was being manipulated in a way that England, looking on with fascinated ambivalence and primal hostility, had not witnessed since the indictment of Oscar Wilde. Indeed, that Bowie's Glam rock could turn barrow boys into screaming queens was the greatest triumph, and irony, of its period. The trappings of transvestism, thanks to Bowie, were granted the broadest currency of street fashionability. He had set up a sociological template, by accident or intention, which pushed England's buttons; it would reach its apotheosis with wedge haircuts and eye-shadow for a generation of teenage boys. Added to this, Bowie projected himself as a serious artist, for whom rock-'n'-roll was simply another medium in which to work. Bowie was the first English pop performer fully to utilize the language of fine art in the glittering construction of his celebrity; he was the ultimate product of the Mod to Art School vector that the Creation had described in their charting single of 1966, 'Painter Man'. And, as such, Bowie demanded cultural seriousness in a way that only the Beatles had previously received. Hence *The Times* comparison with Eliot. Pop idols can be artists – official.

From the platform of Bowie's ground-breaking androgyny, the ragged history of English dandyism's nervous flirtation with actual homosexuality can be seen as an elderly branch line on England's counter-cultural Underground map. It's a well-worn route, from the terminal prejudice of Victorian society's incarceration of Wilde, through the misplaced jingoism of World War One (the health-bringing purge of Wildean decadence), on to the inter-war flippancy of Mayfair's born-again hedonists, into the long tunnel of World War Two's eventual reorganization of the class system, and out into the delinquency and exploitation fictions of the early pop age. Over the sixty-odd years that it actually took for the rigid formality of Victorian England to break down (or reveal the neurosis beneath the ruddy exterior), the homosexual dandy as a fictional type had acquired the shamanistic role of the amused outsider whose cynicism reveals the wisdom of a brutally realist philosophy. Best defined by the character of Anthony Blanche, in Waugh's *Brideshead Revisited*, who sees right through the superficiality of artist Ryder's fashionable imitations of Gauguin, the type is an impious Buddha to youth who codes his theology as wit. Doomed by his sexuality to solitude or a secret world (pansy bars and Piccadilly) he plays on the emotional and intellectual curiosity of young men with a Socratic charm and a Jesuitical cleverness, revealing their self-deception with the authority of a social agent who has been prematurely aged, and who rejects the moral orthodoxy. He is the executor of Wilde's philosophical legacy, and he embodies a choice to fervent and impressionable youth.

But Bowie was to blend two mythologies of outsiderdom to create his persona of the mutant pop star. The first of these was the cult of the sexually ambiguous dandy (hence the *succès de scandale* of his wearing a dress on the original cover of *The Man Who Sold the World* or the camp peevishness of 'Queen Bitch') which achieved a fashionable credibility at the hands of Bowie's intellectualized stylishness. To reject heterosexuality – albeit as a dramatic device – was to distance him from the old-fashioned machismo of rock-'n'-roll. It also tapped into the underground world of Warhol's Factory and Lindsay Kemp's hugely influential interpretations of Wilde, Lorca and Genet – all three of which, as the hymning of homosexual outsiderdom as the last act of Glam aesthetics and the tense pause before the storm of punk, were staged as mimes at the Roundhouse, in Camden Town, during the mid 1970s.

Kemp, reputedly the descendant of Shakespeare's favourite fool, would launch his massively influential mimes in London at a time, 1975, when the legacy of the art school temperament of Bowie and Roxy Music was poised to influence the founding aesthetic of punk rock. At the Roundhouse, murky with potent incense, Kemp's febrile mingling of symbolist decadence, powdered androgyny and blood-soaked poetics would forge a link between *fin-de-siècle* and *fin-de-millennium* notions of decadence. Kemp had worked with Bowie in 1972, as the choreographer of the Astronettes for the Ziggy Stardust concerts, but playing with his own company (including the defiantly beautiful David Haughton, and eerily dame-like Incredible Orlando) he presented, through interpretations of the lives and work of Genet, Lorca and Wilde, a cast of romantic heroes who were historic opponents of social, sexual and political orthodoxy. Genet's merging of high aesthetics and petty criminality, Lorca's homosexuality and execution at the hands of the Spanish fascists during the Civil War, and Wilde's downfall (his play, *Salome*, had originally been refused performance in England on the grounds that it depicted biblical figures on stage) provided a triptych of iconic martyrs for Kemp, and by dramatizing their legends in the sensual, doom-laden aesthetic of late Glam he linked the anti-heroes of cultural history to the rehearsal for a new cult of artifice. A slight, white-painted figure, rising from a debris of mirrored coffin lids in a mist of dry-ice and talcum powder, drooling stage blood, Kemp's beckoning curtain call at the end of *Flowers* positioned him as a household god of punk rock and an ancestor of the Scottish dancer Michael Clark – a cross between Puck and Oberon to stimulate a court of Ziggy fans and momentarily lost souls.

English dandies had drawn their strength from foreign exotica (public school spies in Moscow, Lindsay Kemp choosing to live in Barcelona, Anthony Blanche a cosmopolitan cocktail of nationalities which allowed him to play up his Englishness while mocking its anal formality) and Bowie took the trait to its limit. By suggesting himself as an existential, unisexual and ultimately vulnerable alien, Bowie's adoption of the persona of a messianic dandy from another planet was the trump card of exotica. Science fiction, as a vital component of pop culture, had since the 1950s been using aliens either as corny horror characters or as metaphors for communist infiltration. Aliens provided a good line in spooky entertainment while addressing the Gothic need for mysteries beyond the ever-expanding frontiers of science and technology. And this tied in, directly, with the experience of the first American teenagers as a new social group, brought up on the evangelism for science which had its practical demonstration in the dropping of the Atomic bomb on Hiroshima, in 1946 – an education in paranoia that was noted by William S. Burroughs. Over in the New World, away from rationing and rain, teenagers had been instructed that the apocalypse could really happen; history could end, and their perception of the future would always be tinged with a sense of death and a science fiction afterlife. In America, home of Pop Art, the future was fetishized during the 1950s as both the bringer of a benign technological society and as an Utopia under threat from either Russians or robots, or both. All of those Cadillac tail-fins and big white fridges had to mean something: the future was here today, and aliens, crudely speaking, were the darker siblings of the eagerly anticipated hover-cars and dome-homes.

And Bowie's Major Tom, floating around his tin can, would signify the astronaut not as hero, but as seeker after truth on the verge of an existential crisis – drifting away from the applause of a nervous nation. Far from astronauts being the cowboys of the space range as suggested in the innocence of the 1950s, a film such as *Marooned* (1969) in which three astronauts become stranded in space, joined with Kubrick's *2001: A Space Odyssey* (1968) to show Major Toms as vulnerable, quasi-corporate pioneers into altered states of consciousness and the philosophical unknown – in English terms they were like so many Reggie Perrins at the ass-end of space.

Received as mere hearsay in England, but incorporated into our Wellsian notion of Doomsday in Dorking, the Atomic Age cult of aliens and astronauts (the latter being the heroic version of the former) was at odds with our sense of history and as a consequence even more exotic. Martians in New York sounded plausible, Martians in Margate, however, were unthinkable. Hence the potency of Bowie's impact on England: the marriage of alien and dandy giving birth to the ultimate outsider figure for the modern age, the queer messiah from space – the definitive rebel.

Pallid as opposed to tanned, skinny as opposed to muscular, Bowie was Beaton with a bouffant and reversed the idea of what a pop idol and sex symbol might look like. Launched in a pantomime of bisexual other-worldliness on an England still recovering from Gilbert O'Sullivan's flannel shorts, Bowie became the Pied Piper of Handbag to a younger generation out of patience with cheesecloth. Above all, being a dedicated follower of Bowie was self-defining; it could be seen as a liberation from mere fandom into a cult of mass individualism, and thousands of Bowie imitators were acting out their own sense of alienation or narcissism in pubs, clubs and bedrooms. Cynically, this might create a conservative idea of individualism, but to Bowie, as an extremist from Beckenham, the army of impersonators represented a triumph for suburbia and the provinces as the home of revolt through style. And, however fluent in the styles of Japan, Germany or Hollywood Bowie might become, he was always touched by the hand of South Croydon. Boots and the new Miss Selfridge, with their neon white counters, were meeting the demand for henna and lip-gloss, re-routeing space age glamour back to the precinct and the High Street, where it seemed to blossom in the rain.

Hot on Bowie's stacked heels were Roxy Music, who mingled science and artifice into a cabaret futura of decadent romance – playing with nostalgia as Bowie played with the future. Roxy Music played their debut concert at the Royal College of Art, which was only right for a group comprised of former art students, and they joined with Bowie at playing clever pop stars – and none was more clever than keyboardist Brian Eno (who had also claimed to be an alien) – who knew how to manipulate their cultural reference points. Luxurious and melodramatic, Roxy Music, like Bowie, were essentially time-travellers – a point made in the purple prose of Simon Puxley's sleeve notes to their self-titled, unsurpassable, first LP: 'And in inner space . . . the mind loses its bearings. What's the date again (it's so dark in here) 1962? or twenty years on?' Roxy Music, as their name explained, took their cue from the elegance of the 1930s and 1940s, but the real mission of their cool theatricality was a kind of *fin-de-siècle* swoon into the arms of technology; Ferry's artful caricature of the matinée idol as doomed romantic (Jay Gatsby meets Marcello Mastroianni on Tyneside) always seemed to suggest a fancy dress party in the not-too-distant future. This was playing with history as a cosmetic version of itself: the apocalyptic cityscapes on Bowie's *Diamond Dogs* were as florid and stylized as Roxy Music's inter-war glamour, and this was the greater part of their strangeness, charm and relevance. Bowie's shock of the new was Roxy Music's shock of the old, but they shared a dandyism which thrived on artifice; it suggested the present as an amalgam of the past and the future, in which the pop star was a cross between Dirk Bogarde, Noël Coward and Mr Spock – a point made in 1973 by David Bowie's *Pin-Ups* collection of rampant thrash Mod covers and Ferry's response, elegantly titled with a nod to the 1930s, *These Foolish Things*. The glamour of such time-travelling, in turn, brought with it a certain internationalism – a short-lived but passionate love affair between English pop and European sophistication.

And yet Roxy Music and David Bowie, throughout the first half of the 1970s, as the ghosts of Christmas Past and Future respectively, propounded notions of time travel that were heavily tinged with death, disorientation and decay. From Bowie's 'Five Years', as an imagined response to the imminent end of the world, to Roxy Music's 'The Bob Medley' (1972) in which the strains of an interior elegance are drowned out by gun-fire, the ultimate destination of their glamour was shaped by a romantic sense of mortality – a plastic Keatsian 'half in love with easeful death'. This strong theme of death beneath glamour – the Petronian role of the *arbiter elegantiae* being sentenced to commit suicide at his leisure – would be crucial to those post-punks who looked to the Glam age for their own aesthetic of death, dehumanization and Weimar decadence. As the sensual images of pin-up girls and swooning sirens on the covers of Roxy Music's first four LPs hovered close to pornography, so too did their music move closer to the gloriously lurid, subverted by an arcane knowingness which crystallized their luxurious image into a sealed world of erotic melodrama: Edith Piaf meets Helmut Newton. Ferry – ever the trend-setter – would drop into German on the goose-stepping chorus line of 'Lullabye' (1974), to proclaim that the end of the world was nothing when one was stranded between love and art, thus setting in place, more or less, the entire agenda of New Romanticism.

In terms of drama, David Bowie and Roxy Music turned pop concerts into rallies and Goth-Futurist theatre, with the trashy rock-'n'-roll finding a natural home between the atmospheric, synthesized soliloquies on love and loss. Bowie singing 'Sweet Thing', as a lover lost in an urban future, could compete with Bryan Ferry singing 'In Every Dream Home a Heartache' as a lover lost in Harrods; Roxy Music's 'A Song For Europe', with its punning on the Bridge of Sighs, fitted nicely with Bowie's double serenading of Jean Genet and Iggy Pop in 'Jean Jeanie'. A whole new language had been invented for radical English pop, a kind of neo-Platonic plutonium plush, which was a world and a time away from the previous tyranny of American rockism over pop cool.

If David Bowie and Roxy Music, as the twin architects of Glam rock's influence on post-punk morbidity, were openly flirting with death and despair – attempting a futuristic rumba on their own imagined graves as it were – then these themes were also being put forward in the less dramatic, but equally complex, songs of Steve Harley & Cockney Rebel. As vital informants of Howard Devoto's second group Magazine, five years later, Cockney Rebel would describe on their LP *The Human Menagerie of Cockney Rebel* (1973) a mixture of soulful melancholy and street-wise impudence that would also bring to mind the earliest suburban urchin poetry of Suede. And, as Bowie's vocal mutated Anthony Newley, and Ferry's swooping vibrato seemed to put Gilbert Becaud into a tonal blender with Noël Coward, so too did Steve Harley's nasal gulps of caricatured intonation appear to cross Bob Dylan with Bob Cratchit in a way that would not be rivalled until Wire's Colin Newman sang 'I Am The Fly' as though chanting surrealist poetry from the terraces of the Shed at Chelsea FC.

Cockney Rebel's reference points were those of impeccable suburban outsiders ('We can go to a hop and do suburban bop, cool and sharply' they sang on 'What Ruthy Said'); and *The Human Menagerie* touched all of the bases of Clockwork Orange pop, culminating in the collaged moods of 'Death Trip' with its repeated question: 'Can you think of one good reason to remain?' Glam rock's ambiguous death wish could be acted out as romantic fantasy by Bowie or Roxy Music, but Harley's version showed the lucid reasoning of a pantomime philosopher for whom the suicidal impulse added the last brush-stroke to a misanthropic portrait of today. On 'Muriel the Actor', he rehearsed the irreverence of punk styling:

> Oh! See her move so right in her big baggy stride,
> And her golden top made of satin.
> See her wriggle her hips, take the almighty piss

while 'Death Trip' itself contains, in precis, Malcolm McLaren's entire blueprint for the *Rock-'n'-Roll Swindle* of punk rock:

> Take a pinch of Schemeland
> And turn it into Dreamland.

There was even a word perfect announcement for the forthcoming attraction of post-punk's obsession with all things Teutonic, synthetic and grey:

> You're wearing grey lady, you're from Berlin
> I'd say; you're a model . . .

And 'she's looking good'? Kraftwerk would let us know in their own efficient way, five years later. Ultimately, *The Human Menagerie of Cockney Rebel* was a record some years ahead of its time, like the first LP by Roxy Music, and within their collected eighty minutes lay the sly, elegant and confrontational agenda which would make post-punk Style culture resemble Glam rock with sunken cheeks and the sparkle sucked out of it.

In 1976, punk rock would be the catalyst that turned the fans of David Bowie and Roxy Music into the stars of post-punk, New Romanticism and electro-pop. Siouxsie and her Banshees first met at a Roxy Music concert at Wembley, and the artful theatricality of Deaf School (Liverpool pub cabaret to Roxy's Palm Court elegance), Adam and the Ants and Bow Wow Wow would continue the tradition of camp flamboyance. But by 1979, with the release of Basildon born Gary Numan and Tubeway Army's stirring hymn to the loneliness of dehumanization, 'Are "Friends" Electric?' (the *Hearts of Oak* of suburban futurists) synthesizer minimalism would have completed the cultural circuit and lipstick and robots would have been fused into the new pop paradigm. With the emergence of the Human League's monolithic synthesizer primitivism, carrying Phil Oakey's strangely hymn-like vocal style ('Circus of Death', as a tune, sounding rather like an old favourite on *Songs of Praise*), the blank expression of robotic performance would suggest inner-city futurism masking operatic passion. The *maquillage* mask, by 1979, would conceal the dandy android frozen in the monochrome lighting of film noir – be he, she or it from Essex or South Yorkshire.

Bowie, once again, had rehearsed this shift in his role as the alien Newton in Nicolas Roeg's *The Man Who Fell To Earth*, who had fallen to Earth with impeccable timing in 1976. Newton, with his androgynous glamour, bird-like delicacy and eventual descent into apathetic alcoholism, was the face that launched a thousand clubs. A sort of Mod from Mars, Newton was not only a cunning portrait of Bowie by Roeg (perhaps the best interpretation of Bowie ever written) but also a traditional, sympathetic hero in the school of Bogart's Rick – another stranger in a strange land. And there, buried deep in the film's theology, was arch time-traveller W. H. Auden, represented by a quotation from his poem 'Musée des Beaux Arts':

> and the expensive delicate ship that must have seen
> something amazing, a boy falling out of the sky.

A grandfather of the robot dandys, Auden had passed on all of the essential traits: sexual difference, residence in pre-War Europe and a fascination with the glamour of science and technology. These were to be the principal reference points, in the late 1970s and early 1980s, of the lipstick and robotics vogue in English pop.

England was an exotic host culture for the pop that dared not squeak its name, which was as linked to images of Weimar decadence as it was to Teutonic Robot Kultur. English clubs were throbbing to a synthesized interpretation of pre-War Berlin decadence or Cold War Berlin greyness. As method actor macho group Microdisney were to point out later, with waspish accuracy, vicariously commenting on the ethos of the Passions' mini-hit of 1981, 'I'm in Love with a German Film Star', English pop was in love with 'Art School, Sulphate, Berlin'. Given a leg up by Bowie and Eno's magnificent recordings at Berlin's Hansa-by-the-Wall studio, and

Bowie's shift into all things grey and expressionist in the late 1970s, the fledgeling New Romantics and robo-groups were all agog at anything with an *umlaut*. *Cabaret* (1972; already a prize influence on Siouxsie Sioux). Louise Brooks, Fritz Lang's *Metropolis* and the Bachs of robot-musik, Kraftwerk, had all found their way into the eerie mists of English post-punk and early New Romanticism. Even the Oxbridge boyishness of Michael York, as Sally's bisexual lover in *Cabaret*, would inform the archaic elegance of the New Romantic male, flicking his fringe towards the Weimar Republic. It was a potent brew of sexuality, pseudo-fascism and technology, popped in the microwave of Style to create a spooky soufflé of fashionable alienation, garnished with more than a pinch of melodrama.

Imported from Germany and Eastern Europe, there was a mythology of robots as both sinister (in the Gothic, Frankensteinian sense of the self-awakening monster) and political, in terms of allegories of Fordism, Communism and Bolshevism. The female robot in *Metropolis* had raised new notions of sexuality, combining eroticism with political allegory to make a Goth–Futurist morality tale that was equally concerned with emotional and sexual relationships. There was also Karel Čapek's 'Robot Play' of 1920, *Rossum's Universal Robots*, which not only provided the word 'robot' but told the story of an army of robots who unite to destroy mankind, thus becoming a critique of totalitarian communism. Peter Wollen, in his essay on 'Robot Kultur', has linked the robot eroticism in the latter half of *Metropolis* with Gramsci's notion of industrialization prompting a sexual crisis: the libido is placed at odds with the need for efficiency in the factory. Translated, as reference points within the robot aesthetic, into Style (rehearsed in the Robo-Warhol confessional of John Foxx's 'I Want To Be A Machine', on the first Ultravox LP, 1977), these precursors provided metaphors for individualism within a bland society, but were neutered, ironically, by the tyranny of fashion-consciousness itself.

As stylized Germanism was to be a principal influence on English popular culture at the end of the 1970s, the role of Kraftwerk (who had been considered little more than eccentric transmitters of a few catchy tunes prior to punk rock, poised somewhere between 'Sparky's Magic Piano' and the BBC Radiophonic Workshop) was enormous. Kraftwerk had been a concept waiting to happen, with their roots in the avant-garde head-music scene around Dusseldorf in the late 1960s, in groups such as Can, Neu, Faust and Tangerine Dream. But where these other groups had taken to Stockhausen or John Cage for the inspiration of their mystical improvisations, Kraftwerk – with or without their tongue in their cheek – chose to celebrate German efficiency and the aesthetics of the power station. They became the Swingle Singers of the Economic Miracle, projecting themselves as technicians as opposed to musicians, and their sublime minimalism made their 'lyrics' sound gloriously child-like: 'We are the robots' or 'I'm the operator with my pocket calculator'. In this much, they connected with the Warholian influence of wanting to be an endlessly repeating machine with seemingly child-like needs. Kraftwerk applied the musical mathematics of Bach to their machine-generated music, and played with the clichés of Teutonic efficiency. They were known to come on stage five minutes before their concert was due to begin, wait, check their watches, and then start at the scheduled time. Similarly, by programming their equipment to play 'Music Non Stop', they could leave the stage in the capable claws of their robot-dummy representatives, and be back at their hotel before the concert had finished. As a group, they were closer to Mercedes Benz than Goethe in terms of their romanticism. Their project was chilling, sensual and comic, simultaneously, and they were the perfect house band for Grey Young Things with a penchant for emotional sub-contraction.

Despite their technology, Kraftwerk were careful to be archaic in their imagery and ironically old-fashioned in their appearance.

Their aesthetic was drawn from the early 1930s and the late 1950s (thus commenting on the periods that book-end the demonized role of Germany in the 1940s), and they played the role of philosopher scientists who had disposed of human problems – which was another link with Warhol's philosophy of seeing all but participating in nothing. Whizzed through the blender of pop fashionability, Kraftwerk suggested a science fiction fable of survival through transcendental dehumanization in an apocalyptic culture; like Bowie being the ghost of a dead future, haunting a dying present, Kraftwerk were emotionless machines for whom the desire, fragmentation and paranoia of an insane consumer culture were just blips to be programmed out. It was a hugely romantic premise, and young, fashionable people all over England began to look like depressed Europeans; being a moody mannequin was suddenly breathlessly modern – or 'modern(e)'.

Thus, between 1979 and 1982, in the *ménage à trois* of fashion, pop and clubbing, there was a rush and a push in English Style Culture (although Style Culture, as a term, was still a twinkle in the eyes of social commentators) to make dandyism and technology the pop accessories for the end of time. There was an inference in all of this – a *fin de siècle* reflex – to regard one phase of history (a Yeatsian vortex) as dead, and youth, therefore, as so many robots or ghosts posing poetically in the ruins.

There was also a political ambiguity at work in this enterprise: either, as Peter York has suggested, the New Romantics were empathizing with the New Right and honing an agenda of elitism and exclusivity; or, equally, the movement was a direct reaction against the social consequences of Thatcherism – a kind of Tory-baiting by way of an autistic obsession with unadulterated style. Like the early-twentieth-century robots, the roboromantics could be seen to critique both ends of the political spectrum. But turning their backs on the use of pop as an energizing political force for the Left, as was also under way in

England with Rock Against Racism, the Anti-Nazi League and
Red Wedge, the fledgeling New Romantics flirted with fascist
imagery and held their parties in an ambience of picturesque
ruins that could house a broken heart or no heart at all. Politics,
when you were dressing like Lord Byron or a member of some
nameless constructivist army, came fairly low down on your list
of social responsibilities – more important than religion but far
less important than shopping. As the 1970s flipped into the 1980s,
the denizens of Billy's, Blitz, Hell and Cabaret Futura were
united in their style-driven Bohemia and its aspirant generation
of fashion designers, stylists and would-be pop stars. Strangely,
for a movement that was so vocal about its individualism, the
two principal Maître ds of the scene – Steve Strange and Richard
Strange – had assumed the same non-conformist surname.

Grey was the colour and alienation was the game. Steve Strange's
group Visage had a hit with 'Fade to Grey', while John Foxx's
Ultravox, on 'Hiroshima Mon Amour', were 'riding InterCity
trains, dressed in European grey'. Grey, as the ghostly non-colour
of urban mist, had popped up in Gary Numan's founding vocabulary in reference to the 'friend' of 'Are "Friends" Electric?', who
was 'dressed in a long coat, grey hat, smoking a cigarette'. (A
fair description of David Bowie during his residence in Berlin,
with Iggy Pop as Isherwood to his Auden.) Grey was also the
shade of film noir and pre-war Europe (on the style index) as
well as the eerie hue of half-life, after-life and indecision. Powdered and heavy-fringed, Japan scored cult hits with 'Ghosts'
and 'Nightporter' (another film reference to sex and Nazism)
while the little-known Metro would pout the lyric to 'Criminal
World' (which was later bound in leather by Bowie) in a breathy
staccato: 'The boys are like baby-faced girls . . .' Spandau Ballet
and New Order both punned on Nazism to convey some screw-
ball sense of historic alienation, while Heaven 17 took their
names from A Clockwork Orange. And the lyrical style of the
movement could be summed up by a line from 'I Want To Be

A Machine': 'From the reservoir of video souls in the lakes beneath my tongue.'

Nineteen eighty became a year in which death, as a theme and metaphor, would figure large in English pop. This was the year that 'Stereotype', as an ultimate doom anthem of provincial adolescence ('wrapped round a lamp-post on Saturday night') reached the Top Five, while the surprise Number one of 'Theme From M*A*S*H (Suicide Is Painless)' was given a far darker shadow in the real world by the tragic suicide of Joy Division's Ian Curtis. This was also the year when Bowie released the funereally titled 'Ashes To Ashes', and it seemed as though English pop was caught between the mood swings of manic depression and the creeping fear of an existential crisis. From the chilling minimalism of Cabaret Voltaire's 'Do The Mussolini (Head Kick)', to the unarguably disturbing and poignant posthumous release of Joy Division's 'Love Will Tear Us Apart', there was a requiem mood of finality and mourning; a stirring of the ashes of the funeral pyre, and a concentration on the symbolism of death, prior to rebirth as robots, or – as with the Specials' timely hit of 1981, 'Ghost Town' – a return as ghosts to haunt the ruins of an England which some factions saw as laid waste by Thatcherism. In this much, 1980 could be described as a year of Death in English pop, and it seemed to serve as a marker – rather than the more obvious choice of 1984 – between two distinct notions of popular culture's identity.

From Gautier's style-journalistic Preface to *Mademoiselle de Maupin* (1835) – a rallying cry for the New Romantics of Paris in the early nineteenth century – through Huysmans' morbid account of artifice and boredom in his novel *Against Nature*, imported to England through the writings of Wilde, an agenda for *fin-de-siècle* decadence as youth's response to the change of century had been established in the 1880s and repeated in the 1980s. Hence the emergence, as latter-day *symbolisme*, of video artist poets maudits, poised between Kempian aesthetics and pop video,

such as John Maybury and Derek Jarman's colleague Cerith Wyn
Evans, or the revival, in the name of transgressive ideologies,
of performance-based art centring on Bataille, occultism and
extreme sexual rituals – as exemplified by COUM and Psychic
TV. This would suggest Style as 'magick', in a febrile formula of
new technology and arcane philosophy, and would be underwritten, ultimately, by the insular, predominantly transvestite
hedonism of the Taboo club at Maximus in unreconstructed
Leicester Square.

The twentieth-century variation on the decadent theme, however,
had not only taken the end of history as a melodramatic backdrop
but also, despite itself, prophesied the irony boom and pop as
Pure Product sensibility that was just around the corner. As
provincial city centres became, in terms of architectural development around precincts, waterfronts, and heritage awareness, so
many miniature Londons (a trend that would accelerate with
the urban regeneration programmes of the 1980s), and St Martins
School of Art became the Paradise Regained for · aspiring
designers and entrepreneurs, New Romanticism was both a wake
for punk rock and a dress rehearsal for the rampant materialism
of the 'Designer Decade'. Fairly soon, the veils and powder would
be exchanged for shorts and vests, Latin American dance music
would take over from synthesizers, and the perfect pop of Trevor
Horn's productions of ABC (Roxy Music revisited) and Dollar
(ironic kitsch or just plain kitsch) would be the soundtrack for
the *cognoscenti* of Stock, Aitken and Waterman's bright young
Britain. Clubbing, having been funereal, would return to being
fun: Culture Clubbing, in fact. And, once through the tunnel
of Techno, the loop of popular culture in England would be
repeating itself, celebrating an ironic nostalgia for every phase
of pop since the middle of the 1950s. Pop would become an
archive for readers in the virtual library, wide open to the Three
Ps of post-modernism: punning, plagiarism and parody.

Spun off the backs of Roxy Music and David Bowie, the post-punk

fade into New Romanticism would remagneti:e London to produce a period, eventually, of effervescent creative hot-housing,
giving rise to a new wave of independent desig.1, publishing and
video art. The dawn of the 1980s took media technology to its
broken heart, virtually rebirthing after the death fixation and
Weimar neuroses of the late 1970s, and turning all the artifice
into artefacts. *i-D* magazine was the first samizdat journal of
the new street fashion, and in its first four issues (refreshingly
amateurish to contemporary eyes used to the slick professionalism of cultural mediation) one was faced with snap after snap
of fey young men and tough young women who were all, paradoxically, spouting the same reference points in the name of
individualism.

'Identity counts more than fashion,' declared issue 1. 'Make a statement, originate don't imitate, find your own I.D.' This was punk
réchauffé, but it also precipitated a nose-dive into the despotism
of cultural commodification and style-mongering that would
mark the *Zeitgeist* for the rest of the 1980s. Individualism, in
fact, was out; cultural materialism, as an art and science of
baroque complexity, was in. Oscar, it transpired, would have the
last laugh at the expense of those dandies who had taken his
maxim 'One should either be a work of art or wear a work of
art' at face value.

selling εnglanð by the sound

> *Gillick*: Why be alternative when the alternative has
> already become the main-stream, and when every-
> thing's turned on its head, and it doesn't make any
> sense? There's no motivation to act in that way. It
> doesn't mean anything any more.
> None of those terms mean anything, so you might as well
> go ahead and just do it for real.
>
> ANDREW RENTON and LIAM GILLICK (eds),
> *Technique Anglaise: Current Trends in
> British Art* (1991)

As the mediation of New Romanticism had given birth to the style
press, in a healthy fanzine-type media typified by the initial,
enthusiastic issues of *i-D* and *The Face* magazines, so the style
press, as the 1980s wore on, would give rise to a new brand of
Fleet Street journalism and periodicals publishing that could
recondition emerging trends in popular culture to suit the taste
and economic values of mainstream advertising and readers alike.
It was rather as though, back in 1960, *Date* magazine had been
produced as a supplement to *The Times*. In the 1980s and 1990s,
however, the gradual dissolution of the boundaries between 'high'
and 'low' culture would become progressively contended, and
the elevation or reduction of their specific values to a common
language would establish factions of opinion that were as open
to the cycle of generational attitudes as they were to intellectual
flexibility. As regards the cultural and pop cultural constitution
of Englishness, however, there was a predominant feeling that

accelerated technology and multi-culturalism were challenging the value of the term. The ambivalence towards 'Englishness', as an attitude and aesthetic of ambiguous meaning, would be as marked as the retreat from Arcady that had run through the first half of the century.

With the rediscovery of pin-up pop from Wham!, Duran Duran and Paul Young taking care of the UK side of the corporate Hit machine, and a pre-heroin Boy George becoming the Vera Lynn of the enterprise economy, the former half-world of English post-punk could be reconstituted for the video age as partially ironic entertainment, free of the portentous significance that had been attached, for instance, to Joy Division's impassioned anxiety and despair. And this was a curious terminus for the cult of artifice and alienation that David Bowie had neatly defined as 'Pictures of Jap girls and synthesists' in his lyric for 'Ashes To Ashes', and which had seen pallid posing as the opt-out clause in the social contract. As New Romantic pop had taken the machine aesthetic as its foundation, celebrating the triumph of cosmetics and computers over convictions, so the heavy layers of irony and analysis with which this foundation was now plastered might set into a mask of commodified values and responses. Neil Tennant, of Pet Shop Boys, summarized the situation during an interview for *Blitz* magazine when he said, with reference to the way in which *Actually* (1987), by Pet Shop Boys, had been taken by some critics to be an ironic concept LP about Thatcherism, that 'Everything has become a "phenomenon" – in inverted commas.' The media, in short, were masquerading as the message – with varying degrees of accuracy – by turning critical theory into a fashion accessory.

And the ubiquitous black polo-neck of the New Look in cultural theorizing was post-modernism. Post-modernism, as a term looted from architectural theory to describe the resultant meanings derived from a collision of styles, had found much broader currency as a concept to describe the cultural, social and psychological results of accelerated technology and the fragmentation of information within media – thus providing an intellectual conduit between consumption and sociology. As a combination of structuralism, applied semiotics and style-watching, post-modernism became both the dominant means of understanding contemporary culture, and, by extension, a creative tool in itself. Advocating the denial of authorship, the supremacy of context and the malleability of meaning, post-modernism was both liberating and reductivist, permitting in its popular form a triumph of style at the expense, some argued, of content.

The gathering momentum of Thatcherism's social and economic campaigns had encouraged irony as the principal means of protest and commentary; the celebration of consumerism could also be taken as its own ironic critique. Even the Human League had colour-coded their 12-inch singles to signify their various moods within the marketplace, and the computer barcode (as the beginning of the visual alphabet delivered by technology) could now be used as a graphical device in its own right. Thus, during the heady build-up to the boom years of the 1980s, the increasing fluency of pop consumers in codified visual argot and the massively expanded access to pop cultural media, had created a situation in which the advert – a product-led, thirty-second blipvert of *Zeitgeist* – would become the ultimate venue for the pop sensibility in deconstructed England.

From architecture to retail engineering to fashion design, the stage, props and costumes for acting out lifestyles had seldom been so cleverly crafted: atria and urban sophistication had colonized pop protest, as typified by the appearance of Pete Murphy, from Bauhaus, in a dramatic advert for Maxell tapes. Hawk-faced yuppies could drift like ghosts though the bare brick walls of their warehouse conversions to advertise building societies, while the pristine mirror-glass of redeveloping Docklands, reflecting the still waters of the former docks, could prompt the slogan 'Looks like Venice, works like Manhattan', as well as providing the location and inspiration for a myriad pop videos. The visual language of New Romanticism – the glamorous solitude of the modern(e) European – had become the template for advertising's concept of the upwardly mobile consumer. We had faded to grey, as Visage had predicted, and pop was indeed poised to eat itself; the gap between an agit-prop slogan and an advert, as the American display artist Barbara Kruger would demonstrate, was almost too subtle to be noticed in a post-modern context. In this much, 'Frankie Says . . .', as pop protest, would not be that far removed – as a strategy – from the 'Ask Sid . . .' share flotation later in the same decade. Despite the glorious trashiness of electro-pop anthems by Soft Cell or the Human League, their cultural by-product, 'Style', was put into harness for the designer decade.

The alchemical skill with which a Wilde or a Warhol could manipulate surface values to create deeply moral ways of seeing was co-opted by the expanding needs of cultural materialism to build a pop cultural hall of mirrors in which irony and intention were reflected to an infinity of endless advertising and consumption. With an equally infinite capacity to absorb resistance, response or deviation, this hall of mirrors became the white-knuckle ride of the *Zeitgeist*-surfers, in which the reduction or elevation of a cultural value was only as interesting as its last self-created reference point on the loop. This was the Age of the List (proliferating within the new print media, from reconstructed organs of the upper classes such as *Tatler* and *Harpers & Queen* to the *Sunday Times*) as a sub-cultural directory to maintaining lifestyle – a Flaubertian Dictionary of Received Ideas locked in the amber of irony. Courting opulence, the elitism of the designer consciousness played with notions of aristocracy and status which blurred afresh the boundaries between yob and snob, as pointed out by Julie Burchill's coruscating maxim: 'Can a Burchill look at a Churchill?' England (as broadcast from London at least) was no longer a nation of shop-keepers but a nation of shoppers

– as suggested in 'Shopping' by the Pet Shop Boys, a comment on the nationalized industries that might well have been construed as a hymn to Next and Marks & Spencer. It wasn't so much that anything was art; rather, read the right way, everything either was or looked like an advert for aspirational lifestyle – a theory concretized by the increased power of MTV over the production and sale of pop.

This, too, was the age of clever pop, from Paul Morley's wittily intellectual sleeve notes to Frankie Goes To Hollywood's *Welcome To The Pleasure Dome* LP, through to Scritti Politti's breathy pop song 'Jacques Derrida' and the lyrically nimble and authorially self-aware songs from Prefab Sprout and Momus. Posing as makers of commercially-minded perfect pop, the subtextual cleverness of Nick Currie (aka Momus), Paddy McAloon (of Prefab Sprout) or Green Gartside (of Scritti Politti) was both whimsical and knowing, suggesting a tertiary-educated sensibility that was equally related to the techniques of literary composition and the manipulation of pop glamour. These were the metaphysical poets of early middle-age – troubadors for thirtysomethings – and their contribution to English pop seemed just as concerned with deconstruction as it was with dancing away the heartache; their subject was the problem of being too clever. Ultimately, their pop seemed to flirt with self-consciousness at a time (the Me Decade) when self-consciousness was precariously balanced on the edge of self-obsession.

Writing in *The Face* magazine, in December 1985, in an essay entitled 'The Toytown Nihilists', Jon Savage offered a devastating analysis of what he saw as the simultaneous deliquescence of style culture and rise of new pop cultural media whose cynicism was matched only by their voraciousness.

Style culture's biggest canard now appears to be the idea of unfettered mass media access, where it's enough to enter and to skate across the surface of the media, without worrying about what it is you have to say and what effect it has on the people who consume it. Into this black hole rush the Toytown Nihilists, whose 'novel' postures, in their more extreme forms, mask an old-fashioned and self-destructive pathology. Their ways of saying 'No!' are even worse than the saying of nothing.

For Savage, witnessing the 'Age of Style over Content', the advance of a blinkered yet self-serving nihilism could be seen in the unquestioning appropriation of Malcolm McLaren's 'You have to destroy in order to create!' – only this time, in 1985, there was little creativity following the destruction. Nihilism had replaced negation, in the terminology which Savage had cited from the American music critic Greil Marcus, and the ultimate nihilism of style culture – an 'emptiness at the heart of style over content, a philosophical black hole' – played right into the hands of 'the new media economy': 'the symptom-laden saying of nothing falls in with the profound cynicism of the new media owners and the government which fosters them.' The importance of this essay lay not only in its overtly political assessment of a trend that more or less denied the existence of politics, but also its element of prophecy.

While style-watching, as a sophisticated decoding of the bleeps and squeaks of the Zeitgeist, could be taken as a form of progressive naturalism – revealing the interior of society by a close study, mimetically, of its surface (as practised in the ground-breaking essays by Anne Barr and Peter York for Harpers & Queen magazine), it also paved the way for an alliance between market research as a self-serving influence on culture and, by extension, for a cultural media largely led by market research. As a complex algebra of irony and intention, this was all meat for a conceptual stew, but as the decade wore on to a cultural complicity with market forces above all else, it would make for what Savage described as 'the manipulator who takes industry, artist and punter for a ride. This is not cleverness but contempt.' Style for style's sake, however ironic, within this perception, could be an effective tyrant.

With Style Culture, which had emerged from a deeply romantic sense of European history, midwifed by Bowie and sent up the Top Ten by Ultravox's self-confessedly meaningless exclamation in 1981, 'This means nothing to me! Oh, Vienna!', English popular culture appeared to have synthesized itself into a moodily lit corner. The popular cult of Style was typified by reinvented Soho, the reconstruction of advertising as art and the jazz–pop fusion of Blue Rondo a la Turk & Animal Nightlife, or the surfer-surrealism of Sigue Sigue Sputnik. But as a hot-housed reworking of *fin-de-siècle* decadence, that would eventually become *fin-de-millennium* neurosis, the potency of the post-modern age was also being analysed in psychiatric terms as a galloping loss of identity.

The erosion of identity by a bombardment of signs, levelling mean-ing into an outwardly seductive kaleidoscope of styles and intentions, was described in 1986 by Brandon Taylor in an essay entitled 'After Post-modernism', and his observations, while drawn from international sources, revived the conceit of illness that has marked the history of cultural change within Englishness:

As one New York analyst wrote recently, a propos this new frenzied consumer consciousness, there is 'now a new type of patient who is presenting himself. The classical neurotic for whom psychiatry was invented suffered from symptoms which were lodged in a self that was otherwise intact. By contrast, the new patient of the post-modern period has not even progressed to the point where a stable identity structure has coalesced.' Typically, 'he or she suffers from feelings of emptiness, isolation and futility, pre-Oedipal rage and primitive separation, which are masked by grandiose narcissistic fantasies.' These are 'fuelled by the marked intensification of the pursuit of material success, power and status, an increased preoccupation with youth, health and glamour, accompanied by difficulty in form-ing relationships with emotional depth.' Excessive alienated narcissism, frequently masked by social adaptability has come to dominate our era, according to this perception, just as hysteria and (later) neurosis did Freud's.

Translated back into the sensibility of popular culture in England, which was opening further and further to regional and international influence, even as the boundaries between supposedly 'high' and 'low' culture became increasingly irrelevant, one can see in Taylor's reported assessment of the post-modern 'patient' a set of needs that could be answered only by a complete reversal of all that Style culture was proposing. Indeed, according to this paradigm, the seeds of the post-modern malaise (if malaise it was) might well have been sown in the advance of a popular culture that took first robotics, artifice, despair and romanticized European angst as its aesthetic, and then, sealing the mask with what Savage would describe as 'Toytown Nihilism', offered nothing save a celebratory scrutiny, in the new media, of that same mask. Frankie said 'Relax' to a generation on the verge of a nervous breakdown. The influential groups of the late 1970s and early 1980s, composing dark anthems on sequencers or synthesizers, sang songs which often took 'emptiness, isolation and futility' (to use Taylor's description) as their principal theme – reaching an apotheosis in New Order's darkling 'How does it feel?' on *Blue Monday* (1983). It was almost as though a portion of the audience who had grown up with punk rock or the commodified pop of the Style era were suffering from the depressive symptoms that would be laid out in Taylor's account of the post-modern patient – rage, separatism, loneliness and lost bearings – and were failing to find sufficient therapy (cathartic or otherwise) in the style-bound legacy of post-punk. What was required was a new therapy for English pop's lost children, and the therapist arrived in the shape of Morrissey – 'Manchester's answer to the H-Bomb', as he would later claim he would like to be remembered.

Arriving in a pop medium that had been dominated by synthesizers, metropolitan stylishness as pop's ultimate ambition, chic or robotic internationalism and a predominance of narcissistic glamour (chilled in the fridge of cool alienation), Morrissey's first strategic triumph was to reverse all of the current values of fashionable pop, thus reclaiming realism and the undisguised sincerity of awkward emotions as the province of the three-minute pop song – itself an archaic form. After the modern(e) naming of post-punk groups – the Human League, Orchestral Manoeuvres in the Dark, Spandau Ballet – even the title of Morrissey's group, the Smiths, eschewed fashionability for an ordinariness which exuded its own perverse glamour; similarly, electronics and sequencers were wholeheartedly rejected in the group's choice of the traditional pop format of bass, lead guitar and drums – made musically sublime by Johnny Marr's reinvention of pop composition. As such, Morrissey's project was organically English, at a time when popular culture was synthetically international.

With formidable literary brilliance, Morrissey chose to make a creative virtue of his semi-suburban northern upbringing; this was recast, in his writing, by an epicurean selection of minutely studied and darkly romantic fables from English mythology (Billy Fury, *The Leather Boys*, *George and Mildred*, the Moors murderers, kitchen-sink cinema, to name but a few), whose presence informed the comedy or violence of his language as the socially and emotionally imprisoned aesthete. This was a revolutionary reworking of English pop, strip-mining the half-forgotten icons of Englishness in the face of post-punk alienation as a stylism mask, and re-routeing, through their resonance, the power of the romantic imagination back to the undefended self – gauche, ordinary, lonely, misunderstood or frustrated. In the late Tim Broad's promotional video for 'Stop Me If You Think You've Heard This One Before', from the last LP by the Smiths, *Strangeways Here We Come* (1987), Morrissey was filmed cycling on an old-fashioned bicycle around an area of derelict terraces in

Manchester, accompanied – also on their bicycles – by a group of the famously loyal fans who would imitate his clothing and appearance to the last detail. The essence of Morrissey's cult of awkwardness occurs when one of the fans, attempting to dismount from her bicycle, gets the hem of her jeans caught and is forced to stumble as the bike topples over. Filmed on a damp, overcast day, with the cliché of the star being pursued by his fans converted into a parody of the aimless bike ride, in which star and fan are united but wholly separated by the ritual of impersonation, the image of a fan stumbling in her idol's video seemed to typify the loop of identification upon which Morrissey's earlier work was based.

By projecting himself as the ultimate patient, Morrissey's alternately heroic and mock-heroic declamation of his symptoms ('I am sick and I am dull and I am plain' or 'It's time the tale were told, of how you took a child and you made him old') established him as the one sympathetic analyst and confessor. And, in what could be described as a classic case of psychiatric transference and counter-transference, his equally 'ill' audience of analysands fell hopelessly in love with their analyst – a passion kept enflamed by Morrissey's simultaneous pleas for understanding and the denial that he could ever be understood, as in 'The Boy With The Thorn In His Side', with its bereft questioning:

How can they hear me say those words, and still they don't believe me?
And if they don't believe me now, will they ever believe me?

One clue to Morrissey's concept of self-diagnosis could be found in Radclyffe Hall's lesbian romance of 1928, *The Well of Loneliness*; Morrissey had cited Hall as one of his favourite authors in a *Sunday Correspondent* questionnaire, and her best-known novel contains a proclamation of difference and fortitude which seems central to Morrissey's own identity as a writer and performer, and to the reassurance through identification that he was passing on to his loving fans:

You're neither unnatural, nor abominable, nor mad; you're as much part of what people call nature as anyone else; only you're unexplained as yet – you've not got your niche in creation. But some day that will come, and meanwhile don't shrink from yourself, but just face yourself calmly and bravely. Have courage; do the best you can with your burden. But above all be honourable. Cling to your honour for the sake of those others who share the same burden. For their sakes show the world that people like you and they can be quite as selfless and fine as the rest of mankind. Let your life go to prove this – it really would be a great life-work, Stephen.

The fact that Hall's heroine shares the same Christian name (phonetically, at least) with Morrissey, is a poignant coincidence, but the similarities between Morrissey's claimed predicament within the social orthodoxy and Hall's charge for the 'unexplained' to have courage is marked as a theme throughout Morrissey's writing. The extended isolation of the lone, social failure, converted into a romantic cell of unrequited passion, could be heard with clarion clearness in songs such as 'How Soon Is Now', 'These Things Take Time' and, most importantly, 'There Is A Light That Never Goes Out', in which the solidarity of failure becomes a soaring claim for love – held in place, as ever, by Morrissey's sharpening use of mordant comedy:

> And if a ten-ton truck
> kills the both of us,
> To die by your side
> The pleasure and the privilege is mine.

Morrissey's subject was his own ill-treatment at the hands of fate, and his complaints became articulations of common suffering by his deft mingling of comedy and tragedy – again a northern trait, but rendered unique by his Wildean understanding of

paradox. 'I had a really bad dream,' he wrote on 'Never Had No
One Ever': 'It lasted twenty years, seven months and twenty-
seven days.' Similarly, when the pop monolith that the Smiths
had become broke up in 1987, Morrissey described their controversial demise in the language reserved for a lately expired family
pet: the group was 'buried in a shoe-box in the garden'.

In its return to the cat's cradle of English ordinariness, the impact
on English pop of Morrissey's writing and performance could
be likened to the revolution caused in English theatre in 1956
by John Osborne's *Look Back in Anger*. The sophisticated tragedy
and the ironic comedy of manners had been usurped. And a
return to the glamour of the ordinary, in the face of honed
sophistication, could be achieved only by a writer who knew
how to lift poetic truths out of the mass of common experience;
a novelistic skill which had never been applied with such constancy and literary use of language within the English pop song.
Tony Parsons, writing in *Vox* magazine in 1993, would suggest
that 'Morrissey sings of England and something black, absurd
and hateful at its heart'; and there was also a sense that Morrissey
was repeating the same concept of Englishness that Philip Hoare
establishes in his definitive *Noël Coward: A Biography* (1995):
'He [Coward] spoke of his ambivalence towards his native land,
"I *am* England, and England is me. We have a love–hate relationship with each other. It's everything I stand for, but day by day
the place changes."'

Due partly to the enshrinement of the mythology of Englishness
that was growing around him in the middle of the 1980s, and
partly to his determined choice, within his lyrics, of the local as
the venue for heightened emotional states, Morrissey was both
applauded and condemned for his reinvention of Englishness
within popular culture. Morrissey's England was recognizably
within the vision of early Auden and late Larkin – the Auden
of 'Get There if You Can' and the Larkin of 'Going, Going' –
and he shared with them an ambivalence towards the English

landscape which seemed always to be mourning something lost – hence the ambiguous meaning of 'The Queen is Dead' (1986) as both a political statement and a personal lament: 'Some nine year-old tough who peddles drugs, I swear to God, I swear I never even knew what drugs were.'

But it was the constancy of Morrissey's Englishness, his aesthetic roaming from 'a rented room in Whalley Range' to the resonance, as a song title, of 'Jack The Ripper', which made him, in his own words, 'a living sign' – the pop cultural embodiment of a century or more of English sensibility. ('But compared to John Mills,' he once said, 'I'm scarcely born.') Morrissey, in this sense, is an accumulation of personae whom he casts as the players in a dynastic drama of his own life. And there is a rich seam of Victorian Gothic in Morrissey's writing, one quality of which is to find personal romance in archaism and seek – as had the French convict and novelist Jean Genet – a source of love and meaning in the arcane workings of a half-forgotten underworld. Morrissey, like Genet, combines the temperament of an aesthete with a yearning to identify with the passionate failure of society's criminal outsiders.

Vital to Morrissey's aesthetic, this equation between looking back and the social underworld was well defined by Graham Greene, in his travel book, *Journey Without Maps* (1936). 'Seediness has a very deep appeal, it seems to satisfy, temporarily, the sense of nostalgia for something lost; it seems to represent a stage further back.' Repeated by Greene in his handling of character and atmosphere in *Brighton Rock*, a version of this sentiment would also develop in Morrissey's writing subsequent to his departure from the Smiths, and was deeply informed by his renewed residence in London – as conveyed by his use of the voicetrack from an English documentary from the 1950s, about youths on a South London council estate, as the eerie underpinning of 'Spring-Heeled Jim' on *Vauxhall & I* (1994). This formula of archaic Englishness (particularly as expressed in the undeveloped areas of the City of London and the East End) and the romanticized defiance or hopelessness of working-class youth, were also central to the work in the 1980s of the artists Gilbert & George. Their large-scale, colour-treated photographs depicted eerily lit London streets around their home in Fournier Street, with full-length self-portraits – besuited as ever, in the uniforms of old-fashioned office clerks or civil servants – flanked by similar portraits of tough-looking young men. These were ambiguous statements about sexuality and Englishness, as removed from Morrissey's aesthetic by their opacity as they were related to it in their themes. Arguably, this particular combination of imagery was far closer to Greene's 1936 formula of seediness as a portal of nostalgia – and, most importantly, of nostalgia as an erotic or romantic ideal – than it was to any simple and misguided statements about nationalism. Morrissey, however – particularly in the wake of his 'National Front Disco' track on *Your Arsenal* (1992), the title of which echoes a chapter heading in Bill Buford's *Among the Thugs* study of football hooliganism – would join Gilbert & George in finding his every move monitored for crypto-fascistic tendencies by a vogue for political correctitude.

For Morrissey, the replacement of characters from northern kitchen-sink cinema (created by the intellectual Left of the 1950s) with the mythology surrounding London's skinhead tribalism, showed a further development of his search for stylized outsiders who represented a bygone era, and the alienation within rites of passage. Nick Knight, in his study *Skinhead* (1982), combined sociology with investigative journalism to present what appears to be an apologia for skinhead nationalism, and raised the relationship between Englishness, nostalgia and hopelessness that becomes bogged down in political complexity:

> the skinheads often see themselves as victims of almost Biblical proportions – as a stricken race of Jobs, as modern wanderers cast out into a cheerless world . . . And, as with all myths, there's a kernel of truth in the skinheads' perception of themselves as

outcasts. They aren't welcome anywhere. They are denied any useful role in the present. So instead they turn to the past, to an idea of what the unspoiled working class community might have looked like . . .

[He concludes:] The irony is that the skins in trying to be 'authentic' have ended up reviving an idea of working class culture which is frozen at precisely the point when a 'real', 'authentic' working class identity was being positively eaten away from outside.

As an aesthetic within the popular culture of the 1980s, Englishness *per se* – beyond the safe haven of commodified heritage culture and costume drama, reviving the Arcadian reflex to look back to soft-core Edwardiana – would be regarded as questionable. The Union Jack had become a discredited emblem of Little Englander nationalism, within the post-modern index of signs. In the thirty-odd years of English pop's dalliance with the Union Jack, since Michael English's Union Jack sunglasses for the 'Gear' boutique in 1965, or Geoff Reeve's Union Jack textile design, printed at the Royal College of Art's textiles department in 1960 (to make a subsequent appearance in John Entwistle's Union Jacket on the cover of the Who's *My Generation*, 1966), the English flag had been perhaps the ultimate icon of English pop's ambivalence towards Englishness. As David Mellor, who chronicled this etymology in his *The Sixties Art Scene in London*, wrote with regard to Gear's Union Jack sunglasses: 'The sunglasses had Union Jacks printed across the lenses and became a ubiquitous prop and fashion accessory with a multitude of connotations: principally the tension between patriotic sign and its decontextualized transgressive identity, as one more "hard edge" colour abstract pattern'; and Reeve's Union Jack textile: 'In this case the flag was given a serial meaningless, a repetition out of context, festive only in the announcement of the carnival-like circulation of a sign that had previously signified "correct" behaviour, within the mental boundaries of the British state.'

Thus, Pop Art's use of the Union Jack as a principal image within

Mod and Swinging London was already loaded with an ambivalence that would be somewhat sedated by the time Christmas
Top of the Pops 1973 decked out the studio in a Glam Union
Jack motif, and wholly reconstructed, by 1978, in its use by
extreme right-wing movements attempting to infiltrate popular
culture through skinhead tribalism – a situation which, in terms
of pop's relationship to Englishness, would make the Union
Jack motif synonymous with the minority politics of the British
Movement or the National Front. In this much, within the
reflexive workings of pop's agenda, Englishness as a theme, label
or aesthetic would be reinvented by a generational shift in sensibility that read the surface of its particular sign and found it
irrelevant at best and politically abhorrent at worst.

It would be ironic that Wilde and Morrissey, both Anglo-Irishmen,
would be England's underground analysts at either end of the
century; the English equivalents, perhaps, of Whitman and Warhol in America. It would be doubly ironic that they would find
themselves first fêted and then pilloried for going too far by the
respective generations who had found wit, solidarity or guidance
in their philosophies. If Morrissey (like Wilde) had sat by the
psychoanalyst's couch to accept the troubles of a nation's youth,
receiving first adoration and then blame as the soother of a
collectively troubled brow ('And when you're dancing, and laugh-
ing, and finally living, hear my voice in your head and think of
me kindly,' he had sung), then it was the conviction with which
he undertook this role that would eventually place him as an
outsider beyond the outsiders.

A case could be made for describing Morrissey, romantically, as
the Last English Pop Star. His looking back to a sensibility of
Englishness has been driven by a singular aesthetic and ambivalence, in which the deliquescence of national identity becomes
a metaphor for personal identity, again linking him to Larkin or
Auden. And, as an artistic position, this use of Englishness
has been conscious in its sincerity as a sealed world, in which

Morrissey himself becomes a force of nature: 'Panic on the streets of London, panic on the streets of Birmingham, I wonder to myself – could life ever be sane again?' For Morrissey, as the prodigal son of 'Maudlin Street' (the location of the school in *Carry on Teacher*), but with no home left to come to, there is a sense in which his country is the past (as nostalgia, or memories) and as such he can have no faith in the future ('And the year 2000, won't change anyone here'), and little spiritual nourishment in the present.

These are the convictions of a writer tethered to the end of an ancestral chain; the last representative of a nation in decline, for whom affairs of state are synonymous with affairs of the heart. By donning again the mantle of Billy Fury's gold lamé jacket (already inherited by Mick Travis in *O Lucky Man!*) at his controversial appearance (with Union Jack) at an open-air concert in Finsbury Park, it could seem as though Morrissey was positioned at the end of a particular sensibility, marking the shift of Englishness away from the tradition of ambivalence signified by Greene's empathetic description of Dallow, Spicer, Pinkie, Cubitt (the teenage gangsters of *Brighton Rock*, whom Morrissey listed under his few friends on *Vauxhall & I*) and on to an infantilist comedy of recognition – the Britishness of 'Brit Pop' – in which referral to the popular culture of the early 1970s, in particular, would be a virtual compound of irony and emulation based largely on stylistic cleverness.

As the cultural commodification that Jon Savage had predicted in 1985 gained new strength from corporate- and advertising-controlled entertainment, so the protesting gene within English popular culture seemed to be not so much silenced as coaxed into partial tokenism. The charitable rock spectaculars and tele-thon philanthropy inspired by the success of 1985's 'Live Aid' were defended by their undoubted altruism, putting the power of corporate rock to good use. And, as the underground became mainstream with increasing speed, so the protesting voice of popular culture could be bought off to be a further commodity within the social orthodoxy. Pop outrage, inevitably, would become a standard entry in the cultural index, and appeared to be complicit with this new role. Indeed, as the bullish ethos of the 1980s gave way to the fiscal neurasthenia of the 1990s, delivering a mixed legacy of hedonism, insecurity and materialism to a new generation of pop consumers brought up within Thatcherism, so the political basis of protest might be seen as comprised of raised awareness clichés, reflexively acknowledged as though to authorize the financial business of providing commercially-minded entertainment.

Within pop, the teeny-bopper mentality of the early 1970s was applied to groups such as Blur or Supergrass, whose jaunty amiability made them perfect pop cartoons for an infantilist culture: 'We are young! We are free!' These were like an English revival of The Monkees, with professional pop slickness augmented by a personable boyishness. Similarly, despite their lyrical or musical accomplishments, Pulp (whose 'Common People', 1995, caught a rare moment of defiance aimed at cultural tourists taking a cheap holiday in other people's misery) and Oasis referred back to the Kinks and the Beatles respectively, thus prompting Simon Reynolds's observation, in an essay for *Frieze* magazine in 1995, that BritPop's very nostalgia denied it the quality of determined modernity that was required to justify its label as the 'new Mod'. Ironically, the overwhelming popularity of Oasis seemed to be a reworking of England's need for the Beatles (northern, working-class lads with vivid personalities) at a time when the surviving Beatles themselves were being cast in marble by their annotated, institutionalized history, *Anthology* (1995–6). Oasis would collage footage of themselves with footage of the Beatles from the 'Sgt Pepper' era on their video for 'Don't Look Back in Anger', while 'Free As A Bird' (1995) as a 'new' Beatles single was in fact an exercise in 'virtual' Beatles, collaging the late Lennon's voice into new material. It seemed appropriate that Oasismania should occur at the time when the National Grid announced a power surge caused by the broadcast, within one hour, of the video for 'Free As A Bird' by the Beatles and Princess Diana's *Panorama* interview. This, it could be argued, was a triumph for 1960s revivalism in which the Royal Family and the Beatles were once more united in focusing the consciousness and conscience of England, with Noel and Liam Gallagher being the acknowledged heirs to the dusty throne of national pop – or the princes in pop's tower. And this dialogue, applauded and publicized, between Oasis and the Beatles was the kernel of Britishness in BritPop – an example of England's nostalgia for Englishness as a kind of heritage pop, in which Oasis were a cultural hologram of their heroes.

Simultaneous with BritPop, the renaissance of London as the world capital for contemporary art – which had stemmed from the success of the 'Freeze' exhibition, curated by Damien Hirst at the PLA building in 1988, and would provide, eventually, a metropolitan export to the Venice Biennale of 1995 and, as 'Brilliant!: New Art from London' to the Walker Art Center in Minneapolis (1995) or 1997's 'Sensation' – saw a generational response to the legacy of Thatcherism in what the *Evening Standard* would hail, in another reference to the England of the 1960s, as 'London Swings Again!' Seen as a creative *ménage à trois* between popular culture, fine art and metropolitan fashionability, in which Damien Hirst would direct a video for Blur, Gavin Turk would make a disturbing effigy of himself as the late Sid Vicious and Sam Taylor-Wood would propose making a film with Kylie Minogue, this latest version of Swinging London declared itself as consumed by popular culture in what the novelist Gordon Burn described, in an essay on Hirst in 1996, as 'the post-object, neo-Swinging, post-modern world'.

Derived from video art, computer technology and neo-conceptualism, the new generation of British artists had taken irony and punning – on materials, roles and titles – as the keynote of their projects, frequently mediating their own biographies as pop consumers (as in Gillian Wearing's video 'Dancing in Peckham', 1994, or Georgina Starr's 'Hypnodreamstuff', 1996, video-based installation at the Tate Gallery) or creating transgressive cartoons to question the boundaries of the sayable; as in Jake and Dinos Chapman's mutated child dummies ('Chapmanland', ICA, 1996) or their fibreglass and resin model of the physicist Stephen Hawking ('Ubermensch', 1995). Whether this was a rampant complicity with the blanding of meaning invoked by cultural commodification, or a grapeshot expression of violent alienation in the face of it, remained the fulcrum upon which much of its ambiguity – in terms of a generational solidarity – was balanced. On the one hand, a generation of British artists were united (on this one point only) in making work which seemed relevant to a distancing of perceptive certainty; on the other, within their manifold mixing of media and imaging, a frequent choice was the conceptual gag with an ironic punchline – Angus Fairhurst's 'A Cheap and Ill Fitting Gorilla Suit' (1995) or Michael Landy's 'Make a Clean Sweep with Scrapheap Services' (1996), to cite two works from 'Brilliant!' In a media-literate age of some sophistication, the immediacy or obscurity of British neo-conceptualism was either the first test of its intention or the last, releasing a vast quantity of new work, in appropriated or non-gallery spaces, which rejected the 'big money for big paintings' ethos that had typified the London art world in the mid- to late-1980s (as Scottish painting and the importation of Jeff Koons's morbid kitsch had vied for prominence) and seemed most concerned with allegories of muteness or conceptual mischief-making. This situation was compounded in 1993 when Rachel Whiteread was awarded the Turner Prize for her casts of interior spaces, and a conceptual booby prize (worth more than the Turner award) from former rock musicians the KLF, who had literalized – as conceptual protest – the expression 'having money to burn' by allegedly burning £1 million in cash of their royalties.

And yet, the direction of the first wave of works by young neo-conceptualists, at least, had already been questioned back in 1991, in a dialogue between the dealer Karsten Schubert and the curator Andrew Renton, recorded in the Introduction to *Technique Anglaise: Current Trends in British Art*:

> Renton: It is like a language which has been worn out. Part of the irony about these artists is that they belong to a very fertile field which should be completely barren, because there is something that tells you, 'Well, it's all been said, and we've out-minimalised each other and out-conceptualised each other. So where now?'
>
> Schubert: But the term that springs to my mind about these artists is they're playing for time and they're doing it very, very successfully.

With the inevitable elevation of the underground (warehouse exhibitions, agit-prop sloganeering, post-techno indie music) to the overground (mass media access, advertising, youth television programming, BritPop) and the replacement of Englishness, as a current cultural term, with the multi-culturalism of Britishness, the baton in the cultural relay race between fine art, literature, music, film and drama, could be said to have been exchanged for a basketball and a pair of Nikes. Whatever expressions of 'Englishness' might have become ('a boxed jig-saw turning yellow in the window of a closed sub-post office' as one journalist put it), they had less to do with a specific cultural etymology and more in common with responding to pre-mediated phenomena – be that Mark Wallinger's reverse playing of a video of Tommy Cooper ('Regard a Mere Mad Rager', 1993), Douglas Gordon's 'Twenty-four Hour Psycho' (1994), the appropriation of Damien Hirst's tanked halves aesthetic to advertise Ford cars, or the creative use of computer technology in the collaging of images or music. But there had been another route to follow.

In 1986, when Morrissey had struck the rocks of controversy by declaring, on 'Panic', that 'The music they constantly play, it says nothing to me about my life; Hang the blessed DJ!', he had both laid down an historic marker for one sensibility and pronounced disaffection with the then proliferating dance music scene, which would sub-sectionally mutate at break-neck speed according to the sampling and mixing preferences, internationally, of a thousand DJ artists. The dance music scene, as complex and self-referential as modern jazz, had emerged towards the middle of the 1980s as a coming together, in terms of social attitude and musical enthusiasms, of the black underground and white electro-pop, combining funk, dub-reggae, and imported black American music (from Grandmaster Flash to DJs such as Frankie Knuckles) to create an entirely new musical vocabulary out of sampled, collaged and vocally reworked beats and phrases. And, as the critic Stuart Maconie would point out in his radio documentary about the influence of Kraftwerk, the philosopher-scientists of robot music had also been seminal in the import and export of perfect beats to Brooklyn or Detroit and back to London or Manchester.

Dance music, in keeping with the greater history of pop music, was the product of an essentially black sensibility that was both laundered by a white society and maintained within its own underground to assure its development. But herein lay a creative marriage. As the labels under which dance music progressed from one form to another – house, garage, hip-hop, techno, acid, ambient, trance and so forth – were bewildering to the sub-cultural tourist, so its primary function as dance music made it open to all-comers as a social 'phenomenon' (to borrow Neil Tennant's loaded term) above all. Rejecting introspection and the post-modern glamour of anxiety (or anxiety of glamour), dance music, by definition, was a communal celebration within a sub-world of clubs and parties concerned solely with dancing itself. The new drug Ecstasy, as it became the principal icon of the dance scene, could be seen to define an attitude that was anti-analysis and pro-sensuality (be that drug-induced mind-gazing), physicality and hedonism; the point was to party, or there was no point at all. Coupled with a fetishizing of the latest sportswear, cyber-technology and new age philosophies, dance music took the body as a metaphor for the party and the party as a metaphor for the global society. Bleeps, squeaks and beats, received through chemical enhancement in the body, were the route to extreme states of mind. An energetic version of the relationship between Prog Mod Psychedelia and hallucinogenics, the ethos of dance music was a stripped down and computerized variation of the Happenings of the 1960s. Simultaneously autistic and tribal, its influence passed in and out of the osmotic membrane of mainstream popular culture to inform the retail industry of commercial fashionability while retaining an underground edge – that edge being dependent on 'blackness' or musical extremism.

In this much, the dance scene had little to do with Englishness, and everything to do with multi-culturalism and the portability, via technology, of a unifying attitude to different regional centres – be that Bristol, Leeds, Birmingham or Brighton – as defined by their local club nights and DJs. Most importantly, as the legality of raves was challenged by licensing laws (in an attempt to police drug abuse, allegedly), so the dance scene disposed of regional venues as a founding necessity and made a sub-political protest out of squatting rurally obscure locations reached by convoy in complex cat-and-mouse games with the police up and down the motorways of Britain. Fields, derelict mansions or abandoned warehouses could all house the house for a night, prior to reconvening in Reykjavik or Ibiza.

In the decade of its development as a pervasive sub-strand of popular culture, from the influence of New Order's *Blue Monday* to the elevation to commercial success of Goldie's *Metal Headz Platinum Breakz* compilation of drum & bass DJs or Roni Size's 'New Forms', dance music has articulated a vivid notion of the black experience of modern Britain while extending the project of white psychedelia. Ironically, for a form and movement that seemed to exist in the stateless physics of 'virtual' society, it is intensively crafted and aesthetically refined as music, sharing similarities with classical minimalism in terms of the blocking of beats within silence and the generation of musical loops.

Dance music's eventual mutation into jungle (itself sub-sectioned into 'intelligence', 'drum & bass' or 'hard-step') extended a movement of sealed complexity which was so musically radical that it confounded easy commodification. With an encylopaedia of tracks to sample and the constant refinements of computer technology, dance music's capacity for reinvention within its own form maintained its modernity on a weekly basis. Hence the critic Simon Reynolds's assertion that 'It's these kids – the kind you'll find at drum & bass hang-outs like Speed and AWOL – who are today's mods.' Jungle, as a paring down of sampled music and percussive beats, with few 'stars' but a rota of competing practitioners, could be seen as pop culture's ultimate acknowledgement of post-modernism's assertion that authorship, context and narrative have been wholly reinvented. For the Jungle DJ, as artist, the signature of authorship was already obscured or codified into semi-anonymity, prior to a collaging of found sound across a minimalist framework of break-beat percussion. As such, jungle in its various permutations – from the 'hardness' of Goldie or Dillinja to the 'Haunted Science' of OmniTrio or eerie minimalism of Photek's 'The Hidden Camera' – is a musical form which expresses, with deliberate resistance to quantification, the soundscape of 'post-postmodern' Britain as a clandestine cartography beneath the official map.

But England had been crossed by underground tunnels throughout the twentieth century, establishing patterns of action and reaction which, in the pop age, were well defined by the portentous narration of a 1973 *Nationwide* television report on David Bowie, delivered over the synthesized last movement of Beethoven's Ninth Symphony that had been bent sinister in Kubrick's *A Clockwork Orange*:

Ten years ago when the Beatles and the Stones created scenes like this, the young saw them as rebels in an adult world. Bowie's appeal lies in rebellion too, only he must be more outrageous, for public tastes have changed. When he dresses up and plasters his face, the kids of today see it as his way of flouting convention and they respect him for it. It's worth wondering though, what the Beat Age will spawn next, when someone like David Bowie isn't even freakish enough to shock us any more.

The stars of English pop, like Wilde's Remarkable Rocket, would have time to gasp, 'I knew that I would cause a sensation' before they went out; but twenty years later, *Nationwide*'s fearful questioning of the pop future would simply cue archive footage of the Sex Pistols, or Hi 8 video of an 'E'-sodden rave. And so the loop would continue, of England sub-contracting its need to identify an idea of Englishness to those artists, performers or consumers most articulate, by desire or not, of its cultural contradictions. Now, as we excavate the tunnels which have crossed English culture, making their effective underground out of so many connections or dead-ends, there is a sense in our archival condition, as nostalgic consumers scavenging for bargain rarities of the past, that a car boot sale can double as a faculty of Cultural Studies: the ditched record collection, still neatly named in a teenage hand, or the pile of last decade's style magazines bound with string beneath a trestle table.

In an age of cultural sampling, when yesterday's gauche enthusiasm can be recycled as tomorrow's distinguishing label, there is little distance between the hidden source and the public destination of England's unofficial commentary upon itself. As the pop soundscape of modern England, this commentary fades in and out of audibility and effectiveness, like a weak current on a remote rural circuit, amplified or submerged within a myriad simultaneous transmissions. And at night, as jungle stations send Respect to junglists whose identity is defined by little more than the names of towns – to Torquay, Carlisle, Ipswich, Wigan –

there is the momentary sense, before that movement too becomes absorbed into the loop of cultural history, that England is being broadcast as an outlaw sonic sculpture. Flying Officer Trubshawe, tuning in on the celestial wireless, might raise an eyebrow.

acknowledgɛments

The Publishers have made every effort to trace all copyright holders of quoted material and apologise for any omissions. The Publishers are happy to receive any emendations from copyright holders.

The Author and Publishers are grateful to the proprietors listed below for permission to quote from the following material: the Specials' songs *Nite Klub* (Dammers/Hall /Panter/Golding/Bradbury/Staples /Byers) © 1979 Plangent Visions Music Limited; *Too Much, Too Young* (Dammers) © 1979 Plangent Visions Music Limited; *Friday Night, Saturday Morning* (Hall) © 1981 Plangent Visions Music Limited. The Pet Shop Boys' songs *So Hard*, words and music by Neil Tennant and Christopher Lowe © 1990 reproduced by permission of Cage Music Ltd/ EMI Music Publishing Ltd, London WC2H 0EA; *Decadence*, words and music by Neil Tennant and Christopher Lowe © 1993 reproduced by permission of Cage Music Ltd/EMI Music Publishing Ltd, London WC2H 0EA; and *I Wouldn't Normally Do That Kind of Thing*, words and music by Neil Tennant and Christopher Lowe © 1990 reproduced by permission of Cage Music Ltd/EMI Music Publishing Ltd, London WC2H 0EA. The Bonzo Dog Band's song *My Pink Half of the Drainpipe*, words and music by Neil Innes and Vivien Stanshall © 1968 reproduced by permission of EMI Music Publishing Ltd, London WC2H 0EA. Crass' *A Series of Shock Slogans and Mindless Token Tantrums* © Penny Rimbaud, Exitstencil Press. Sham 69's song *Hurry Up Harry* © Maxwood Music. Cockney Rebel's songs *Muriel The Actor* (1974) and *Death Trip* (1974) are reproduced by kind permission of Steve Harley and Rak Publishing. Human League's song *Don't You Want Me?* (1981) words and music by Callis, Oakey and Wright, reproduced by kind permission of EMI Music Publishing Ltd, London WC2H 0EA and Warner Chappell Music Ltd, London W1Y 3FA. The Smiths' songs *There's A Light That Never Goes Out* (1986) words and music by Morrissey and Marr and *The Boy With the Thorn In His Side* (1985) words and music by Morrissey and Marr, are reproduced by kind permission of Warner Chappell Music Ltd, London W1Y 3FA. Morrissey's song *Every Day is like Sunday* (1988) words and music by Stephen Street and Morrissey reproduced by kind permission of Warner Chappell Music Ltd, London W1Y 3FA and EMI Music Publishing Ltd, London WC2H 0EA. The Fall's songs, *Mark'll Sink Us* (1987) words and music by Smith, Hanley and Scanlon; *Room To Live* (1982) words and music by Smith and Scanlon; and *Wings* (1983) words and music by Smith and Hanley, are reproduced by kind permission of Minder Music Ltd, London W9 2JQ.

indεx